Improving Vocabulary Skills

Fourth Edition

Improving Vocabulary Skills

Fourth Edition

Sherrie L. Nist
Professor Emerita, University of Georgia

Townsend Press Reading Series
Groundwork for College Reading with Phonics
Groundwork for College Reading
Ten Steps to Building College Reading Skills
Ten Steps to Improving College Reading Skills
Ten Steps to Advancing College Reading Skills
Ten Steps to Advanced Reading

Townsend Press Vocabulary Series
Vocabulary Basics
Groundwork for a Better Vocabulary
Building Vocabulary Skills
Building Vocabulary Skills, Short Version
Improving Vocabulary Skills
Improving Vocabulary Skills, Short Version
Advancing Vocabulary Skills
Advancing Vocabulary Skills, Short Version
Advanced Word Power

Supplements Available for Most Books
Instructor's Edition
Instructor's Manual and Test Bank
Online Exercises
PowerPoint Presentations
Blackboard Cartridges

ISBN-13 (Student Edition): 978-1-59194-190-3
ISBN-10 (Student Edition): 1-59194-190-3
ISBN-13 (Instructor's Edition): 978-1-59194-195-8
ISBN-10 (Instructor's Edition): 1-59194-195-4

Send book orders and requests for desk copies or supplements to:

Townsend Press Book Center
439 Kelley Drive
West Berlin, New Jersey 08091

For even faster service, contact us in any of the following ways:
By telephone: 1-800-772-6410
By fax: 1-800-225-8894
By e-mail: cs@townsendpress.com
Through our website: www.townsendpress.com

Contents

NOTE: Twenty-six of the chapters present ten words apiece. The other four chapters each cover ten word parts and are so marked. For ease of reference, the title of the selection that closes each chapter is included.

Unit Four

Unit Five

Appendixes

Preface: To the Instructor

The problem is all too familiar: *students just don't know enough words.* Reading, writing, and content teachers agree that many students' vocabularies are inadequate for course demands. Weak vocabularies limit students' understanding of what they read and the clarity and depth of what they write.

The purpose of *Improving Vocabulary Skills* and the other books in the Townsend Press vocabulary series is to provide a solid, workable answer to the vocabulary problem. In the course of 30 chapters, *Improving Vocabulary Skills* teaches 260 important words and 40 common word parts. Here are the book's distinctive features:

1 **An intensive words-in-context approach.** Studies show that students learn words best by reading them repeatedly in different contexts, not through rote memorization. The book gives students an intensive in-context experience by presenting each word in **six** different contexts. Each chapter takes students through a productive sequence of steps:

   ● Students infer the meaning of each word by considering two sentences in which it appears and then choosing from multiple-choice options.
   ● On the basis of their inferences, students identify each word's meaning in a matching test. They are then in a solid position to deepen their knowledge of a word.
   ● Finally, they strengthen their understanding of a word by using it three times: in two sentence-length practices and in a passage practice.

   Each encounter with a word brings it closer to becoming part of the student's permanent word bank.

2 **Abundant practice.** Along with extensive practice in each chapter, there are a crossword puzzle and a set of unit tests at the end of every six-chapter unit. The puzzle and tests reinforce students' knowledge of the words in each chapter. In addition, Chapters 2 through 30 reuse words from earlier chapters (such repeated words are marked with small circles, like this°), allowing for more reinforcement. Last, there are supplementary tests in the *Instructor's Manual and Test Bank* and the online exercises that accompany the book. All this practice means that students learn in the surest possible way: by working closely and repeatedly with each word.

3 **Controlled feedback.** The opening activity in each chapter gives students three multiple-choice options to help them decide on the meaning of a given word. The multiple-choice options also help students complete the matching exercise that is the second activity of each chapter. A limited answer key at the back of the book then provides answers for the third activity in the chapter. All these features enable students to take an active role in their own learning.

4 **Focus on essential words.** A good deal of time and research went into selecting the words and word parts in each book in the TP vocabulary series. Word frequency lists were consulted, along with lists in a wide range of vocabulary books. In addition, the authors and editors each prepared their own lists. A computer was used to help in the consolidation of the many word lists. A long process of group discussion then led to final decisions about the words and word parts that would be most helpful for students on each reading level.

5 **Appealing content.** Dull practice materials work against learning. On the other hand, meaningful, lively, and at times even funny sentences and passages can spark students' attention and thus enhance their grasp of the material. For this reason, a great deal of effort was put into creating sentences and passages with both widespread appeal and solid context support. We have tried throughout to make the practice materials truly enjoyable for teachers and students alike. Look, for example, at the selection on page 27 that closes the fifth chapter of this book.

6 Clear format. The book has been designed so that its very format contributes to the learning process. Each chapter consists of two two-page spreads. In the first two-page spread (the first such spread is on pages 8–9), students can easily refer to all ten words in context while working on the matching activity, which provides a clear meaning for each word. In the second two-page spread, students can refer to a box that shows all ten words while they work through the fill-in activities on these pages.

7 Supplementary materials.

a A convenient *Instructor's Edition* is available at no charge to instructors using the book. It is identical to the student book except that it contains answers to all of the activities and tests.

b A combined *Instructor's Manual and Test Bank* is also offered at no charge to instructors who have adopted the book. This supplement contains a general vocabulary placement test, along with a pretest and a posttest for the entire book as well as for each of its five units. It also includes teaching guidelines, suggested syllabi, an answer key, and an additional mastery test for each chapter as well as an additional mastery test for each unit.

c *PowerPoint presentations and a Blackboard cartridge* are available for the book and may be downloaded from the "Supplements" area for instructors at **www.townsendpress.com**.

d *Online exercises,* available in the Online Learning Center at **www.townsendpress.com**, also accompany the book. These exercises consist of two additional tests for each vocabulary chapter in the book. In addition, they include—at the instructor's option—some of the practice material in the book itself. The program includes a number of user- and instructor-friendly features: brief explanations of answers, a sound option, frequent mention of the user's first name, a running score at the bottom of the screen, a record-keeping file, and actual pronunciation of each word.

Probably in no other area of reading instruction is the computer more useful than in reinforcing vocabulary. These online exercises take full advantage of the computer's unique capabilities and motivational appeal. Here's how the program works:

- Students are tested on the ten words in a chapter, with each word in a sentence context different from any in the book itself.

- After students answer each question, they receive immediate feedback: The program states that the answer is right or wrong and why, frequently using the student's first name and providing a running score.

- When they complete each test, students receive their scores. If they repeat the test, they then receive a new score, labeled "R" on the scores report, with a number following the "R" indicating how many times they have taken the same test. What is so valuable about this, of course, is that the program gives students immediate additional practice with the words they need to review.

- In addition, the online exercise program offers a second, more challenging "Word Definitions" test in which students must identify the meanings of the chapter words without the benefit of context. This test is a final check that students have really learned the words. And, again, there is the option of a retest, with its own score.

- Finally, if the instructor so chooses, the online program will provide the student with two of the exercises in the book—Sentence Check 2 and the Final Check. Students can take these exercises online and receive immediate feedback and the option of a retest.

Once students complete these exercises, their knowledge of each word in the chapter will have been carefully reinforced. And this reinforcement will be even more effective for having occurred in an electronic medium that especially engages today's students.

To obtain a copy of either the *Instructor's Edition* or the *Instructor's Manual and Test Bank*, instructors may contact Customer Service at 1-800-772-6410 or at **cs@townsendpress.com**.

8 **Realistic pricing.** As with the previous editions, the goal has been to offer the highest possible quality at the lowest possible price. While *Improving Vocabulary Skills* is comprehensive enough to serve as a primary text, its modest price also makes it an inexpensive supplement.

9 **One in a sequence of books.** The most fundamental book in the Townsend Press vocabulary series is *Vocabulary Basics*. It is followed by *Groundwork for a Better Vocabulary* (a slightly more advanced basic text) and then by the three main books in the series: *Building Vocabulary Skills* (also a basic text), *Improving Vocabulary Skills* (an intermediate text), and *Advancing Vocabulary Skills* (a more advanced text). The most advanced book in the Townsend Press vocabulary series is *Advanced Word Power*. There are also short versions of the *Building, Improving*, and *Advancing* books. Suggested grade levels for the books are included in the *Instructor's Manual*. Together, the books can help create a vocabulary foundation that will make any student a better reader, writer, and thinker.

Notes on the Fourth Edition

A number of changes have been made in the fourth edition of *Improving Vocabulary Skills:*

- **A full-color design.** Color has been carefully used throughout, not as window dressing but to add clarity and readability to the different parts of each chapter and the different sections of the book.

- **Thirty new graphics.** To engage today's visual learners, a full-color illustration has been added to the Final Check passage in each chapter.

- **Additional multicultural names and repeated words.** To broaden both the appeal and the effectiveness of the practice materials, ethnic names have been used more frequently, and even more vocabulary words have been repeated in the Final Checks.

- **Revised and updated practice items.** As always, a number of practice items throughout the book have been revised or updated to ensure that each item works as clearly and effectively with students as possible.

Acknowledgments

I am grateful for the enthusiastic comments provided by users of the Townsend Press vocabulary books over the life of the first three editions. I appreciate as well the work done on earlier editions by Eliza Comodromos, Beth Johnson, John Langan, and, in particular, Carole Mohr. I would also like to thank Kathryn Bernstein, Denton Cairnes, and Rick Moore for design, editing, and proofreading assistance with the fourth edition. And I owe special thanks to two TP editors who brought their exceptional talents to this revision. Barbara Solot is responsible for a full-color text design that is as clear as it is inviting. The result of her artistry is a strikingly attractive book that both students and teachers will enjoy. Janet Goldstein, in addition to providing significant design and content input, has lent her extraordinary editing and proofreading skills to this project. Under her guidance, the vocabulary series has been in the best possible hands.

Sherrie L. Nist

Introduction

Why Vocabulary Development Counts

You have probably often heard it said, "Building vocabulary is important." Maybe you've politely nodded in agreement and then forgotten the matter. But it would be fair for you to ask, "*Why* is vocabulary development important? Provide some evidence." Here are four compelling kinds of evidence.

1 Common sense tells you what many research studies have shown as well: **vocabulary is a basic part of reading comprehension.** Simply put, if you don't know enough words, you are going to have trouble understanding what you read. An occasional word may not stop you, but if there are too many words you don't know, comprehension will suffer. The content of textbooks is often challenge enough; you don't want to work as well on understanding the words that express that content.

2 **Vocabulary is a major part of almost every standardized test,** including reading achievement tests, college entrance exams, and armed forces and vocational placement tests. Test developers know that vocabulary is a key measure of both one's learning and one's ability to learn. It is for this reason that they include a separate vocabulary section as well as a reading comprehension section. The more words you know, then, the better you are likely to do on such important tests.

3 Studies have indicated that **students with strong vocabularies are more successful in school.** And one widely known study found that **a good vocabulary, more than any other factor, was common to people enjoying successful careers in life.** Words are in fact the tools not just of better reading, but of better writing, speaking, listening, and thinking as well. The more words you have at your command, the more effective your communication can be, and the more influence you can have on the people around you.

4 **In today's world, a good vocabulary counts more than ever.** Far fewer people work on farms or in factories. Far more are in jobs that provide services or process information. More than ever, words are the tools of our trade: words we use in reading, writing, listening, and speaking. Furthermore, experts say that tomorrow's workers will be called on to change jobs and learn new skills at an ever-increasing pace. The keys to survival and success will be the abilities to communicate skillfully and learn quickly. A solid vocabulary is essential for both of these skills.

Clearly, the evidence is overwhelming that building vocabulary is crucial. The question then becomes, "What is the best way of going about it?"

Words in Context: The Key to Vocabulary Development

Memorizing lists of words is a traditional method of vocabulary development. However, you are likely to forget such memorized lists quickly. Studies show that to master a word (or a word part), you must see and use it in various contexts. By working actively and repeatedly with a word, you greatly increase the chance of really learning it.

The following activity will make clear how this book is organized and how it uses a words-in-context approach. Answer the questions or fill in the missing words in the spaces provided.

Inside Front Cover and Contents

Turn to the inside front cover.

● The inside front cover provides a _____ that will help you pronounce all the vocabulary words in the book.

Now turn to the table of contents on pages v–vi.

● How many chapters are in the book? _____

● Most chapters present vocabulary words. How many chapters present word parts? _____

● Four sections follow the last chapter. The first of these sections provides a limited answer key, the second gives helpful information on using _____, the third contains _____, and the fourth is a list of the 260 words and 40 word parts in the book.

Vocabulary Chapters

Turn to Chapter 1 on pages 8–11. This chapter, like all the others, consists of five parts:

● The *first part* of the chapter, on pages 8–9, is titled _____.

The left-hand column lists the ten words. Under each **boldfaced** word is its _____ (in parentheses). For example, the pronunciation of *absolve* is _____. For a guide to pronunciation, see the inside front cover as well as "Dictionary Use" on page 181.

Below the pronunciation guide for each word is its part of speech. The part of speech shown for *absolve* is _____. The vocabulary words in this book are mostly nouns, adjectives, and verbs. **Nouns** are words used to name something—a person, place, thing, or idea. Familiar nouns include *boyfriend, city, hat,* and *truth*. **Adjectives** are words that describe nouns, as in the following word pairs: *former* boyfriend, *large* city, *red* hat, *whole* truth. All of the **verbs** in this book express an action of some sort. They tell what someone or something is doing. Common verbs include *sing, separate, support,* and *imagine*.

To the right of each word are two sentences that will help you understand its meaning. In each sentence, the **context**—the words surrounding the boldfaced word—provides clues you can use to figure out the definition. There are four common types of context clues: examples, synonyms, antonyms, and the general sense of the sentence. Each is briefly described below.

1 Examples

A sentence may include examples that reveal what an unfamiliar word means. For instance, take a look at the following sentence from Chapter 1 for the word *eccentric*:

> Bruce is quite **eccentric**. For example, he lives in a circular house and rides to work on a motorcycle, in a three-piece suit.

The sentences provide two examples of what makes Bruce eccentric. The first is that he lives in a circular house. The second is that he rides to work on a motorcycle while wearing a three-piece suit. What do these two examples have in common? The answer to that question will tell you what *eccentric* means. Look at the answer choices below, and in the answer space provided, write the letter of the one you think is correct.

___ *Eccentric* means   A. ordinary.   B. odd.   C. careful.

Both of the examples given in the sentences about Bruce tell us that he is unusual, or odd. So if you wrote *B*, you chose the correct answer.

2 Synonyms

Synonyms are words that mean the same or almost the same as another word. For example, the words *joyful, happy*, and *delighted* are synonyms—they all mean about the same thing. Synonyms serve as context clues by providing the meaning of an unknown word that is nearby. The sentence below from Chapter 2 provides a synonym clue for *irate*.

> If Kate got angry only occasionally, I could take her more seriously, but she's always **irate** about something or other.

Instead of using *irate* twice, the author used a synonym in the first part of the sentence. Find that synonym, and then choose the letter of the correct answer from the choices below.

___ *Irate* means   A. thrilled.   B. selfish.   C. furious.

The author uses two words to discuss one of Kate's qualities: *angry* and *irate*. This tells us that *irate* must be another way of saying "angry." (The author could have written, "but she's always angry about something or other.") Since *angry* can also mean *furious*, the correct answer is *C*.

3 Antonyms

Antonyms are words with opposite meanings. For example, *help* and *harm* are antonyms, as are *work* and *rest*. Antonyms serve as context clues by providing the opposite meaning of an unknown word. For instance, the sentence below from Chapter 1 provides an antonym clue for the word *antagonist*.

> In the ring, the two boxers were **antagonists**, but in their private lives, they were good friends.

The author is contrasting the boxers' two different relationships, so we can assume that *antagonists* and *good friends* have opposite, or contrasting, meanings. Using that contrast as a clue, write the letter of the answer that you think best defines *antagonist*.

___ *Antagonist* means   A. a supporter.   B. an enemy.   C. an example.

The correct answer is *B*. Because *antagonist* is the opposite of *friend*, it must mean "enemy."

4 General Sense of the Sentence

Even when there is no example, synonym, or antonym clue in a sentence, most of the time you can still figure out the meaning of an unfamiliar word. For example, look at the sentence from Chapter 1 for the word *malign*.

> That vicious Hollywood reporter often **maligns** movie stars, forever damaging their public images.

After studying the context carefully, you should be able to figure out what the reporter does to movie stars. That will be the meaning of *malign*. Write the letter of your choice.

___ *Malign* means   A. to praise.   B. to recognize.   C. to speak ill of.

Since the sentence calls the reporter "vicious" and says she damages public images, it is logical to conclude that she says negative things about movie stars. Thus answer *C* is correct.

By looking closely at the pair of sentences provided for each word, as well as the answer choices, you should be able to decide on the meaning of a word. As you figure out each meaning, you are working actively with the word. You are creating the groundwork you need to understand and to remember the word. *Getting involved with the word and developing a feel for it, based upon its use in context, is the key to word mastery.*

It is with good reason, then, that the directions at the top of page 8 tell you to use the context to figure out each word's _____. Doing so deepens your sense of the word and prepares you for the next activity.

● The *second part* of the chapter, on page 9, is titled _____.

According to research, it is not enough to see a word in context. At a certain point, it is helpful as well to see the meaning of a word. The matching activity provides that meaning, but it also makes you look for and think about that meaning. In other words, it continues the active learning that is your surest route to learning and remembering a word.

Note the caution that follows this activity. Do not proceed any further until you are sure that you know the correct meaning of each word as used in context.

Keep in mind that a word may have more than one meaning. In fact, some words have quite a few meanings. (If you doubt it, try looking up the word *make* or *draw* in a dictionary.) In this book, you will focus on one common meaning for each vocabulary word. However, many of the words have additional meanings. For example, in Chapter 13, you will learn that *devastate* means "to upset deeply," as in the sentence "The parents were devastated when they learned that their son had been arrested." If you then look up *devastate* in the dictionary, you will discover that it has another meaning—"to destroy," as in "The hurricane devastated much of Florida." After you learn one common meaning of a word, you will find yourself gradually learning its other meanings in the course of your school and personal reading.

● The *third part* of the chapter, on page 10, is titled _____

Here are ten sentences that give you an opportunity to apply your understanding of the ten words. After inserting the words, check your answers in the limited answer key at the back of the book. Be sure to use the answer key as a learning tool only. Doing so will help you to master the words and to prepare for the last two activities and the unit tests, for which answers are not provided.

● The *fourth and fifth parts* of the chapter, on pages 10–11, are titled _____ and _____.

Each practice tests you on all ten words, giving you two more chances to deepen your mastery. In the fifth part, you have the context of an entire passage in which you can practice applying the words.

At the bottom of the last page of this chapter is a box where you can enter your score for the final two checks. These scores should also be entered into the vocabulary performance chart located on the inside back cover of the book. To get your score, count the number of items that you answered correctly in each section. Then add a zero. For example, if you got seven answers right in Sentence Check 2, you would write "70" on the first line in the score box.

Word Parts Chapters

Word parts are the building blocks of many English words. Learning word parts can help you spell and pronounce words, unlock the meanings of unfamiliar words, and remember new words.

This book covers forty word parts—prefixes, suffixes, and roots. **Prefixes** are word parts that are put at the beginning of words. When written separately, a prefix is followed by a hyphen to show that something follows it. For example, the prefix *non* is written like this: *non-*. One common meaning of *non-* is "not," as in the words *nontoxic* and *nonfiction*.

Suffixes are word parts that are added to the end of words. To show that something always comes before a suffix, a hyphen is placed at the beginning. For instance, the suffix *ly* is written like this: *-ly*. A common meaning of *-ly* is "in a certain manner," as in the words *easily* and *proudly*.

Finally, **roots** are word parts that carry the basic meaning of a word. Roots cannot be used alone. To make a complete word, a root must be combined with at least one other word part. Roots are written without hyphens. One common root is *cycl*, which means "circle," as in the words *motorcycle* and *cyclone*.

Each of the four chapters on word parts follows the same sequence as the chapters on vocabulary. Keep the following guidelines in mind as well. To find the meaning of a word part, you should do two things.

1 First decide on the meaning of each **boldfaced** word in "Ten Word Parts in Context." If you don't know a meaning, use context clues to find it. For example, consider the two sentences and the answer options for the word part *quart* or *quadr-* in Chapter 6. Write the letter of your choice.

Let's cut the apple into **quarters** so all four of us can share it.

The ad said I would **quadruple** my money in two months. But instead of making four times as much money, I lost what I had invested.

____ The word part *quart* or *quadr-* means   A. overly.   B. two.   C. four.

You can conclude that if four people will be sharing one apple, *quarters* means "four parts." You can also determine that *quadruple* means "to multiply by four."

2 Then decide on the meaning each pair of boldfaced words has in common. This will also be the meaning of the word part they share. In the case of the two sentences above, both words include the idea of something multiplied or divided by four. Thus *quart* or *quadr-* must mean _____.

You now know, in a nutshell, how to proceed with the words in each chapter. Make sure that you do each page very carefully. *Remember that as you work through the activities, you are learning the words.*

How many times in all will you use each word? If you look, you'll see that each chapter gives you the opportunity to work with each word six times. Each "impression" adds to the likelihood that the word will become part of your active vocabulary. You will have further opportunities to use the word in the crossword puzzle and tests that end each unit and in the online exercises available at **www.townsendpress.com**.

In addition, many of the words are repeated in context in later chapters of the book. Such repeated words are marked with a small circle (°). For example, which words from Chapter 1 are repeated in the Final Check on page 15 of Chapter 2?

_____   _____

Analogies

This book also offers practice in word analogies, yet another way to deepen your understanding of words. An **analogy** is a similarity between two things that are otherwise different. Doing an analogy question is a two-step process. First you have to figure out the relationship in a pair of words. Those words are written like this:

LEAF : TREE

What is the relationship between the two words above? The answer can be stated like this: A leaf is a part of a tree.

Next, you must look for a similar relationship in a second pair of words. Here is how a complete analogy question looks:

LEAF : TREE ::

A. pond : river   C. page : book
B. foot : shoe   D. beach : sky

And here is how the question can be read:

___ LEAF is to TREE as

    A. *pond* is to *river.*   C. *page* is to *book.*
    B. *foot* is to *shoe.*   D. *beach* is to *sky.*

To answer the question, you have to decide which of the four choices has a relationship similar to the first one. Check your answer by seeing if it fits in the same wording as you used to show the relationship between *leaf* and *tree:* A ___ is part of a ___. Which answer do you choose?

The correct answer is *C.* Just as a leaf is part of a tree, a page is part of a book. On the other hand, a pond is not part of a river, nor is a foot part of a shoe, nor is a beach part of the sky.

We can state the complete analogy this way: *Leaf* is to *tree* as *page* is to *book.*

Here's another analogy question to try. Begin by figuring out the relationship between the first two words.

___ COWARD : HERO ::

    A. soldier : military   C. actor : famous
    B. infant : baby   D. boss : worker

Coward and *hero* are opposite types of people. So you need to look at the other four pairs to see which has a similar relationship. When you think you have found the answer, check to see that the two words you chose can be compared in the same way as *coward* and *hero:* ___ and ___ are opposite types of people.

In this case, the correct answer is *D; boss* and *worker* are opposite kinds of people. (In other words, *coward* is to *hero* as *boss* is to *worker.*)

By now you can see that there are basically two steps to doing analogy items:

1 Find out the relationship of the first two words.
2 Find the answer that expresses the same type of relationship as the first two words have.

Now try one more analogy question on your own. Write the letter of the answer you choose in the space provided.

___ SWING : BAT ::

    A. drive : car   C. catch : bat
    B. run : broom   D. fly : butterfly

If you chose answer *A,* you were right. *Swing* is what we do with a *bat,* and *drive* is what we do with a *car.*

Here are some other relationships often found in analogies:

- **Synonyms:** freedom : liberty (*freedom* and *liberty* mean the same thing)
- **Item to category:** baseball : sport (baseball is one kind of sport)
- **Item to description:** school bus : yellow (*yellow* is a word that describes a school bus)
- **Producer to product:** singer: song (a singer is the person who produces a song)
- **Time sequence:** January : March (January occurs two months before March)

A Final Thought

The facts are in. A strong vocabulary is a source of power. Words can make you a better reader, writer, speaker, thinker, and learner. They can dramatically increase your chances of success in school and in your job.

But words will not come automatically. They must be learned in a program of regular study. If you commit yourself to learning words, and you work actively and honestly with the chapters in this book, you will not only enrich your vocabulary—you will enrich your life as well.

Unit One

absolve	antagonist
adamant	eccentric
amiable	encounter
amoral	epitome
animosity	malign

Ten Words in Context

In the space provided, write the letter of the meaning closest to that of each **boldfaced** word. Use the context of the sentences to help you figure out each word's meaning.

1 absolve
(ăb-zŏlv′)
-verb

- Since there was not enough evidence of his guilt, the jury had to **absolve** Mr. Melman of the murder.
- Accused of taking bribes, the mayor said, "In the end, I'll clear my name and be **absolved** of any wrongdoing."

__ *Absolve* means   A. to accuse.   B. to clear of guilt.   C. to inform.

2 adamant
(ăd′ə-mənt)
-adjective

- Ron is **adamant** about not changing plans. He insists we should still camp out even though the weather report now says it will be cold and rainy.
- **Adamant** in his support of gun control, Senator Keen won't give in to pressure from powerful opponents.

__ *Adamant* means   A. firm.   B. uncertain.   C. flexible.

3 amiable
(ā′mē-ə-bəl)
-adjective

- My **amiable** dog greets both strangers and old friends with a happy yip and energetic tail-wagging.
- At first, our history teacher doesn't seem very friendly, but once you get to know her, she shows her **amiable** side.

__ *Amiable* means   A. intelligent.   B. uncaring.   C. good-natured.

4 amoral
(ā-mŏr′əl)
-adjective

- Jerry is almost totally **amoral**. He cares only about making money and having fun and couldn't care less about right or wrong.
- A former president of Uganda, Idi Amin, was truly **amoral**. He jailed, tortured, and killed innocent opponents without the slightest feeling of guilt.

__ *Amoral* means   A. cowardly.   B. lazy.   C. lacking ethical principles.

5 animosity
(ăn′ə-mŏs′ə-tē)
-noun

- I was shocked when Sandy said she hated Lionel. I'd never realized she felt such **animosity** toward him.
- The bad feelings between the two families go back so many generations that nobody remembers what originally caused the **animosity**.

__ *Animosity* means   A. strong dislike.   B. admiration.   C. great fear.

6 antagonist
(ăn-tăg′ə-nĭst)
-noun

- At the divorce hearing, the husband and wife were such bitter **antagonists** that it was hard to believe they had once loved each other.
- In the ring, the two boxers were **antagonists**, but in their private lives, they were good friends.

__ *Antagonist* means   A. a supporter.   B. an enemy.   C. an example.

7 eccentric
(ĭk-sĕn′trĭk)
-adjective

● Bruce is quite **eccentric**. For example, he lives in a circular house and rides to work on a motorcycle, in a three-piece suit.

● Florence Nightingale, the famous nursing reformer, had the **eccentric** habit of carrying a pet owl around in one of her pockets.

__ *Eccentric means*   A. ordinary.   B. odd.   C. careful.

8 encounter
(ĕn-koun′tər)
-noun

● My **encounter** with Malik in a Los Angeles supermarket surprised me, since I thought he still lived in Chicago.

● I dislike returning to my small hometown, where I am likely to have **encounters** with people who knew me as a troubled kid.

__ *Encounter means*   A. a thought.   B. a dinner.   C. a meeting.

9 epitome
(ĭ-pĭt′ə-mē)
-noun

● To many, the **epitome** of cuteness is a furry, round-eyed puppy.

● The great ballplayer and civil rights leader Jackie Robinson was the **epitome** of both physical and moral strength.

__ *Epitome means*   A. a perfect model.   B. an opposite.   C. a main cause.

10 malign
(mə-līn′)
-verb

● That vicious Hollywood reporter often **maligns** movie stars, forever damaging their public images.

● Stacy refuses to **malign** her ex-husband, even though he was the one who insisted on the divorce.

__ *Malign means*   A. to praise.   B. to recognize.   C. to speak ill of.

Matching Words with Definitions

Following are definitions of the ten words. Clearly write or print each word next to its definition. The sentences above and on the previous page will help you decide on the meaning of each word.

1. _____ Not giving in; stubborn

2. _____ Lacking a moral sense; without principles

3. _____ Differing from what is customary; odd

4. _____ To find innocent or blameless

5. _____ A brief or an unexpected meeting

6. _____ A perfect or typical example

7. _____ An opponent; one who opposes or competes

8. _____ Bitter hostility

9. _____ To make evil and often untrue statements about; speak evil of

10. _____ Good-natured; friendly and pleasant

CAUTION: Do not go any further until you are sure the above answers are correct. Then you can use the definitions to help you in the following practices. Your goal is eventually to know the words well enough so that you don't need to check the definitions at all.

Sentence Check 1

Using the answer line provided, complete each item below with the correct word from the box. Use each word once.

A. **absolve**	B. **adamant**	C. **amiable**	D. **amoral**	E. **animosity**
F. **antagonist**	G. **eccentric**	H. **encounter**	I. **epitome**	J. **malign**

_____ 1. Lilly was ___ in her belief that Sam was a genius at business. Even after his first two companies failed, she still had faith in him.

_____ 2. My brothers had planned to meet in the restaurant, but their ___ took place in the parking lot.

_____ 3. I'm tired of hearing the two candidates for governor ___ each other with stupid insults.

_____ 4. Because he doesn't want to lose a sale, Mac remains polite and ___ even when he's annoyed with a customer.

_____ 5. Some criminals are truly ___—they don't see that some actions are right and that others are wrong.

_____ 6. The ___ of refreshment is drinking an ice-cold lemonade on a sizzling hot day.

_____ 7. Jed was ___(e)d of stealing money from the company, but the damage the accusation did to his reputation remained.

_____ 8. The owners of the department store were always competing with each other. They acted more like ____s than partners.

_____ 9. I avoid serious discussions with my sister because she shows great ___ toward me if I don't share her opinion.

_____ 10. Today it's not odd for females to learn carpentry, but when my mother went to high school, girls who took wood shop were considered ___.

NOTE: Now check your answers to these items by turning to page 177. Going over the answers carefully will help you prepare for the next two practices, for which answers are not given.

Sentence Check 2

Using the answer lines provided, complete each item below with **two** words from the box. Use each word once.

_____
_____ 1–2. The ___ millionaire dressed so shabbily that every ___ with him convinced us that he was poor.

_____
_____ 3–4. Hiroshi feels such ___ toward his sister that he never says a single kind thing about her; he only ___s her.

_____
_____ 5–6. Since the congresswoman was ___ in opposing the nuclear power plant, the plant's owners regarded her as their toughest ___.

_____ 7–8. Wayne is so ___ that he doesn't even want to be ___(e)d of guilt for all the
_____   times he has lied, cheated, and stolen.

_____ 9–10. With his friendly air, good-natured laugh and generosity, Santa Claus is the
_____   ___ of the ___ grandfather.

Final Check: *Joseph Palmer*

Here is a final opportunity for you to strengthen your knowledge of the ten words. First read the following selection carefully. Then fill in each blank with a word from the box at the top of the previous page. (Context clues will help you figure out which word goes in which blank.) Use each word once.

    In 1830, a Massachusetts farmer named Joseph Palmer moved to the city, only to find that people continually reacted to him with anger and hatred. Why? Palmer certainly wasn't a(n) (1)_____ man—no, he had a strong sense of right and wrong. He was a friendly and (2)_____ person as well. And on the whole, Palmer was the (3)_____ of a normal citizen, living a typical life with his family. Yet his neighbors crossed to the other side of the street to avoid an (4)_____ with him. Children insulted Palmer and sometimes threw stones at him. Grown men hurled rocks through the windows of his house. Even the local minister (5)_____(e)d Palmer, telling the congregation that Palmer admired only himself.

    One day, four men carrying scissors and a razor attacked Palmer and threw him to the ground. Pulling out a pocketknife, Palmer fought back, slashing at their legs. His (6)_____s fled. Afterward, Palmer was the one arrested and jailed. While in jail, he was attacked two more times. Both times, he fought his way free. After a year—although his accusers still wouldn't (7)_____ him of guilt—he was released.

    Palmer had won. The cause of all the (8)_____ and abuse had been his long, flowing beard. Palmer, (9)_____ to the end, had refused to shave.

    Thirty years after Palmer's difficulties, it was no longer considered (10)_____ to wear whiskers. Among the many who wore beards then was the President of the United States, Abraham Lincoln.

Scores	Sentence Check 2 _____%	Final Check _____%

Enter your scores above and in the **Vocabulary Performance Chart** on the inside back cover of the book.

curt	retort
demoralize	sabotage
dilemma	subsequent
inclination	wary
irate	zeal

Ten Words in Context

In the space provided, write the letter of the meaning closest to that of each **boldfaced** word. Use the context of the sentences to help you figure out each word's meaning.

1 curt
(kûrt)
-adjective

● The fast-food manager trained workers to give polite, full answers to customers, not **curt** responses.

● Betsy doesn't mean to be **curt**. When she's with other people, she often says just a few quick words to them because she's so shy.

___ *Curt* means   A. cautious.   B. courteous.   C. rudely brief.

2 demoralize
(dĭ-môr'ə-līz')
-verb

● Cara's refusal to date my brother **demoralized** him so completely that for months, he lacked the confidence to ask another woman out.

● When Bonita gained a pound during her diet, it so **demoralized** her that she ate a banana split.

___ *Demoralize* means   A. to cheat.   B. to discourage.   C. to excite.

3 dilemma
(dĭ-lĕm'ə)
-noun

● The store manager faced a **dilemma**: either having an elderly, needy man arrested or ignoring store rules about shoplifters.

● In old romantic movies, the heroine's **dilemma** often involves choosing between a rich boyfriend and the poor man she really loves.

___ *Dilemma* means   A. a hard choice.   B. a great danger.   C. a benefit.

4 inclination
(ĭn-klə-nā'shən)
-noun

● My **inclination** is to major in nursing, but I'm going to speak to a few nurses before I make my final decision.

● That two-year-old has some irritating habits, such as her **inclination** to say "no" to everything.

___ *Inclination* means   A. a preference.   B. a reason.   C. a fate.

5 irate
(ī-rāt')
-adjective

● If Kate got angry only occasionally, I could take her more seriously, but she's always **irate** about something or other.

● Ray gets mad when his wife misplaces the TV's remote control, and she becomes equally **irate** when he writes a check and forgets to record it in the checkbook.

___ *Irate* means   A. thrilled.   B. selfish.   C. furious.

6 retort
(rĭ-tôrt')
-verb

● When I told my parents I'd put the dishes in the dishwasher the next morning, my father **retorted**, "Maybe we should serve you dinner in the mornings, too."

● "What do you want?" the young woman asked Dracula. "Only to drink in your charms," he **retorted**.

___ *Retort* means   A. to approve.   B. to reply.   C. to ask.

7 sabotage
(săb′ə-tŏzh′)
-verb

● Terrorist groups train their members to **sabotage** airports and other public places.

● A fired programmer **sabotaged** the company's network by infecting it with a computer virus.

___ *Sabotage* means   A. to develop.   B. to invest in.   C. to do harm to.

8 subsequent
(sŭb′sĭ-kwənt′)
-adjective

● "I was hired as a stock boy," said the company president. "My **subsequent** jobs took me steadily up the company ladder."

● The first few times Janet drove on a highway, she was terrified, but on **subsequent** trips, she felt more relaxed.

___ *Subsequent* means   A. first.   B. following.   C. previous.

9 wary
(wâr′ē)
-adjective

● "There's no such thing as a free lunch" means that we should be **wary** about promises of getting something for nothing.

● I'm a little **wary** of people who, when they first meet me, treat me as if I'm their best friend.

___ *Wary* means   A. careful.   B. tired.   C. welcoming.

10 zeal
(zēl)
-noun

● Velma attacked her food with such **zeal** that I thought she hadn't eaten for a week!

● My neighbor has so much **zeal** about keeping our neighborhood clean that he sweeps our sidewalk if we don't do it ourselves.

___ *Zeal* means   A. resistance.   B. passion.   C. skill.

Matching Words with Definitions

Following are definitions of the ten words. Clearly write or print each word next to its definition. The sentences above and on the previous page will help you decide on the meaning of each word.

1. _____ A tendency, or preference, to think, act, or behave in a certain way; a leaning

2. _____ Rudely brief when speaking to someone; abrupt

3. _____ Cautious; on guard

4. _____ To reply, especially in a quick, sharp, or witty way

5. _____ To lower the spirits of; weaken the confidence or cheerfulness of

6. _____ A situation requiring a difficult choice

7. _____ Following, in time or order; next; later

8. _____ Enthusiastic devotion; intense enthusiasm

9. _____ To deliberately destroy or damage

10. _____ Very angry

CAUTION: Do not go any further until you are sure the above answers are correct. Then you can use the definitions to help you in the following practices. Your goal is eventually to know the words well enough so that you don't need to check the definitions at all.

Sentence Check 1

Using the answer line provided, complete each item below with the correct word from the box. Use each word once.

A. **curt**	B. **demoralize**	C. **dilemma**	D. **inclination**	E. **irate**
F. **retort**	G. **sabotage**	H. **subsequent**	I. **wary**	J. **zeal**

_____ 1. Rob's ___ was whether to go to work feeling sick or to stay home and lose a day's pay.

_____ 2. Be ___ when something sounds too good to be true—it probably is.

_____ 3. I have to watch my budget because I have a(n) ___ to overspend.

_____ 4. The director cut off most of the auditioning singers with a(n) ___ response: "Thank you. That will be all."

_____ 5. The striking miners planned to ___ one of the mines by blowing up the main entrance.

_____ 6. Because Devan expected to get an A on his research paper, receiving a grade of C truly ___(e)d him.

_____ 7. The team played miserably in the first game of the season, but they managed to win all ___ games.

_____ 8. My father always became ___ when any of his children came home after curfew. One time he began yelling at me even before my date had left.

_____ 9. If adolescents could apply to their studies just a bit of the ___ they feel for music and video games, their grades would improve dramatically.

_____ 10. When the wisecracking waiter said, "That hat looks ridiculous, lady," the woman stated, "I didn't come here to be insulted." "That's what you think!" ___(e)d the waiter.

NOTE: Now check your answers to these items by turning to page 177. Going over the answers carefully will help you prepare for the next two practices, for which answers are not given.

Sentence Check 2

Using the answer lines provided, complete each item below with **two** words from the box. Use each word once.

_____
_____ 1–2. Already angry, the customer became even more ___ when he received only this ___ response: "No returns."

_____
_____ 3–4. When I answer my phone and hear someone demand, "Who is this?" my ___ is to ___, "I'm the person whose phone was ringing. Who is *this*?"

_____
_____ 5–6. Because of terrorist attempts to ___ flights, airline security workers are ___ of even innocent-looking passengers.

_____   7–8. I began the semester with great ___ for my chemistry class, but the
_____   realization that I didn't have the necessary background quickly ___(e)d me.

_____   9–10. Margo intended to accept the job offer to be a salad chef, but a(n) ___ offer
_____   for an office position has presented her with a(n) ___: Should she take the
                                  interesting restaurant job, which pays poorly, or the higher-paying job that
                                  may not interest her much?

Final Check: *Telephone Salespeople*

Here is a final opportunity for you to strengthen your knowledge of the ten words. First read the following
selection carefully. Then fill in each blank with a word from the box at the top of the previous page.
(Context clues will help you figure out which word goes in which blank.) Use each word once.

If my carpets need cleaning or I want a new cellphone plan, I will do some comparison shopping first. I am not likely to buy anything suddenly just because a complete stranger has phoned—usually during the dinner hour—to sell it. For this and other reasons, I have always been (1)_____ of telephone salespeople. I don't like their cheerful, overly amiable° voices and their nervy suggestions as to how I might easily pay for whatever it is they are selling. My (2)_____ is to get off the phone as soon as possible.

My husband, however, creates a(n) (3)_____ for me when he takes these calls. He doesn't want what is being sold either, but he feels sorry for the telemarketers. He doesn't want to (4)_____ them with such a(n) (5)_____ reply as "No." When they begin their sales pitches, he is overcome by their (6)_____ for their products and therefore listens politely. Then he (7)_____s my efforts to discourage (8)_____ calls by suggesting that the salespeople call back later to talk to his wife! I don't know who gets more (9)_____ when that happens—I or the salespeople, disappointed when they realize we never intended to buy a thing. More than once, when I've finally said "No sale" for the last time to an adamant° telemarketer who had been refusing to take "no" for an answer, he or she has (10)_____(e)d, "Well, thanks for wasting my time."

Scores   Sentence Check 2 _____%   Final Check _____%

Enter your scores above and in the **Vocabulary Performance Chart** on the inside back cover of the book.

acclaim	exploit
adjacent	methodical
elicit	obsolete
engross	tangible
escalate	terminate

Ten Words in Context

In the space provided, write the letter of the meaning closest to that of each **boldfaced** word. Use the context of the sentences to help you figure out each word's meaning.

1 acclaim
(ə-klām′)
-noun

● Any subway system that is clean, quiet, and safe deserves **acclaim**.

● Although Vincent Van Gogh's paintings are now worth millions of dollars, the artist received little **acclaim** in his lifetime and died in poverty.

___ *Acclaim* means   A. criticism.   B. praise.   C. change.

2 adjacent
(ə-jā′sənt)
-adjective

● Because their desks are **adjacent**, Jeff and Kellie often exchange looks and comments.

● If you keep your dishes in a cupboard that's **adjacent** to the dishwasher, you won't have to walk too far when putting away the clean dishes.

___ *Adjacent* means   A. close.   B. similar.   C. separated.

3 elicit
(ĭ-lĭs′ĭt)
-verb

● The movie star's violet eyes always **elicit** admiration and wonder.

● The basketball player's three-point shot to win the game in its final seconds **elicited** a roar of delight from the excited fans.

___ *Elicit* means   A. to stop.   B. to follow.   C. to bring out.

4 engross
(ĕn′grōs′)
-verb

● The suspenseful TV movie so **engrossed** Bryan that he didn't even budge when he was called to dinner.

● The fascinating single-file march of black ants along the sidewalk **engrossed** me for several minutes.

___ *Engross* means   A. to hold the interest of.   B. to disgust.   C. to bore.

5 escalate
(ĕs′kə-lāt′)
-verb

● The fight between the two hockey players **escalated** into an all-out battle among members of both teams.

● "We need to **escalate** our fund-raising efforts," the theater manager said. "Otherwise, the company won't survive."

___ *Escalate* means   A. to expand.   B. to delay.   C. to weaken.

6 exploit
(ĕks-ploit′)
-verb

● At the turn of the century, factory owners **exploited** children by making them work in terrible conditions for as many as eighteen hours a day.

● Although Ricky is the English teacher's son, he refuses to **exploit** his status. He works as hard as anyone else in the class.

___ *Exploit* means   A. to forget.   B. to take advantage of.   C. to be sad about.

7 methodical
(mə-thŏd'ĭ-kəl)
-adjective

● A **methodical** way to store spices is to shelve them in alphabetical order.
● Juanita is so **methodical** about her diet that she classifies the foods in each meal into different nutritional categories.

___ *Methodical* means   A. accidental.   B. out-of-date.   C. orderly.

8 obsolete
(ŏb'sə-lēt')
-adjective

● Cellphones are so common now that they have made pagers almost **obsolete**.
● In the United States, the automobile quickly made travel by horse and carriage **obsolete**.

___ *Obsolete* means   A. popular.   B. useful.   C. extinct.

9 tangible
(tăn'jə-bəl)
-adjective

● The sculptor loved making her ideas **tangible** by giving them form in metal and stone.
● Corn-chip crumbs, empty soda bottles, and dirty napkins were **tangible** evidence that a party had taken place the night before.

___ *Tangible* means   A. clever.   B. solid.   C. hidden.

10 terminate
(tûr'mə-nāt')
-verb

● As the clock's hands inched toward 3:00, the students waited impatiently for the bell to **terminate** the last class before spring vacation.
● The referee should have **terminated** the boxing match when he first saw the weaker fighter losing the ability to defend himself.

___ *Terminate* means   A. to end.   B. to revive.   C. to begin.

Matching Words with Definitions

Following are definitions of the ten words. Clearly write or print each word next to its definition. The sentences above and on the previous page will help you decide on the meaning of each word.

1. _____ To draw forth

2. _____ To stop; bring to an end

3. _____ Orderly; systematic

4. _____ Close; near (to something)

5. _____ Able to be touched; having form and matter

6. _____ No longer active or in use; out of date

7. _____ To increase or intensify

8. _____ Great praise or applause; enthusiastic approval

9. _____ To hold the full attention of; absorb

10. _____ To use selfishly or unethically; take unfair advantage of

CAUTION: Do not go any further until you are sure the above answers are correct. Then you can use the definitions to help you in the following practices. Your goal is eventually to know the words well enough so that you don't need to check the definitions at all.

Sentence Check 1

Using the answer line provided, complete each item below with the correct word from the box. Use each word once.

A. acclaim	B. adjacent	C. elicit	D. engross	E. escalate
F. exploit	G. methodical	H. obsolete	I. tangible	J. terminate

_____ 1. A wedding ring is a(n) ___ expression of a couple's commitment to each other.

_____ 2. If solar energy becomes as cheap and plentiful as sunshine, nuclear energy, which is expensive, may become ___.

_____ 3. With movies like *Saving Private Ryan, Forrest Gump, Cast Away,* and *Charlie Wilson's War* to his credit, actor Tom Hanks has won Oscars and the ___ of admiring critics.

_____ 4. Our house is ___ to one with a high wooden fence, so our view on that side is completely blocked.

_____ 5. The shouting match between Rose and her brother ___(e)d until it was so loud that the neighbors complained.

_____ 6. Sometimes an article I'm reading on the bus will ___ me so much that I'll pass my stop.

_____ 7. When workers feel ___(e)d by their employers, they often go on strike for larger salaries and better working conditions.

_____ 8. Diana is very ___ when it comes to cooking. She reads the recipe carefully, gathers all the ingredients, and gets out the utensils before beginning.

_____ 9. When Luke was caught stealing money on the job, the company ___(e)d his employment and brought him up on criminal charges.

_____ 10. In one disturbing survey, the question "Which do you like better, TV or Daddy?" ___(e)d this response from a number of children: "TV."

NOTE: Now check your answers to these items by turning to page 177. Going over the answers carefully will help you prepare for the next two practices, for which answers are not given.

Sentence Check 2

Using the answer lines provided, complete each item below with **two** words from the box. Use each word once.

_____
_____ 1–2. The gifted ice skater's routine ___(e)d the audience. It was the epitome° of grace and power combined. At the end, a long, rapid spin ___(e)d a burst of applause.

_____
_____ 3–4. Although hand-crafted furniture is almost ___, mass production hasn't yet ___(e)d all demand for it.

_____
_____ 5–6. Workers want ___ rewards such as a good salary and a health-care program, but they also welcome less concrete benefits, such as ___ for a job well done.

_____   7–8. The more the British ___(e)d the American colonies by taxing them unfairly,
_____   the more the colonists' animosity° toward the British ___(e)d.

_____   9–10. Patty's ___ approach to gardening is to arrange all the plants in a row, with
_____   each one ___ to the one that will be planted after it.

Final Check: *A Cruel Sport*

Here is a final opportunity for you to strengthen your knowledge of the ten words. First read the following selection carefully. Then fill in each blank with a word from the box at the top of the previous page. (Context clues will help you figure out which word goes in which blank.) Use each word once.

As Alex sat down in the carnival tent, the lights dimmed. A spotlight revealed a short, heavy man holding a thick chain. He tugged the chain, and an old, muzzled bear appeared. The man, the animal's owner, announced that the bear's name was Sally. He said he would give a hundred dollars to anyone who wrestled Sally to the floor.

"That's disgusting! You have no right to (1)_____ an animal that way!" a woman called out. Several voices joined her in protest. A number of people walked out of the tent. Alex wanted to leave, too, but he was too shocked to move. He had thought bear wrestling was (2)_____, given up long ago as a cruel sport.

But the man's offer (3)_____(e)d one drunken response. "I'll do it!" a big man yelled, winning the (4)_____ of Sally's owner, who congratulated him warmly. The drunk began swinging at Sally. She backed away. "Knock her on her rear!" the owner shouted with zeal°. When Sally finally raised a paw to defend herself, her antagonist° could see that she had no claws. Feeling very brave now, he (5)_____(e)d his attack.

The horrible scene (6)_____(e)d Alex, who could barely believe his eyes. The man sitting (7)_____ to Alex rose to his feet and left, muttering "This shouldn't be allowed. I'm calling the police."

Meanwhile, the drunken man knocked Sally over. Her owner then (8)_____(e)d the match and handed Sally a bucket of food. The (9)_____ way in which he conducted his act showed Alex he had done it many, many times before.

Finally, the owner led Sally away. The animal's drooping head and her labored walk were (10)_____ expressions of her misery. As Sally passed him, Alex saw two police officers enter the tent. He hoped with all his heart that the law could prevent another such amoral° display of cruelty to this living creature.

Scores   Sentence Check 2 _____%   Final Check _____%

Enter your scores above and in the **Vocabulary Performance Chart** on the inside back cover of the book.

4

deterrent	innovation
implication	revitalize
inequity	sparse
infirmity	subjective
infringe	succinct

Ten Words in Context

In the space provided, write the letter of the meaning closest to that of each **boldfaced** word. Use the context of the sentences to help you figure out each word's meaning.

1 deterrent
(dĭ-tûr′ənt)
-*noun*

● As a **deterrent** to burglars, my father put a sign on our lawn that says, "Beware of pit bull."

● If the dangers of skydiving aren't a big enough **deterrent** for Ben, maybe the high cost will be.

___ *Deterrent* means   A. a reward.   B. a prevention.   C. a reason.

2 implication
(ĭm-plĭ-kā′shən)
-*noun*

● When the boss said that company profits were down, the **implication** was that nobody would be getting a raise.

● When the salesman winked, the **implication** was that he would give Joaquin a special deal on a car.

___ *Implication* means   A. a minor fault.   B. a demand.   C. something suggested.

3 inequity
(ĭn-ĕk′wĭt-ē)
-*noun*

● In South Africa, Mahatma Gandhi experienced an **inequity** that was all too common at the time—he was thrown off a "whites only" train.

● Most Americans consider it an **inequity** that some millionaires pay less in taxes than ordinary citizens do.

___ *Inequity* means   A. an injustice.   B. a physical weakness.   C. a question.

4 infirmity
(ĭn-fûr′mə-tē)
-*noun*

● Rick uses a wheelchair, but he doesn't let his **infirmity** keep him from traveling.

● Certain **infirmities**, such as arthritis and diabetes, are more likely to affect the elderly.

___ *Infirmity* means   A. a relationship.   B. a disability.   C. a secret.

5 infringe
(ĭn-frĭnj′)
-*verb*

● The protesters may picket the nuclear power plant as long as they don't **infringe** on other people's right to enter and exit freely.

● When my mother is doing her homework, no one is allowed to **infringe** on her quiet time.

___ *Infringe on* means   A. to interfere with.   B. to protect.   C. to recognize.

6 innovation
(ĭn′ə-vā′shən)
-*noun*

● When commercial bakers first offered sliced bread, it was considered an exciting **innovation**.

● The high cost of college has led to such financial **innovations** as savings accounts for children's education begun while the children are still infants.

___ *Innovation* means   A. something new.   B. a weakness.   C. an imitation.

20

7 revitalize
(rē-vĭt′əl-īz′)
-verb

- When DeShawn is tired after work, he finds a brief nap **revitalizes** him for an evening out with friends.
- The City Council hopes to **revitalize** the currently lifeless shopping district by offering tax breaks for new businesses.

___ *Revitalize* means   A. to refresh.   B. to amuse.   C. to tire out.

8 sparse
(spărs)
-adjective

- There are thick pine forests at the foot of the mountain, but higher up, the trees become **sparse**.
- Unfortunately, the turnout for the team's first pep rally was **sparse**. Organizers hope to have better attendance at the next one.

___ *Sparse* means   A. long.   B. thin.   C. crowded.

9 subjective
(səb-jĕk′tĭv)
-adjective

- Martina, a highly **subjective** judge of her son's abilities, feels he's brilliant in every respect. The boy's father, however, has a less emotional view of him.
- The reporter refused to write about his friend's trial. He knew any story he wrote would be too **subjective** to be published as an unbiased article.

___ *Subjective* means   A. one-sided.   B. boring.   C. impersonal.

10 succinct
(sək-sĭngkt′)
-adjective

- Text messages are usually **succinct**. People don't want to type any more words than necessary to get their messages across.
- "What's new?" is a **succinct** way of asking, "Has anything of interest happened to you lately, my friend?"

___ *Succinct* means   A. wordy.   B. prejudiced.   C. brief and clear.

Matching Words with Definitions

Following are definitions of the ten words. Clearly write or print each word next to its definition. The sentences above and on the previous page will help you decide on the meaning of each word.

1. _____   Injustice; unfairness; an instance of injustice

2. _____   A new custom, method, or invention; something newly introduced

3. _____   Based on personal opinions, feelings, and attitudes; not objective

4. _____   Something that discourages or prevents a certain action

5. _____   Expressed clearly in a few words; to the point; concise

6. _____   To renew the strength and energy of; restore to a vigorous, active condition

7. _____   A physical weakness or defect; ailment

8. _____   Distributed thinly; not thick or crowded

9. _____   To intrude or trespass on; to go beyond the limits considered proper

10. _____   An idea that is communicated indirectly, through a suggestion or hint

CAUTION: Do not go any further until you are sure the above answers are correct. Then you can use the definitions to help you in the following practices. Your goal is eventually to know the words well enough so that you don't need to check the definitions at all.

Sentence Check 1

Using the answer line provided, complete each item below with the correct word from the box. Use each word once.

A. deterrent	B. implication	C. inequity	D. infirmity	E. infringe
F. innovation	G. revitalize	H. sparse	I. subjective	J. succinct

_____ 1. Although Marie joked about her broken leg, it was an ___ that kept her from work for a month.

_____ 2. When a restaurant's tables have ashtrays, the ___ is that smoking is permitted.

_____ 3. Our democratic rights do not include the freedom to ___ on other people's rights.

_____ 4. "Now" is a ___ way of saying, "At this particular point in time."

_____ 5. Our grass is ___ along a path at the corner of the lot, where kids take a shortcut through our yard.

_____ 6. An interesting ___ in food packaging is a bottle from which salad dressing is sprayed, rather than poured.

_____ 7. The seminar for company employees ___(e)d my aunt's interest in her job by giving her new skills and suggesting new goals.

_____ 8. *The Diary of Anne Frank* is a ___ view of events during World War II, from the point of view of a young Jewish girl in hiding.

_____ 9. The company was accused of creating a(n) ___ by paying women less than men for doing the same work.

_____ 10. The fact that Beethoven was totally deaf by age 50 was not a(n) ___ to his composing, at the age of 53, one of his most ambitious and beloved works, the *Ninth Symphony*.

NOTE: Now check your answers to these items by turning to page 177. Going over the answers carefully will help you prepare for the next two practices, for which answers are not given.

Sentence Check 2

Using the answer lines provided, complete each item below with **two** words from the box. Use each word once.

_____
_____ 1–2. When the candidate for mayor saw the ___ turnout for his speech, he knew he had to do something to ___ his campaign.

_____
_____ 3–4. Future ___s in technology, particularly on the Internet, may make it easier for a government to ___ on the privacy of citizens' computer records.

_____
_____ 5–6. Although arthritis can be a painful ___, Aunt Fern refuses to let it be a(n) ___ to her active lifestyle. For example, she continues to go square-dancing every week.

_____   7–8. All editorials are ___—they represent someone's opinions. In an editorial, for
_____   example, writers are free to argue against the ___ of police brutality, instead
                                          of just reporting on it.

_____   9–10. A sign may be brief and still have several ___s. For example, the ___ sign
_____   "Dangerous Curve" suggests that drivers should be wary° and slow down,
                                          that the curve ahead is sharp, and that bad accidents have happened there
                                          before.

Final Check: *Bald Is Beautiful*

Here is a final opportunity for you to strengthen your knowledge of the ten words. First read the following selection carefully. Then fill in each blank with a word from the box at the top of the previous page. (Context clues will help you figure out which word goes in which blank.) Use each word once.

While I was looking through a men's hair-care magazine, I noticed many ads for toupees and hair thickeners. The (1)_____ seemed to be that a man's baldness is a major (2)_____. Well, I'm not going to let anyone (3)_____ on a man's right to be bald, or to demoralize° those who have already lost their hair. Listen, all you baldies. You may feel it's a serious (4)_____ that some heads have only (5)_____ hair while others are thickly covered, but I think bald men—including my father—are terrifically attractive. Sure, that's just my (6)_____ opinion, but I'm not alone. I know another woman whose boyfriend went so far as to shave his head in order to (7)_____ their tired romance. My thick-haired boyfriend hasn't offered to go quite that far, but I wouldn't offer any (8)_____ to him if he had an inclination° to do the same thing. I know drug companies manufacture medications to produce hair on bald heads, but that's one (9)_____ I would discourage any man from using. I'd even like to see the day when toupees are as obsolete° as hoop skirts. I hate to see all those beautiful, shiny bald heads covered up. Or, to be more (10)_____: bald is beautiful.

Scores   Sentence Check 2 _____%   Final Check _____%

Enter your scores above and in the **Vocabulary Performance Chart** on the inside back cover of the book.

CHAPTER 5

allusion	banal
altruistic	euphemism
appease	mercenary
arbitrary	syndrome
assail	taint

Ten Words in Context

In the space provided, write the letter of the meaning closest to that of each **boldfaced** word. Use the context of the sentences to help you figure out each word's meaning.

1 allusion
(ə-lōō′zhən)
-*noun*

● After I suggested that Monty have fruit for dessert instead of chocolate cake, he responded, "Is that an **allusion** to my weight?"

● Ramon didn't have the courage to come right out and ask Lia to marry him. Instead, he made only an **allusion** to marriage by asking, "Wouldn't it be easier if we had to fill out just one tax return?"

__ *Allusion to* means   A. a contrast to.   B. a hint about.   C. an answer for.

2 altruistic
(ăl′trōō-ĭs′tĭk)
-*adjective*

● When an enemy approaches, ground squirrels show **altruistic** behavior. They risk their own lives to give alarm calls to nearby relatives.

● "I'm not often **altruistic**," Brett admitted. "I usually put my own welfare first."

__ *Altruistic* means   A. unselfish.   B. cheerful.   C. greedy.

3 appease
(ə-pēz′)
-*verb*

● My sister was so outraged when I accidentally dropped and broke her cell phone that nothing I could say or do would **appease** her.

● Roger was furious when he saw me out with another guy, but I quickly **appeased** him by explaining that the "date" was my cousin.

__ *Appease* means   A. to annoy.   B. to heal.   C. to calm.

4 arbitrary
(är′bĭ-trĕr′ē)
-*adjective*

● Professor Miller's students were angry that he graded essays in an **arbitrary** way, rather than using clear-cut standards.

● Parents should not enforce rules according to their moods. Such **arbitrary** discipline only confuses children.

__ *Arbitrary* means   A. steady.   B. slow.   C. impulsive.

5 assail
(ə-sāl′)
-*verb*

● The storm **assailed** us with hail and heavy rain.

● The two candidates continuously **assailed** each other with accusations of dishonesty.

__ *Assail* means   A. to attack.   B. to confuse.   C. to support.

6 banal
(bə-năl′)
-*adjective*

● The film, with its overused expressions and unimaginative plot, was the most **banal** I had ever seen.

● "Nice to see you" may be a **banal** comment, but what it lacks in originality it makes up for in friendliness.

__ *Banal* means   A. greedy.   B. unoriginal.   C. clever.

7 euphemism
(yo͞o′fə-mĭz′əm)
-noun

- Common **euphemisms** include "final resting place" (for *grave*), "intoxicated" (for *drunk*), and "powder room" (for *toilet*).
- The Central Intelligence Agency is on record as having referred to assassination with the **euphemism** "change of health."

__ *Euphemism* means   A. a harsh term.   B. a term that doesn't offend.   C. a foreign term.

8 mercenary
(mûr′sə-něr′ē)
-adjective

- Ed is totally **mercenary**. His philosophy is, "Pay me enough, and I'll do anything."
- The con man pretended to love the wealthy widow, but he actually married her for **mercenary** reasons.

__ *Mercenary* means   A. jealous.   B. angry.   C. greedy.

9 syndrome
(sĭn′drōm)
-noun

- Headaches are usually harmless, but as part of a **syndrome** including fever and a stiff neck, they may be a sign of a serious illness.
- Jet lag is a **syndrome** resulting from flying long distances; it often includes exhaustion, headache, and loss of appetite.

__ *Syndrome* means   A. a group of symptoms.   B. a cause.   C. something required.

10 taint
(tānt)
-verb

- The involvement of organized crime has **tainted** many sports, including boxing and horse racing.
- The government scandal **tainted** the reputations of everyone involved.

__ *Taint* means   A. to benefit.   B. to damage.   C. to start.

Matching Words with Definitions

Following are definitions of the ten words. Clearly write or print each word next to its definition. The sentences above and on the previous page will help you decide on the meaning of each word.

1. _____   Determined by personal judgment, not rule or reason; based on impulse

2. _____   Motivated only by financial gain; greedy

3. _____   An indirect reference

4. _____   A group of symptoms typical of a particular disease or condition

5. _____   A mild or vague term used as a substitute for one considered offensive or unpleasant

6. _____   To calm, especially by giving in to the demands of

7. _____   Lacking originality; overused; commonplace

8. _____   To stain the honor of someone or something

9. _____   To attack physically or verbally

10. _____   Unselfishly concerned for the welfare of others; unselfish

CAUTION: Do not go any further until you are sure the above answers are correct. Then you can use the definitions to help you in the following practices. Your goal is eventually to know the words well enough so that you don't need to check the definitions at all.

Sentence Check 1

Using the answer line provided, complete each item below with the correct word from the box. Use each word once.

A. allusion	B. altruistic	C. appease	D. arbitrary	E. assail
F. banal	G. euphemism	H. mercenary	I. syndrome	J. taint

_____ 1. There have been people ___ enough to sell their own children for the right price.

_____ 2. "Someone hasn't shown me his report card," my mother said, making a(n) ___ to my brother.

_____ 3. It takes a(n) ___ person to adopt a disabled child.

_____ 4. The mugger ___ed his victims with a baseball bat.

_____ 5. The local undertaker insists on using a(n) ___ for the chapel of his funeral parlor. He calls it the "slumber room."

_____ 6. The report that the halfback was addicted to drugs ___(e)d the team's image.

_____ 7. The only thing that would ___ the dead boy's parents was imprisonment of the drunk driver who had killed him.

_____ 8. Abraham Lincoln is thought to have had Marfan's ___, a group of symptoms which includes unusually long bones and abnormal blood circulation.

_____ 9. The judge's harsh sentence was ___. Rather than being based on past similar cases or on the seriousness of the crime, it was based on the judge's opinion of the defendant.

_____ 10. "You're special" probably appears on thousands of greeting cards, but when someone says it to you and means it, it never seems ___.

NOTE: Now check your answers to these items by turning to page 177. Going over the answers carefully will help you prepare for the next two practices, for which answers are not given.

Sentence Check 2

Using the answer lines provided, complete each item below with **two** words from the box. Use each word once.

_____
_____ 1–2. ___ people tend to place the public welfare above their own self-interest. In contrast, ___ people will exploit° anyone for a profit—they will even sell harmful products.

_____
_____ 3–4. The angry customer loudly ___(e)d the salesman for having sold her a broken clock. The salesman quickly ___(e)d her by giving her a full refund.

_____
_____ 5–6. A certain rare ___ includes a very odd symptom—an uncontrollable urge to use obscene language. This disease can ___ a victim's reputation, because some people who hear the foul language won't understand the reason for it.

_____
_____ 7–8. My boss judges performance in a(n) ___ manner, praising and scolding according to his moods. And when he says, "Please stay a few minutes longer today," "a few minutes" is a(n) ___ for "an hour."

_____   9–10. The critic hated stale language. Instead of writing a(n) ___ comment such
_____   as "That ballerina is light on her feet," he made an interesting ___ to the
dancer's movements: "She was never heavier than moonlight."

Final Check: *No Luck with Women*

Here is a final opportunity for you to strengthen your knowledge of the ten words. First read the following
selection carefully. Then fill in each blank with a word from the box at the top of the previous page.
(Context clues will help you figure out which word goes in which blank.) Use each word once.

My older brother, Mark, has no luck with women. He
doesn't understand why. I do.

To begin with, when he first meets a woman, he goes
into one of two styles of conversation. The first is to
(1)_____ her with a stream of personal
questions: "What's your name? Where do you live? Is that
your real hair color? What kind of work do you do? Do you
want to have kids someday? Are you seeing anyone? Would
you like to have dinner with me?" Naturally, most women
find this surprising and annoying. His other approach is to
say the most (2)_____ things imaginable:
"Nice day, isn't it? I thought it might rain this morning,
but it didn't. It might rain tomorrow, but who knows. Last week was nice weather, too." By this time the
poor girl has either walked away or passed out from boredom.

Another thing Mark often does in his encounters° with women is to say things that make him sound
totally (3)_____, as if money were the most important thing in the world to him. He
makes frequent (4)_____s to his own salary, asks the woman how much she makes,
and complains about the prices of everything on a menu. When he takes a date to a movie, he sometimes
embarrasses her by trying to get his money back from the theater manager afterward, claiming he hadn't
liked the movie. Naturally, this sort of behavior somewhat (5)_____s him in the woman's
eyes, and he rarely gets a second date. When one of his former girlfriends complained to me about Mark's
behavior, I tried to (6)_____ her by telling her that underneath it all, Mark is really a nice
guy. She replied by saying that she didn't have the inclination° to dig that far down.

Mark, of course, finds women's reactions to him completely (7)_____.
He shakes his head and says, "Women are just not reasonable. Here I am, as nice as can be, and
they act as if I have some horrible, contagious (8)_____." I try to be a(n)
(9)_____ sister and help the guy out. I point out how his behaviors turn women off,
using gentle (10)_____s such as "You're a special, unusual person, Mark. You're just
a little eccentric°." Maybe I need to come right out and let him hear the truth, even if it makes him mad:
"You're *weird*, Mark."

Scores   Sentence Check 2 _____%   Final Check _____%

Enter your scores above and in the **Vocabulary Performance Chart** on the inside back cover of the book.

ann, enn	-ly
audi, audio-	non-
cycl, cyclo-	path, -pathy
-hood	pend
hyper-	quart, quadr-

Ten Word Parts in Context

Common word parts—also known as *prefixes*, *suffixes*, and *roots*—are used in forming many words in English. Figure out the meanings of the following ten word parts by looking *closely* and *carefully* at the context in which they appear. Then, in the space provided, write the letter of the meaning closest to that of each word part.

1 ann, enn

- This year's **annual** family reunion will be held at a campground.
- Our town is having a big **bicentennial** parade exactly two hundred years after the day the town was founded.

___ The word part *ann* or *enn* means
    A. four.   B. year.   C. hang.

2 audi, audio-

- The bride's softly spoken wedding vows were not **audible** to those at the back of the church.
- The sound system in the new **auditorium** is so good that music can be heard clearly even in the upper balconies.

___ The word part *audi* or *audio-* means
    A. condition.   B. feeling.   C. hearing.

3 cycl, cyclo-

- When Bob asked his parents if he could buy a new "two-wheeler," they didn't realize he meant a **motorcycle**.
- A **cyclone** travels in a circular motion.

___ The word part *cycl* or *cyclo-* means
    A. circle.   B. four.   C. condition.

4 -hood

- When children reach **adulthood**, how much help should their parents give them?
- For my great-grandmother, **womanhood** began early—she was married at 15.

___ The word part *-hood* means
    A. state of.   B. sound.   C. not.

5 hyper-

- Trina is **hypersensitive** to conflict. When people disagree with her, she thinks they are rejecting her personally.
- On the Internet, pages are written in **hypertext**—a special language that includes links to related text, images, and sound.

___ The word part *hyper-* means
    A. opposite of.   B. more than normal.   C. fourth.

6 -ly

- One cannot **easily** drown in Utah's Great Salt Lake because the lake's high percentage of salt helps people float.
- During the American Revolution, many brides **proudly** wore red, instead of white, as a symbol of rebellion.

___ The word part *-ly* means
    A. fourth.   B. in a certain way.   C. opposite of.

7 non-

● The paints used in elementary schools are **nontoxic** so that a child who might swallow some won't be poisoned.

● The story about the aliens was supposed to be **nonfiction**, but it sounded made-up to me.

___ The word part *non-* means   A. condition.   B. not.   C. overly.

8 path, -pathy

● When Ricardo's marriage fell apart, Ben's reaction was very **empathic** because he had also been rejected by a loved one.

● Felicia and her mother claim to have powers of **telepathy**. They say that they know each other's feelings and thoughts without being told.

___ The word part *path* or *-pathy* means   A. feeling.   B. hearing.   C. the opposite.

9 pend

● The children's swing is an old tire that's **suspended** from a strong oak branch.

● I can't sit and watch the swinging **pendulum** of a grandfather clock without starting to feel sleepy.

___ The word part *pend* means   A. suffering.   B. to listen.   C. to hang.

10 quart, quadr-

● Let's cut the apple into **quarters** so all four of us can share it.

● The ad said I would **quadruple** my money in two months. But instead of making four times as much money, I lost what I had invested.

___ The word part *quart* or *quadr-* means   A. overly.   B. two.   C. four.

Matching Word Parts with Definitions

Following are definitions of the ten word parts. Clearly write or print each word part next to its definition. The sentences above and on the previous page will help you decide on the meaning of each word part.

1. _____ Four, fourth

2. _____ Feeling, suffering

3. _____ In a certain manner

4. _____ Hearing, sound

5. _____ To hang

6. _____ State, condition

7. _____ Year

8. _____ More than normal; overly; excessively

9. _____ Circle

10. _____ Not; the opposite of

CAUTION: Do not go any further until you are sure the above answers are correct. Then you can use the definitions to help you in the following practices. Your goal is eventually to know the word parts well enough so that you don't need to check the definitions at all.

Sentence Check 1

Using the answer line provided, complete each *italicized* word below with the correct word part from the box. Use each word part once.

A. ann	B. audi, audio-	C. cycl, cyclo-	D. -hood	E. hyper-
F. -ly	G. non-	H. path, -pathy	I. pend	J. quart, quadr-

_____ 1. Chen loves playing the piano, especially when he has a(n) (. . . *ence*) ___ listening to him.

_____ 2. It's hard for me to be (*sym . . . etic*) ___ when my sister complains, because she causes so many of her problems herself.

_____ 3. Because of therapy, Grace is a well-adjusted adult, but her (*child . . .*) ___ years were troubled and unhappy.

_____ 4. When I lost one of my diamond earrings, I had the other one made into a(n) (. . . *ant*) ___ to hang around my neck.

_____ 5. The children's odd (. . . *et*) ___ consisted of a toy-drum player, a building-block clapper, a piano player, and a bell ringer.

_____ 6. We were told to bring only necessary equipment on our camping trip, so I was surprised to see how much (. . . *essential*) ___ gear others brought.

_____ 7. Mrs. Baker said she and her husband had been (*happi . . .*) ___ married for forty-seven years. But Mr. Baker, correcting her, said 1977 wasn't so great.

_____ 8. One of the most difficult vehicles to ride is also one of the simplest: a (*uni . . . e*) ___, a vehicle with only one wheel.

_____ 9. The supervisor said that workers would be evaluated (. . . *ually*) ___ for possible promotions. So if they don't get a promotion one year, they might get one the next.

_____ 10. My grandmother has (. . . *tension*) ___, which is abnormally high blood pressure.

NOTE: Now check your answers to these items by turning to page 177. Going over the answers carefully will help you prepare for the next two practices, for which answers are not given.

Sentence Check 2

Using the answer line provided, complete each *italicized* word in the sentences below with the correct word part from the box. Use each word part once.

_____
_____ 1–2. Some males act as if their (*man . . .*) ___ really (*de . . . s*) ___ on how many touchdowns they score or home runs they hit, rather than on maturity and strength of character.

_____
_____ 3–4. The (. . . *ist*) ___ stood (*helpless . . .*) ___ staring at the tire he had chained to the tree. The rest of the bike had been stolen.

_____
_____ 5–6. Stan, a (. . . *drinker*) ___, is (. . . *critical*) ___ of anyone who touches alcohol. He is adamant° in his belief that taking even a single drink is the sign of a self-destructive personality.

_____   7–8.   The nursing class watched an (. . . *visual*) ___ show about the horrible conditions in a mental institution of the 1950s. The patients looked (. . . *etic*) ___; clearly, they were suffering.

_____   9–10.   For my research report, I used two online articles—one from a (. . . *erly*) ___, posted four times a year; and the other from an (. . . *ual*) ___ that appears only every January.

Final Check: *A Taste of Parenthood*

Here is a final opportunity for you to strengthen your knowledge of the ten word parts. First read the following selection carefully. Then complete each *italicized* word in the parentheses below with a word part from the box at the top of the previous page. (Context clues will help you figure out which word part goes in which blank.) Use each word part once.

I have a lot of (*sym* . . .) (1)_____ for parents of twins, triplets, and (. . . *uplets*) (2)_____. I just spent the weekend baby-sitting for my four nieces and nephews.

First, I altruistically° offered to watch my brother's two children so that he and his wife could go away for the weekend for their sixth wedding (. . . *iversary*) (3)_____. Then my sister called and said that her husband, an actor, had a chance to (. . . *tion*) (4)_____ for a big part in a TV drama. He had to fly to California for the weekend. She said she'd love to go along if I could watch their children, aged two and three. I (*willing* . . .) (5)_____ agreed.

What a time I had! I soon learned that the word *baby-sitting* has a false implication°—I did very little sitting that weekend. The children's activity was (. . . *stop*) (6)_____. It seemed as if they never sat down, and nothing engrossed° them for more than a few minutes. They went from pedaling their tiny (*tri* . . . *es*) (7)_____ to building with their blocks to banging their toy drums. They "washed" the dishes, let the dog loose, and made mud pies in the tomato garden. By Sunday, I was convinced they were all (. . . *active*) (8)_____. In addition, all weekend I was assailed° with endless questions: "Why can't I stay up late?" "Do I have to brush my teeth?" "What do ants eat?"

Besides all the activity and questions, I had to cope with the knowledge that four little ones were entirely (*de* . . . *ent*) (9)_____ on me for their needs. What if one got hurt? What if they got sick? Fortunately, we survived without a disaster.

I can't imagine what it must be like for parents with two or more children. I guess I'm not ready to have kids yet—not even one. At least my responsibilities were terminated° on Sunday night. But (*parent* . . .) (10)_____ is for keeps. I think I'll wait.

Scores	Sentence Check 2 _____%	Final Check _____%

Enter your scores above and in the **Vocabulary Performance Chart** on the inside back cover of the book.

The box at the right lists twenty-five words from Unit One. Using the clues at the bottom of the page, fill in these words to complete the puzzle that follows.

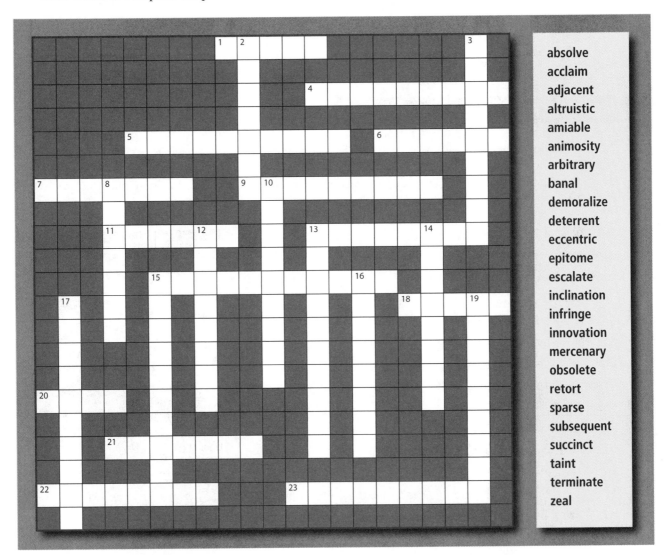

absolve
acclaim
adjacent
altruistic
amiable
animosity
arbitrary
banal
demoralize
deterrent
eccentric
epitome
escalate
inclination
infringe
innovation
mercenary
obsolete
retort
sparse
subsequent
succinct
taint
terminate
zeal

ACROSS

1. To stain the honor of someone or something

4. To stop; bring to an end

5. To lower the spirits of

6. To reply, especially in a quick, sharp, or witty way

7. Friendly and pleasant

9. Motivated only by financial gain; greedy

11. Distributed thinly

13. Close; near (to something)

15. A tendency to think, act, or behave in a certain way

18. Lacking originality; overused

20. Enthusiastic devotion; intense enthusiasm

21. A perfect or typical example

22. To intrude or trespass on; to go beyond proper limits

23. Determined by personal judgment; based on impulse

DOWN

2. Great praise or applause; enthusiastic approval

3. Something that prevents or discourages a certain action

8. To find innocent or blameless

10. Differing from what is customary; odd

12. Expressed clearly in a few words

13. Unselfishly concerned for the welfare of others; unselfish

14. To increase or intensify

15. A new custom, method, or invention; something newly introduced

16. No longer active or in use; out-of-date

17. Following in time or order; next; later; succeeding

19. Bitter hostility

PART A

Choose the word that best completes each item and write it in the space provided.

_____ 1. In the winter, the price of tomatoes ___ while their quality goes down.

    A. elicits   B. appeases   C. escalates   D. absolves

_____ 2. A common ___ for *corpse* is "remains."

    A. syndrome   B. dilemma   C. euphemism   D. zeal

_____ 3. The taxi driver was so ___ that he charged his own mother for a ride.

    A. mercenary   B. amiable   C. curt   D. wary

_____ 4. Do you consider it an ___ that only one percent of Americans own 40 percent of the nation's wealth?

    A. allusion   B. inclination   C. inequity   D. acclaim

_____ 5. You probably thought that mail delivery by mule was ___, but it still exists in the Grand Canyon.

    A. adamant   B. curt   C. tangible   D. obsolete

_____ 6. You can make your essays ___ by going through them carefully to remove all unnecessary words.

    A. succinct   B. adamant   C. tangible   D. eccentric

_____ 7. New York's firefighters and police were the ___ of courage during the attack on the World Trade Center on September 11, 2001. Many of them lost their lives while attempting to save others.

    A. encounter   B. epitome   C. animosity   D. innovation

_____ 8. As a(n) ___ to stealing, a chain of restaurants requires its employees to wear uniforms without pockets.

    A. deterrent   B. acclaim   C. innovation   D. inference

_____ 9. The suspect realized that if she wanted to be ___ of the charges, she'd better hire a detective to find the real murderer.

    A. assailed   B. demoralized   C. tainted   D. absolved

_____ 10. You might have a stronger ___ to work for high grades if you were a student in a special program in the Cleveland public high schools, where each A earns forty dollars toward college tuition.

    A. animosity   B. infirmity   C. inclination   D. syndrome

(Continues on next page)

PART B

On the answer line, write the letter of the choice that best completes each item.

_____ 11. You would have an **encounter** with an old friend from grade school if you
    A. contacted him by e-mail.
    B. missed him.
    C. forgot about him.
    D. ran into him at the mall.

_____ 12. The office manager **maligned** her boss by saying,
    A. "He's not only stupid but also dishonest."
    B. "I wish I had a sports car like his."
    C. "He's the nicest boss I've ever had."
    D. "I think he could be a little more efficient."

_____ 13. Which of the following would be considered an **innovation** if it were put on the market today?
    A. An electric blanket
    B. A fax machine
    C. An automobile that drives itself
    D. A hand plow

_____ 14. Our English teacher says spring fever is a **syndrome** that includes
    A. March through June.
    B. beautiful daffodils.
    C. an urge to stare sleepily out the window.
    D. allergy pills.

_____ 15. "You have **tainted** the name of our family forever," Ellen's father told her, "and you should be
    A. proud."
    B. ashamed."
    C. amused."
    D. thanked."

_____ 16. The nurse **exploited** her elderly patient by
    A. giving him a bath and changing his sheets.
    B. reading aloud to him every day.
    C. complaining to her husband about him.
    D. tricking him into giving his fortune to her.

_____ 17. A **curt** response when someone asked you to dance would be
    A. "No way."
    B. "That'd be great. Thanks."
    C. "I'd really like to, but I've already been asked by someone else."
    D. "I wouldn't dance with you if we were the last two human beings left alive on Earth."

_____ 18. When the Lees moved to a new neighborhood, they were faced with an unfortunate **dilemma**:
    A. They discovered that a large family of squirrels was living in the attic of their new home.
    B. They had to choose between a terrible public school or a private one that was very expensive.
    C. They had friendly neighbors on one side and rude ones on the other.
    D. There was enough sun in their back yard for good-sized vegetable and flower gardens.

_____ 19. When we put out a can of tuna for the stray cat in our yard, the **wary** animal
    A. gobbled it down as though it were starving.
    B. sniffed it suspiciously and took a long time before deciding to eat it.
    C. didn't seem hungry.
    D. ate it and promptly fell asleep.

_____ 20. When the teacher smiled at the class and said, "If I were you, I'd study Chapter 2 tonight," the **implication** was that
    A. most of the students had already studied that chapter.
    B. most of the class members were poor students.
    C. the teacher would test the class on that chapter the next day.
    D. the chapter was not very interesting.

Score   (Number correct) _____ x 5 = _____%

Enter your score above and in the **Vocabulary Performance Chart** on the inside back cover of the book.

PART A

Complete each item with a word from the box. Use each word once.

A. acclaim	B. adamant	C. allusion	D. antagonist	E. appease
F. demoralize	G. elicit	H. infringe	I. retort	J. revitalize
K. sabotage	L. sparse	M. zeal		

_____ 1. An unhappy employee ___(e)d the company's assembly line by spilling coffee on a gear box.

_____ 2. Do you think that supermarket tabloids ___ on celebrities' privacy?

_____ 3. The ___s in the debate took opposing sides on the question of outlawing cigarettes.

_____ 4. Today's children develop a ___ for electronic devices early. Even two-year-olds spend several hours a day in front of a TV or computer screen.

_____ 5. Apparently, the chance to be President of the United States doesn't ___ much enthusiasm from most Americans—89 percent say they wouldn't want the job.

_____ 6. A "perm" involves the contradictory steps of burning hair to a lifeless state and then smearing on conditioners to ___ it.

_____ 7. Although Marilyn Monroe received great ___ from adoring fans and critics, she never received an Academy Award.

_____ 8. Our congressional representative, ___ in her opposition to pesticides, often reminds voters that pesticides kill about fourteen thousand people each year.

_____ 9. When a woman told Winston Churchill, "If you were my husband, I'd put poison in your tea," he ___(e)d, "If I were your husband, I'd drink it."

_____ 10. Although failure ___s some people, it encourages others to try harder.

_____ 11. The plants look ___ now, but within a year or two they'll multiply and fill in the empty spaces.

_____ 12. "Gina isn't the only athlete in the family," Clarence said, making a(n) ___ to Gina's father, a bowling champion.

_____ 13. When Kathleen stood Evan up for the prom, an apology did not ___ him. He's suing her for the cost of his rented tux and the prom tickets.

(Continues on next page)

PART B

Write **C** if the italicized word is used **correctly**. Write **I** if the word is used **incorrectly**.

_____ 14. Ants have the *infirmity* of being able to survive under water for up to two weeks.

_____ 15. When the evidence in a case is unclear, a jury's decision may be *arbitrary*, based on only the jurors' "gut feeling."

_____ 16. Movie reviews are never *subjective*—they represent the personal opinions of critics.

_____ 17. If you worry about the environment, you're *eccentric*. According to a recent poll, over three-fourths of Americans are concerned about the environment.

_____ 18. Phyllis is very *methodical* in her efforts to be the life of any party. She keeps a file box of jokes, indexed by occasion.

_____ 19. A wedding ring is a *tangible* expression of a couple's commitment to each other.

PART C

On the answer line, write the letter of the word that is the **synonym** of the boldfaced word.

Example: __A__ **irate**   A. angry   B. calm   C. well-informed

_____ 20. **terminate**   A. begin   B. end   C. grow

_____ 21. **amoral**   A. ethical   B. costly   C. unprincipled

_____ 22. **amiable**   A. friendly   B. natural   C. unfriendly

PART D

On the answer line, write the letter of the word that is the **antonym** of the boldfaced word.

Example: __B__ **irate**   A. angry   B. calm   C. well-informed

_____ 23. **assail**   A. flow   B. attack   C. defend

_____ 24. **subsequent**   A. previous   B. hidden   C. following

_____ 25. **animosity**   A. liveliness   B. hatred   C. sympathy

Score   (Number correct) _____ x 4 = _____%

Enter your score above and in the **Vocabulary Performance Chart** on the inside back cover of the book.

Each item below starts with a pair of words in CAPITAL LETTERS. For each item, figure out the relationship between these two words. Then decide which of the choices (A, B, C, or D) expresses a similar relationship. Write the letter of your choice on the answer line.

_____ 1. ABSOLVE : BLAME ::
    A. reduce : enlarge   C. trial : verdict
    B. blame : punish   D. wish : desire

_____ 2. AMORAL : CRIMINAL ::
    A. pastor : church   C. uneducated : professor
    B. murderer : victim   D. brave : explorer

_____ 3. ANTAGONIST : TEAMMATE ::
    A. coworker : relative   C. scholar : athlete
    B. opponent : supporter   D. teammate : coach

_____ 4. DILEMMA : SOLUTION ::
    A. puzzle : piece   C. breakdown : repair
    B. confusion : bewilderment   D. size : color

_____ 5. SABOTAGE : TERRORIST ::
    A. entertain : magician   C. terrorize : frighten
    B. destroy : carpenter   D. magic : illusion

_____ 6. WARY : CAUTIOUS ::
    A. jealous : envious   C. jealous : rival
    B. excessive : minimal   D. minimize : exaggerate

_____ 7. IRATE : FRIENDLY ::
    A. peaceful : calming   C. sweet : sour
    B. plentiful : abundant   D. warrior : weapon

_____ 8. ACCLAIM : CRITIC ::
    A. test : question   C. loyalty : dog
    B. statement : silence   D. symptom : disease

_____ 9. ADJACENT : NEARBY ::
    A. neighboring : distant   C. optimistic : cheerful
    B. familiar : strange   D. optimist : whiner

_____ 10. ENGROSS : FASCINATING ::
    A. popular : well-known   C. boring : thrilling
    B. common : rare   D. bore : monotonous

(Continues on next page)

_____ 11. INFIRMITY : STRENGTH ::
       A. joy : unhappiness   C. sadness : depression
       B. disappointment : emotion   D. depression : suicide

_____ 12. METHODICAL : ORGANIZED ::
       A. careful : sloppy   C. simple : elaborate
       B. careful : orderly   D. insult : anger

_____ 13. OBSOLETE : MODEL T ::
       A. well-known : Disney World   C. spotlight : flashlight
       B. old-fashioned : modern   D. nutritious : chewing gum

_____ 14. TANGIBLE : DREAMS ::
       A. weather : snowy   C. frequent : often
       B. probable : likely   D. intentional : accident

_____ 15. TERMINATE : EMPLOYMENT ::
       A. chimney : house   C. remember : forget
       B. begin : commence   D. quit : school

_____ 16. ESCALATE : INTENSIFY ::
       A. labor : work   C. enlarge : preserve
       B. compliment : insult   D. increase : adjust

_____ 17. SPARSE : THICK ::
       A. acorn : oak tree   C. confusing : clear
       B. recent : modern   D. amusing : intelligent

_____ 18. SUCCINCT : WORDY ::
       A. talkative : chatty   C. alarming : frightening
       B. brief : hurried   D. welcome : unwanted

_____ 19. ALTRUISTIC : UNSELFISH ::
       A. saint : holy   C. generous : stingy
       B. artist : painting   D. wealthy : rich

_____ 20. BANAL : UNORIGINAL ::
       A. surprising : unexpected   C. copied : original
       B. pleasant : distasteful   D. match : fire

Score   (Number correct) _____ x 5 = _____%

Enter your score above and in the **Vocabulary Performance Chart** on the inside back cover of the book.

PART A

Listed in the left-hand column below are ten common word parts, followed by words in which the parts are used. In each blank, write in the letter of the correct definition on the right.

Word Parts	Examples	Definitions
____ 1. **ann, enn**	annual, bicentennial	A. In a certain manner
____ 2. **audi, audio-**	audible, auditorium	B. Feeling, suffering
____ 3. **cycl, cyclo-**	motorcycle, cyclone	C. Circle
____ 4. **-hood**	adulthood, womanhood	D. To hang
____ 5. **hyper-**	hypersensitive, hypertext	E. Year
____ 6. **-ly**	easily, proudly	F. Four, fourth
____ 7. **non-**	nontoxic, nonfiction	G. State, condition
____ 8. **path, -pathy**	empathic, telepathy	H. Not; the opposite of
____ 9. **pend**	suspend, pendulum	I. Hearing, sound
____ 10. **quart, quadr-**	quarter, quadruple	J. More than normal; overly

PART B

Using the answer line provided, complete each *italicized* word in the sentences below with the correct word part from the box. Not every word part will be used.

A. **ann**	B. **audi-**	C. **cycl-**	D. **-hood**	E. **hyper-**
F. **-ly**	G. **non-**	H. **-pathy**	I. **pend**	J. **quadr-**

_____ 11. Mickey Mouse had no (*boy . . .*) ___ —he was "born" as an adult.

_____ 12. I enjoy riding an exercise bike because I don't have to (*. . . e*) ___ uphill.

_____ 13. My dog didn't know why I was crying, but I could tell that she felt (*sym . . .*) ___ for me—she began to whine softly.

_____ 14. The spider, (*sus . . . ed*) ___ from the ceiling on its own silken thread, dangled above a bowl of popcorn.

_____ 15. Children's rhymes include such (*. . . sense*) ___ words as "Hickory, dickory, dock."

(Continues on next page)

PART C

Use your knowledge of word parts to determine the meaning of the **boldfaced** words. On the answer line, write the letter of each meaning.

_____ 16. Ned **secretly** slipped a note under Anna's plate.

      A. in a secret manner   B. at a secret time   C. without being secret

_____ 17. Should I buy a **quart** or a gallon of chocolate milk?

      A. a third of a gallon   B. a fourth of a gallon   C. a half gallon

_____ 18. The public library's **biennial** hobby show will take place next month.

      A. happening every two weeks   B. happening every two months   C. happening every two years

_____ 19. My mother was troubled by **hyperthyroidism**.

      A. too little activity   B. too much activity   C. a missing thyroid gland
of the thyroid gland   of the thyroid gland

_____ 20. There's a problem at the television station. Only the **audio** portion of the show is coming through.

      A. sound   B. picture   C. top

Score   (Number correct) _____ x 5 = _____%

Unit Two

calamity	persevere
comprehensive	ponder
conventional	rehabilitate
flagrant	turmoil
fluctuate	venture

Ten Words in Context

In the space provided, write the letter of the meaning closest to that of each **boldfaced** word. Use the context of the sentences to help you figure out each word's meaning.

1 calamity
(kə-lăm′ĭ-tē)
-noun

● The survivors of the earthquake slowly rebuilt their homes and lives after the **calamity**.

● Our neighbor's house burned down one night in May. Ever since that **calamity**, some of the children on our street have been afraid to go to bed at night.

___ *Calamity* means   A. an activity.   B. a tragedy.   C. a risk.

2 comprehensive
(kŏm′prē-hĕn′sĭv)
-adjective

● That article on sightseeing in Charleston was not **comprehensive**. It failed to mention many points of interest in that wonderful city.

● The company's **comprehensive** insurance plan covers most health services, including hospitals, doctors, and dentists.

___ *Comprehensive* means   A. complete.   B. familiar.   C. continuous.

3 conventional
(kən-věn′shə-nəl)
-adjective

● Two **conventional** Valentine's Day gifts are roses and chocolates.

● Jorge wanted to propose to Ramona in the **conventional** manner, so in the middle of a restaurant, he got down on one knee and asked, "Will you marry me?"

___ *Conventional* means   A. out-of-the-way.   B. useful.   C. usual.

4 flagrant
(flā′grənt)
-adjective

● The use of campaign funds for the congressman's private business was a **flagrant** violation of the law.

● In **flagrant** disregard of his parents' stated wishes, Art wore a T-shirt and jeans to their dinner party.

___ *Flagrant* means   A. obvious.   B. acceptable.   C. minor.

5 fluctuate
(flŭk′chōo-āt′)
-verb

● My weight used to **fluctuate** between 150 and 190 pounds. Now it's steady, at 170 pounds.

● Desert temperatures can **fluctuate** by as much as fifty degrees between daytime and nighttime.

___ *Fluctuate* means   A. to continue.   B. to vary.   C. to follow.

6 persevere
(pûr′sə-vîr′)
-verb

● "I know you're tired," Jack said, "but we've got to **persevere** and get to the camp before the storm hits."

● It was not easy to attend English classes while working at two jobs, but Nina **persevered** until she could speak English well.

___ *Persevere* means   A. to surrender.   B. to hold back.   C. to keep going.

7 ponder
(pŏn′dər)
-verb

- Too often we don't take time to **ponder** the possible consequences of our actions.
- Over the years, Mr. Madigan rarely took time to **ponder** the meaning of life. Since his heart attack, however, he's thought a lot about what is important to him.

___ *Ponder* means   A. to wait for.   B. to ignore.   C. to think about.

8 rehabilitate
(rē′hə-bĭl′ə-tāt)
-verb

- Most prisons make little effort to **rehabilitate** inmates so that they can lead productive, wholesome lives after their release.
- My grandfather learned to walk, write, and speak again in a program that **rehabilitates** stroke victims.

___ *Rehabilitate* means   A. to pay back.   B. to return to normal life.   C. to depend upon.

9 turmoil
(tûr′moil)
-noun

- Without a teacher, the sixth-grade class was in **turmoil**, until the principal entered the room and the students quickly came to order.
- After the **turmoil** of crying babies, active children, and trying to feed 120 people, I'm glad when our family reunions end.

___ *Turmoil* means   A. discussion.   B. disorder.   C. harmony.

10 venture
(vĕn′chər)
-verb

- "I'll **venture** going on any ride in this amusement park except the Twister," said Nick. "I'll risk getting sick to my stomach, but I won't risk my life."
- "At tomorrow's staff meeting," my older sister said, "I will **venture** to say what I really think—and cross my fingers that I don't get fired."

___ *Venture* means   A. to dare.   B. to remember.   C. to imagine.

Matching Words with Definitions

Following are definitions of the ten words. Clearly write or print each word next to its definition. The sentences above and on the previous page will help you decide on the meaning of each word.

1. _____ Shockingly obvious; outrageous

2. _____ To take the risk of; dare

3. _____ Including all or much

4. _____ To restore to a normal life through therapy or education

5. _____ To continue with an effort or plan despite difficulties

6. _____ Complete confusion; uproar

7. _____ An event bringing great loss and misery

8. _____ To vary irregularly; to go up and down or back and forth

9. _____ To consider carefully; think deeply about

10. _____ Customary; ordinary

CAUTION: Do not go any further until you are sure the above answers are correct. Then you can use the definitions to help you in the following practices. Your goal is eventually to know the words well enough so that you don't need to check the definitions at all.

Sentence Check 1

Using the answer line provided, complete each item below with the correct word from the box. Use each word once.

A. calamity	B. comprehensive	C. conventional	D. flagrant	E. fluctuate
F. persevere	G. ponder	H. rehabilitate	I. turmoil	J. venture

_____ 1. Tracy is so vain that she considers it a ___ if a pimple appears anywhere on her face.

_____ 2. Too many people have a child without taking time to ___ parenthood. They give less thought to having a baby than to buying a sofa.

_____ 3. When Charlene lost her job because she spoke up for a fellow employee, it was a ___ violation of her rights.

_____ 4. Our history exam will be ___; it will cover everything we've studied since September.

_____ 5. Nobody in Doug's family has a ___ job. His mother is a drummer, his father is a magician, and his uncle is a wine taster.

_____ 6. Learning the new software program was difficult, but when Maria saw how useful it would be in her work, she was glad she had ___(e)d.

_____ 7. It took many months of therapy to ___ my aunt after she lost her sight, but now she can get around her home and neighborhood on her own.

_____ 8. The day we moved, the apartment was in ___. Boxes and people were everywhere, and the baby wouldn't stop crying.

_____ 9. The way my dog's appetite ___(e)d this week worries me. One day she hardly ate anything, and the next day she gulped down everything I gave her.

_____ 10. Instead of hiring a lawyer, the defendant will ___ to plead her own case in court.

NOTE: Now check your answers to these items by turning to page 177. Going over the answers carefully will help you prepare for the next two practices, for which answers are not given.

Sentence Check 2

Using the answer lines provided, complete each item below with **two** words from the box. Use each word once.

_____
_____ 1–2. The one time my cousin ___(e)d skydiving, the result was a ___. Her parachute didn't open, and she was injured so badly in the fall that she almost died.

_____
_____ 3–4. A drug-treatment center can ___ most addicts. Among the failures are addicts who don't ___ with the treatment and leave the center early.

_____
_____ 5–6. When he drives alone, Marshall's behavior is very ___; he obeys all the traffic rules. But when his friends are with him, he shows off with ___ violations of the speed limit.

_____ 7–8. "We need to ___ all we might do to help families in trouble," said the social
_____ worker to her staff. "We must plan a ___ program, not just a narrow plan
dealing with only one part of their lives."

_____ 9–10. The boss's moods and orders ___ so wildly at times that they throw the
_____ department into ___. As a result, productivity is at an all-time low, and it will
take a new boss to revitalize° this office.

Final Check: *Accident and Recovery*

Here is a final opportunity for you to strengthen your knowledge of the ten words. First read the following selection carefully. Then fill in each blank with a word from the box at the top of the previous page. (Context clues will help you figure out which word goes in which blank.) Use each word once.

We tried to stop Anna from jumping, but her (1)_____ disregard of our warnings led to a (2)_____ that would change her life forever. She dove off a rock into a river none of us was sure was deep enough. When she hit the bottom, she broke her back.

I visited Anna at the hospital every day for the next few weeks. I saw her mood (3)_____ between anger and quiet depression. Her whole life seemed in (4)_____; she was too confused and demoralized° to think reasonably about her future.

Within about a month, however, I began to see a change in Anna. She had moved to Henner House to participate in a very (5)_____ program, designed to meet all the needs of patients like Anna. The program (6)_____s accident victims so that they can subsequently° return to fulfilling lives. Anna gained hope once she saw she could learn to do such everyday tasks as cooking, cleaning, and bathing. After learning how to get around indoors, she (7)_____(e)d traveling around the city in her wheelchair. The more she did, the better she felt. The staff also helped Anna plan for her future. They urged her to (8)_____ her goals and how she might meet them. At times, it was difficult for her to (9)_____ with the program, but she didn't quit.

Now, ten months later, Anna is able to live a somewhat (10)_____ life. Her infirmity° is not a deterrent°; she is able to do many of the ordinary things she used to do—work, drive, and live in an apartment with a friend. Yes, her life has changed forever. But Anna is once again glad to be alive.

| Scores | Sentence Check 2 _____ % | Final Check _____ % |

Enter your scores above and in the **Vocabulary Performance Chart** on the inside back cover of the book.

attest	enigma
attribute	exemplify
discern	mobile
dispatch	nocturnal
enhance	orient

Ten Words in Context

In the space provided, write the letter of the meaning closest to that of each **boldfaced** word. Use the context of the sentences to help you figure out each word's meaning.

1 attest
(ə-tĕst′)
-verb

- Anyone who has seen the Golden Gate Bridge in the rose-gold light of sunset can **attest** to its beauty.
- Witnesses **attest** to the fact that rainfall makes the ground of Death Valley so slippery that boulders slide across it.

___ *Attest to* means A. to declare to be true.   B. to wish for.   C. to forget easily.

2 attribute
(ăt′rə-byōot′)
-noun

- A three-hundred-page novel written in 1939 has the odd **attribute** of containing no *e*, the most common letter in English.
- Some cars have computerized **attributes** such as windshield wipers that automatically turn on when it rains.

___ *Attribute* means A. a tendency.   B. a defect.   C. a characteristic.

3 discern
(dĭ-sûrn′)
-verb

- An experienced jeweler can easily **discern** whether a diamond is genuine or fake.
- People who are red-green colorblind can **discern** the colors of traffic lights by recognizing shades of gray.

___ *Discern* means A. to see clearly.   B. to disregard.   C. to change.

4 dispatch
(dĭ-spăch′)
-verb

- I wanted to **dispatch** the letter as quickly as possible, so I took it to the post office instead of dropping it into a mailbox.
- At work Harold is treated like an errand boy. His boss often **dispatches** him to the deli for sandwiches or donuts.

___ *Dispatch* means A. to represent.   B. to send.   C. to drive.

5 enhance
(ĕn-hăns′)
-verb

- Our gym teacher **enhanced** her appearance with a more attractive hairstyle.
- The college catalogue stated that the writing course would "**enhance** all students' writing skills" by improving their grammar and style.

___ *Enhance* means A. to make better.   B. to recognize.   C. to reduce.

6 enigma
(ĭ-nĭg′mə)
-noun

- How the thief entered our house was an **enigma** until we remembered that the cellar door had been left unlocked.
- The "singing sands" of Scotland remained an **enigma** until scientists learned that footsteps caused the round grains of sand and the surrounding air pockets to make musical vibrations.

___ *Enigma* means A. a comfort.   B. a puzzle.   C. an error.

7 exemplify
(ĭg-zĕm′plə-fī′)
-verb

● The many IRS employees who give citizens inaccurate information **exemplify** governmental incompetence.

● Mr. Ramirez, who emphasizes original thinking and freedom of expression, **exemplifies** the best in teaching.

___ *Exemplify* means   A. to illustrate.   B. to save.   C. to oppose.

8 mobile
(mō′bəl)
-adjective

● My parents own a **mobile** home, which can be moved from place to place.

● Every morning when I was in the hospital, a volunteer wheeled a **mobile** library into my room.

___ *Mobile* means   A. active.   B. expensive.   C. movable.

9 nocturnal
(nŏk-tûr′nəl)
-adjective

● I know when my brother has enjoyed one of his **nocturnal** feasts because I find a stack of dishes in the sink in the morning.

● Since owls are **nocturnal**, they are rarely seen during the day.

___ *Nocturnal* means   A. noisy.   B. busy.   C. of the night.

10 orient
(ôr′ē-ĕnt)
-verb

● When coming up from the subway, I often need to look at a street sign to **orient** myself.

● Certain cars let drivers **orient** themselves in unfamiliar places with the help of an electronic map that shows the car's location.

___ *Orient* means   A. to locate.   B. to welcome.   C. to question.

Matching Words with Definitions

Following are definitions of the ten words. Clearly write or print each word next to its definition. The sentences above and on the previous page will help you decide on the meaning of each word.

1. _____ A mystery or puzzle

2. _____ To send to a specific place or on specific business

3. _____ Of, about, or happening in the night; active at night

4. _____ To make a statement about something on the basis of personal experience; bear witness; testify

5. _____ To determine one's location or direction; to locate in relation to a direction (east, west, etc.)

6. _____ To recognize; detect

7. _____ To improve; add to the strength, beauty, or value of something

8. _____ Moving or able to move from place to place

9. _____ A quality or feature of a person or thing

10. _____ To be an example of; represent; be typical of

CAUTION: Do not go any further until you are sure the above answers are correct. Then you can use the definitions to help you in the following practices. Your goal is eventually to know the words well enough so that you don't need to check the definitions at all.

Sentence Check 1

Using the answer line provided, complete each item below with the correct word from the box. Use each word once.

A. **attest**	B. **attribute**	C. **discern**	D. **dispatch**	E. **enhance**
F. **enigma**	G. **exemplify**	H. **mobile**	I. **nocturnal**	J. **orient**

_____ 1. Fresh garlic may not ___ the breath, but it certainly improves spaghetti sauce.

_____ 2. A witness ___(e)d to the truth of the defendant's claim that she had loved the murdered man.

_____ 3. When I was younger, my mother used to ___ me to the store for milk or some missing cooking ingredient as often as twice a day.

_____ 4. The lives of such reformers as Susan B. Anthony, Mahatma Gandhi, and Martin Luther King ___ greatness.

_____ 5. Science does not have enough evidence to solve the ___ of whether or not there is other intelligent life in the universe.

_____ 6. The convicts decided on a(n) ___ escape. The darkness would hide them as they fled through the forest.

_____ 7. Sue's hairpiece is so natural-looking that it's impossible to ___ where the hairpiece ends and her own hair begins.

_____ 8. The positions of the stars help sailors ___ themselves on the open seas.

_____ 9. My mother is unable to walk, but with her wheelchair she is ___ enough to get around her apartment, move along a sidewalk, and even shop at a mall.

_____ 10. Giant kelp, a form of seaweed, has some amazing ___s. Not only is it the world's fastest-growing vegetable, but the more it is cut, the faster it grows.

NOTE: Now check your answers to these items by turning to page 177. Going over the answers carefully will help you prepare for the next two practices, for which answers are not given.

Sentence Check 2

Using the answer lines provided, complete each item below with **two** words from the box. Use each word once.

_____
_____ 1–2. Because Helen Keller could not hear or see, the keenness of her other senses was ___(e)d by use. It is said that she could ___ who was in a room simply by using her sense of smell.

_____
_____ 3–4. A ___ robot that collects and delivers mail throughout the office building ___s itself with electric eyes.

_____
_____ 5–6. In fables, animals often illustrate human ___s. In the story of the race between the tortoise and the hare, the tortoise is meant to ___ the human qualities of being slow but steady. Despite competing against a much speedier antagonist°, he perseveres° and defeats the overly confident hare.

_____   7–8. The reason the boss likes to ___ Oliver on lengthy errands is no ___.
_____   Everyone knows that the office functions better with Oliver out of the way.

_____   9–10. Anyone who has ever gone to college can ___ to the fact that during final
_____   exams, many students become ___ animals. They study all night before an
                                 exam and then, once the test is over, sleep the rest of the day.

Final Check: *Animal Senses*

Here is a final opportunity for you to strengthen your knowledge of the ten words. First read the following
selection carefully. Then fill in each blank with a word from the box at the top of the previous page.
(Context clues will help you figure out which word goes in which blank.) Use each word once.

Animals possess sensory powers that humans lack.
Homing pigeons fly with great speed and accuracy when
(1)_____(e)d with messages to faraway
places. How do pigeons (2)_____
themselves in unfamiliar regions? This remains something of
a(n) (3)_____. The mystery, however, is
partly explained by a pigeon's ability to see ultraviolet light,
which reveals the sun's position even through clouds. In
addition, pigeons can hear sound waves that have traveled
hundreds of miles. These waves (4)_____
a pigeon's sense of direction by indicating distant mountains
and seas. Pigeons even appear to (5)_____ changes in the earth's magnetic field.

Bats have impressive (6)_____s equally worthy of acclaim°. As
(7)_____ animals, they search for food in complete darkness. They do so by screeching
in tones higher than any human can hear and then locating prey by the returning echoes.

Scorpions also (8)_____ the night hunter. Tiny leg hairs enable them to feel
vibrations in the sand made by a (9)_____ insect as far as two feet away.

People with knowledge of the pigeon, bat, and scorpion can (10)_____ to the
fact that such "innovations"° as the magnetic compass, radar, and the motion detector are nothing new.

Scores	Sentence Check 2 _____%	Final Check _____%

Enter your scores above and in the **Vocabulary Performance Chart** on the inside back cover of the book.

concurrent	hypothetical
confiscate	nominal
constitute	predominant
decipher	prerequisite
default	recession

Ten Words in Context

In the space provided, write the letter of the meaning closest to that of each **boldfaced** word. Use the context of the sentences to help you figure out each word's meaning.

1 concurrent
(kən-kûr′ənt)
-*adjective*

● Having mistakenly registered for two **concurrent** classes, Joe had to drop one of them and choose a course that met at a different time.

● **Concurrent** with the closing of the steel mill was the opening of a new toy factory in town. As a result, most of the workers laid off from the mill found jobs at the new factory.

___ *Concurrent* means   A. occurring at the same time.   B. resulting.   C. noticeable.

2 confiscate
(kŏn′fĭs-kāt′)
-*verb*

● "Hand 'em over," my father said. Just as we were really starting to have fun, he **confiscated** our entire supply of water balloons.

● Chinese drug agents once **confiscated** $2 million worth of heroin that had been wrapped in plastic and inserted into live goldfish. The agents seized the drugs as they were being sent out of the country.

___ *Confiscate* means   A. to distribute widely.   B. to take possession of.   C. to overlook.

3 constitute
(kŏn′stĭ-to͞ot)
-*verb*

● In my opinion, a good movie, a pizza, and animated conversation **constitute** a perfect night out.

● Twelve business and professional people **constitute** the board of directors of the women's shelter. Among other things, they help raise funds for the shelter.

___ *Constitute* means   A. to repeat.   B. to oppose.   C. to form.

4 decipher
(dĭ-sī′fər)
-*verb*

● Why do contracts have to use language that's so difficult to **decipher**?

● If your teacher can't **decipher** your handwriting, you'll need to write your papers on a computer.

___ *Decipher* means   A. to figure out.   B. to find.   C. to improve.

5 default
(dĭ-fôlt′)
-*verb*

● We won our case against the appliance repairman because he **defaulted** by failing to appear in court.

● Eli's mother said, "I'll co-sign on your car loan, but you have to make every payment. If you **default**, it will hurt my credit rating."

___ *Default* means   A. to act as expected.   B. not to do something required.   C. to begin.

6 hypothetical
(hī′pō-thĕt′ĭ-kəl)
-*adjective*

● Imagine the **hypothetical** situation of going to live alone on an island. Which books and CDs would you take along?

● Law schools hold pretend court sessions with **hypothetical** cases so that students can practice their skills.

___ *Hypothetical* means   A. sure to happen.   B. dangerous.   C. imaginary.

7 nominal
(nŏm′ə-nəl)
-adjective

● Except for a **nominal** registration fee, the camp for needy children is entirely free.

● Professor Banks gave us only **nominal** extra credit for participating in psychology experiments. She wanted our course grade to be based mainly on our test scores.

__ *Nominal* means   A. enormous.   B. very little.   C. helpful.

8 predominant
(prĭ-dŏm′ə-nənt)
-adjective

● Rock is the **predominant** music on that radio station, but country music is also played.

● Although the **predominant** type of car in New York City in 1900 used gasoline, a third of the cars ran on electricity.

__ *Predominant* means   A. rare.   B. main.   C. temporary.

9 prerequisite
(prē-rĕk′wĭ-zĭt)
-noun

● You can't take Spanish Literature I unless you've taken the **prerequisite**, Spanish III.

● Since she was allergic to cigarette smoke, Kaylin told Troy that his quitting smoking was a **prerequisite** for their marrying.

__ *Prerequisite* means   A. a requirement.   B. a penalty.   C. a method.

10 recession
(rĭ-sĕsh′ən)
-noun

● While seashore businesses in the North suffer a **recession** in the winter, they do very well from spring to fall.

● The department store laid off twenty workers during the **recession**, but it rehired them when business improved.

__ *Recession* means   A. a rapid growth.   B. a sale.   C. an economic setback.

Matching Words with Definitions

Following are definitions of the ten words. Clearly write or print each word next to its definition. The sentences above and on the previous page will help you decide on the meaning of each word.

1. _____ To make up; be the parts of

2. _____ To fail to do something required

3. _____ Most common or most noticeable

4. _____ Something required beforehand

5. _____ To seize with authority; legally take possession of

6. _____ To interpret or read (something confusing or hard to make out)

7. _____ Slight; very small compared with what might be expected

8. _____ Happening or existing at the same time; simultaneous

9. _____ A temporary decline in business

10. _____ Supposed for the sake of argument or examination; imaginary; theoretical

CAUTION: Do not go any further until you are sure the above answers are correct. Then you can use the definitions to help you in the following practices. Your goal is eventually to know the words well enough so that you don't need to check the definitions at all.

Sentence Check 1

Using the answer line provided, complete each item below with the correct word from the box. Use each word once.

A. **concurrent**	B. **confiscate**	C. **constitute**	D. **decipher**	E. **default**
F. **hypothetical**	G. **nominal**	H. **predominant**	I. **prerequisite**	J. **recession**

_____ 1. Anger was the ___ emotion among voters when they first heard that their taxes would be raised again.

_____ 2. Although the two robberies were ___—both occurred at midnight on Friday—one man had planned them both.

_____ 3. One hundred senators and 435 members of the House of Representatives ___ the United States Congress.

_____ 4. A ___ for taking the driver's road test is passing a written test on the state's driving laws.

_____ 5. The town library charges only a ___ fine for late books but a higher fine for late DVDs.

_____ 6. Karim has such terrible handwriting that his wife couldn't ___ his message saying she should meet him at the restaurant.

_____ 7. When the shoe factory closed, our little town went into a ___ because the laid-off workers had no money to spend at local businesses.

_____ 8. The phone company refused to install a phone in Glen's new apartment because he had ___(e)d on several of his previous bills.

_____ 9. After Justine borrowed the family car without permission for the third time, her parents ___(ed) her driver's license.

_____ 10. To teach young children safety, many parents explain what to do in ___ situations, such as if a stranger asks them to go for a ride.

NOTE: Now check your answers to these items by turning to page 178. Going over the answers carefully will help you prepare for the next two practices, for which answers are not given.

Sentence Check 2

Using the answer lines provided, complete each item below with **two** words from the box. Use each word once.

_____
_____ 1–2. This summer, local children can sign up for art or music lessons for a ___ fee of $3. They can't take both, though, since the classes will be ___.

_____
_____ 3–4. Although cancer and heart disease ___ the leading threats to life in the United States, car accidents are the ___ cause of death for teenagers.

_____
_____ 5–6. "It seems as if a degree in accounting is a ___ for understanding our tax laws," said Ken. "How else could anyone ___ the tax codes?"

_____   7–8. The small print on the Bryants' mortgage stated that if they should ___ on
_____   payments, the bank had the right to ___ their house.

_____   9–10. When Ms. Howe was interviewed for the job of store manager, the regional
_____   manager asked her a question about a ___ situation. "Imagine that our
                                  business is in a ___," he said. "What would you do to enhance° sales?"

Final Check: *Money Problems*

Here is a final opportunity for you to strengthen your knowledge of the ten words. First read the following
selection carefully. Then fill in each blank with a word from the box at the top of the previous page.
(Context clues will help you figure out which word goes in which blank.) Use each word once.

My neighbor, Martha, ran into my house crying and angry.
"My car has been stolen!" she gasped. "I saw them take it!"

I called the police for her, and she told an officer the license
number and car model. "The (1)_____ color
of the car is brown," she added, "but it has a black roof. I had it
parked in the lot adjacent° to the beauty shop I own. I saw two
men tow it away."

"You saw them tow it away?" the officer asked. "Have you
(2)_____(e)d on your car loan?"

"What do you mean?" Martha asked.

"If you haven't been making your payments, the bank or
dealer has the right to (3)_____ the car."

Martha admitted that she hadn't made any payments for three months. Later she told me she'd
gotten notices in the mail but threw them away because their language was too complicated to
(4)_____. She also said she was having money problems. (5)_____
with the car loan was a big home-improvement loan. She also had five credit-card bills and regular living
expenses to pay. To top it all off, the city was suffering from a (6)_____, so her income
was down, something her laid-off employees could certainly attest° to. She was about $12,000 in debt.

At my suggestion, Martha visited a debt counselor, who helped her develop a comprehensive°
plan to pay her bills. The only (7)_____s for this free service were a regular
job and a willingness to pay one's debts in full. The counselor and Martha planned what would
(8)_____ a reasonable budget, based on Martha's income and expenses. They then
wrote to the companies she owed to arrange to pay a (9)_____ amount each month until
the whole debt was paid. They also discussed what she would do in several (10)_____
situations, such as if her refrigerator died or her income changed.

Now, Martha is getting back on her feet again—in more ways than one, since she never got the
car back.

Scores	Sentence Check 2 _____%	Final Check _____%

Enter your scores above and in the **Vocabulary Performance Chart** on the inside back cover of the book.

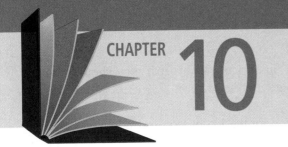

degenerate	sanctuary
implausible	scrutiny
incoherent	sinister
intercede	suffice
intricate	vulnerable

Ten Words in Context

In the space provided, write the letter of the meaning closest to that of each **boldfaced** word. Use the context of the sentences to help you figure out each word's meaning.

1 degenerate
(dĭ-jĕn′ər-āt′)
-*verb*

● Mr. Freedman's family was called to the nursing home when the old man's condition began to **degenerate**. It was feared he didn't have long to live.

● Mel's relationship with his parents **degenerated** when he dropped out of school against their wishes and became a bartender.

___ *Degenerate* means   A. to improve.   B. to remain the same.   C. to get worse.

2 implausible
(ĭm-plô′zə-bəl)
-*adjective*

● As **implausible** as it may sound, southern Florida sometimes does get snow.

● Insurance companies hear such **implausible** excuses for auto accidents as "I hit the telephone pole when I was blinded by the lights of a flying saucer."

___ *Implausible* means   A. unbelievable.   B. acceptable.   C. valuable.

3 incoherent
(ĭn′kō-hîr′ənt)
-*adjective*

● If Mitch doesn't get some sleep soon, he'll become completely **incoherent**. He's so tired that he's already having trouble expressing his thoughts clearly.

● My sister talks a lot in her sleep, but she's so **incoherent** then that we can never figure out what she's saying.

___ *Incoherent* means   A. calm.   B. unclear.   C. inconvenient.

4 intercede
(ĭn′tər-sēd′)
-*verb*

● When the principal said Harry couldn't play in Friday's football game, the coach **interceded**, hoping to change the principal's mind.

● Inez's parents refused to come to her wedding until her brother **interceded** and persuaded them to come after all.

___ *Intercede* means   A. to give in to someone.   B. to plead for someone.   C. to examine closely.

5 intricate
(ĭn′trĭ-kĭt)
-*adjective*

● *War and Peace* is a long, **intricate** novel that weaves together the detailed life stories of many individuals.

● It's amazing to see the **intricate** gold and silver jewelry that ancient Indians made with only simple tools. It obviously required great patience and skill to create such complex ornaments.

___ *Intricate* means   A. simple.   B. uninteresting.   C. complicated.

6 sanctuary
(săngk′chōō-ĕr′ē)
-*noun*

● Old, unused trains in Grand Central Station serve as a nighttime **sanctuary** for some of New York City's homeless.

● When the houseful of children becomes too noisy, Ned finds the laundry room to be a **sanctuary**, a place where he can read in quiet.

___ *Sanctuary* means   A. a reminder.   B. a shelter.   C. a challenge.

7 scrutiny
(skro̅o̅t′ən-ē)
-*noun*

● Store security guards give careful **scrutiny** to people carrying large bags, since the bags may be used for shoplifting.

● Before being published, a book comes under the **scrutiny** of a proofreader, who examines it for grammar and spelling errors.

__ *Scrutiny* means   A. attention.   B. protection.   C. permission.

8 sinister
(sĭn′ĭs-tər)
-*adjective*

● In the movie, a mad scientist thought up the **sinister** scheme of releasing a deadly virus. His evil plot failed when he died from the virus himself.

● The creepy novel *The Boys from Brazil* tells of a **sinister** plot to clone dozens of copies of Adolf Hitler who would then take over the world.

__ *Sinister* means   A. illogical.   B. evil.   C. inconsiderate.

9 suffice
(sə-fīs′)
-*verb*

● The amount of research you've done may **suffice** for a high-school term paper, but not for a college essay.

● I forgot to buy something for lunch tomorrow, but the leftover meatloaf will **suffice**.

__ *Suffice* means   A. to be wasted.   B. to be adequate.   C. to be examined.

10 vulnerable
(vŭl′nər-ə-bəl)
-*adjective*

● Homes in heavily wooded areas are especially **vulnerable** to termites.

● Because they tend to have brittle bones, the elderly are **vulnerable** to fractures.

__ *Vulnerable* means   A. open.   B. safe.   C. attracted.

Matching Words with Definitions

Following are definitions of the ten words. Clearly write or print each word next to its definition. The sentences above and on the previous page will help you decide on the meaning of each word.

1. _____ Having many parts arranged in a complicated way; complex

2. _____ To be good enough

3. _____ To worsen; deteriorate

4. _____ A place of safety, protection, or relief

5. _____ To make a request or plead on behalf of someone else

6. _____ Open to damage or attack; susceptible

7. _____ Difficult to believe; unlikely

8. _____ Evil; wicked

9. _____ Close inspection; careful examination

10. _____ Unable to speak in an orderly, logical way

CAUTION: Do not go any further until you are sure the above answers are correct. Then you can use the definitions to help you in the following practices. Your goal is eventually to know the words well enough so that you don't need to check the definitions at all.

Sentence Check 1

Using the answer line provided, complete each item below with the correct word from the box. Use each word once.

| A. degenerate | B. implausible | C. incoherent | D. intercede | E. intricate |
| F. sanctuary | G. scrutiny | H. sinister | I. suffice | J. vulnerable |

_____ 1. Ken's cartoons ___ for the school newspaper, but they wouldn't be good enough for the city papers.

_____ 2. In the *Batman* movies, the Joker's name is misleading, for he's a(n) ___ man who takes pleasure in doing evil.

_____ 3. People who live in big cities are more ___ to muggings than are residents of small towns.

_____ 4. The leaves outside the window created a(n) ___ lacy shadow on my bedroom wall.

_____ 5. Although it seems ___, the seemingly dead desert really does blossom after a rainstorm.

_____ 6. People who allow an escaped convict to use their home as a ___ may face criminal charges themselves.

_____ 7. My brother was so upset that he was ___. It wasn't until he calmed down that I understood what he was saying: that he had been fired.

_____ 8. Unclaimed bags at airports receive the ___ of security officers watching for drugs or explosives.

_____ 9. When I don't have company, my apartment tends to ___ into a jumble of papers, clothes, and school supplies.

_____ 10. When Dad informed my little sister that she had to be home from her date no later than ten o'clock, Mom ___(e)d and gave her a midnight curfew.

NOTE: Now check your answers to these items by turning to page 178. Going over the answers carefully will help you prepare for the next two practices, for which answers are not given.

Sentence Check 2

Using the answer lines provided, complete each item below with **two** words from the box. Use each word once.

_____
_____ 1–2. Birds feel ___ to attack when they are out in the open where shrubbery is sparse°. To attract them to your bird feeder, put it near a ___ of thickly growing trees and large bushes.

_____
_____ 3–4. To get into the party, Malcolm made up a flagrant° lie—a(n) ___ story about having lost our invitations in a fire. However, the unlikely tale did not ___ to get us in.

_____
_____ 5–6. When a complicated musical piece is played by a talented orchestra, audiences can appreciate the ___ structure. But when poor musicians try the piece, it usually ___s into noise.

_____   7–8. As he left the bank, the robber shot and wounded an elderly man on mere
_____   impulse. Shocked by the ___ act, the bank clerk was at first ___. However,
                                  after calming down, she was able to clearly tell the police about the robbery
                                  and the totally arbitrary° shooting.

_____   9–10. The children's eager ___ of the carefully arranged candies and cookies
_____   brought a curt° warning from their mother: "Look, but don't touch!"
                                  However, their grandmother ___(e)d and convinced her that it would be an
                                  inequity° to give all the goodies to company and none to the children.

Final Check: *The New French Employee*

Here is a final opportunity for you to strengthen your knowledge of the ten words. First read the following
selection carefully. Then fill in each blank with a word from the box at the top of the previous page.
(Context clues will help you figure out which word goes in which blank.) Use each word once.

One summer, Nan worked in a factory with an employee
who had recently arrived from France, a soft-spoken young
man named Jean-Louis. He spoke little English, but Nan's
basic French (1)_____(e)d for simple
conversations and helpful translations.

However, one day when she was called to the foreman's
office, she wished she knew no French at all. FBI agents
were there with Jean-Louis. After explaining that Jean-Louis
may have been more (2)_____ than
the innocent young man he appeared to be, the foreman
left her there to translate for the agents. The agents said
Jean-Louis had been on the run after committing several
jewel thefts in France. They had already been to Jean-Louis's apartment and confiscated° a diamond
necklace and some expensive watches. Nan struggled to translate their questions, which were often
too (3)_____ for her limited vocabulary. At times, she became so nervous that she
was nearly (4)_____. When Jean-Louis finally deciphered° what Nan was saying, he
said the police were maligning° him. He claimed he was being mistaken for his no-good twin brother,
who was responsible for the robberies, and therefore he was innocent—he should be absolved° of all
blame. The angry FBI agents found Jean-Louis's story (5)_____. The conversation soon
(6)_____(e)d into a shouting match, with everyone yelling at poor Nan. When her boss
heard the racket, he (7)_____(e)d, appeased° the agents, and got them to excuse her.

Nan then went to the ladies' room, a (8)_____ from the turmoil° of
all the shouting. After the agents left with Jean-Louis, she was calm enough to go back to work.
But she felt (9)_____ for days as she wondered if she was under the
(10)_____ of jewel thieves who might blame her for Jean-Louis's arrest.

Scores   Sentence Check 2 _____%   Final Check _____%

blatant	gloat
blight	immaculate
contrive	plagiarism
garble	qualm
gaunt	retaliate

Ten Words in Context

In the space provided, write the letter of the meaning closest to that of each **boldfaced** word. Use the context of the sentences to help you figure out each word's meaning.

1 blatant
(blā′tənt)
-*adjective*

- Eva is a **blatant** bargain-hunter. Not only does she wait for end-of season sales, but she chooses an already-reduced item and then asks if the salesperson will accept a lower price.

- The company's disregard of the environment is **blatant**. It makes no effort to stop polluting coastal waters with garbage.

__ *Blatant* means   A. unmistakable.   B. scrambled.   C. not noticeable.

2 blight
(blīt)
-*noun*

- Nothing has hurt our country more than the **blight** of drugs.

- There are two ways of looking at TV: as a valuable source of information or as a **blight** that dulls the mind.

__ *Blight* means   A. something that assists.   B. something that is new.   C. something that harms.

3 contrive
(kən-trīv′)
-*verb*

- My eight-year-old son could write a book titled *101 Ways I Have* **Contrived** *to Stay Up Past My Bedtime.*

- Jill has to **contrive** a way to get a day off from work for her friend's wedding. She's already used up her vacation time.

__ *Contrive* means   A. to think up.   B. to mix up.   C. to avoid.

4 garble
(gär′bəl)
-*verb*

- The new reporter **garbled** the newspaper story; the result was an article that made no sense at all.

- The company had **garbled** the bike's assembly instructions so badly that we were constantly confused about which step to do next.

__ *Garble* means   A. to read.   B. to lose.   C. to jumble.

5 gaunt
(gônt)
-*adjective*

- Abraham Lincoln's beard made his **gaunt** face look fuller.

- Sharon's eating disorder, called anorexia nervosa, has made her so **gaunt** that she looks like a walking skeleton.

__ *Gaunt* means   A. very thin.   B. wide.   C. confused.

6 gloat
(glōt)
-*verb*

- The coach told his team, "There's only one thing worse than a sore loser, and that's a mean winner. Don't **gloat**."

- Neil's sister always tattles on him and then **gloats** when he's punished, saying, "I told you so."

__ *Gloat* means   A. to apologize fully.   B. to be overly self-satisfied.   C. to pay back.

7 immaculate
(ĭ-măk′yə-lĭt)
-*adjective*

- It's amazing that while Carolyn's appearance is always **immaculate**, her apartment often seems very dirty.
- Don't expect a child to come home from a birthday party with **immaculate** clothing. Children usually manage to get as much birthday cake on their clothing as in their mouths.

___ *Immaculate* means   A. uncomfortable.   B. spotless.   C. soiled.

8 plagiarism
(plā′jĕ-rĭz′əm)
-*noun*

- When the author saw a movie with the same plot as one of her novels, she sued for **plagiarism**.
- The teacher warned her students that using an author's exact words as one's own is **plagiarism**.

___ *Plagiarism* means   A. creativity.   B. the stealing of ideas.   C. planning.

9 qualm
(kwôm)
-*noun*

- Lorenzo is so honest that he has **qualms** about telling "little white lies." For instance, it bothers him to say he likes a friend's new haircut when he really doesn't.
- After hiding Kwan's bike as an April Fool's joke, I began to have **qualms**. What if she thought it was stolen and called the police?

___ *Qualm* means   A. a guilty feeling.   B. a proud memory.   C. a clever plan.

10 retaliate
(rĭ-tăl′ē-āt′)
-*verb*

- When I broke my sister's stereo, she **retaliated** by taking my iPod earphones and refusing to give them back.
- When Ron refused to pay his younger brother for washing his car, he **retaliated** by washing it again—with its windows open.

___ *Retaliate* means   A. to forgive.   B. to take revenge.   C. to confuse.

Matching Words with Definitions

Following are definitions of the ten words. Clearly write or print each word next to its definition. The sentences above and on the previous page will help you decide on the meaning of each word.

1. _____ An uneasy feeling about how right or proper a particular action is

2. _____ To mix up or confuse (as a story or message); scramble

3. _____ To feel or express delight or self-satisfaction, often spitefully

4. _____ Something that weakens, damages, or destroys

5. _____ Using someone else's writings or ideas as one's own

6. _____ To plan cleverly; think up

7. _____ To return an injury for an injury; pay back

8. _____ Very obvious, often offensively so

9. _____ Perfectly clean

10. _____ Thin and bony

CAUTION: Do not go any further until you are sure the above answers are correct. Then you can use the definitions to help you in the following practices. Your goal is eventually to know the words well enough so that you don't need to check the definitions at all.

Sentence Check 1

Using the answer line provided, complete each item below with the correct word from the box. Use each word once.

A. **blatant**	B. **blight**	C. **contrive**	D. **garble**	E. **gaunt**
F. **gloat**	G. **immaculate**	H. **plagiarism**	I. **qualm**	J. **retaliate**

_____ 1. A(n) ___ house may be a sign that someone has nothing better to do than clean.

_____ 2. Child abuse is a ___ on the physical and mental health of our youth.

_____ 3. My aunt refuses to drive Mr. Elson to bingo because he ___s so much when he wins, which is often.

_____ 4. The F's and D's on my brother's report card are ___ evidence of how little he has studied this term.

_____ 5. Emilio still hopes to ___ a way to get Rita to go out with him, even though she's refused him four times.

_____ 6. When my friend Jamee left a message with my little brother, inviting me to go to the mall, my brother ___(e)d it so badly that the message I got was "Jamee wants you to go play ball."

_____ 7. Every time the Hatfields harmed the McCoys, the McCoys would ___, so the feud went on for years.

_____ 8. Rescued after being lost at sea for nine days, the men were terribly ___, but they put on weight rapidly.

_____ 9. My parents say it is foolish to give spare change to panhandlers, but I always feel a ___ when I walk by them and give nothing.

_____ 10. Mark Twain joked that charges of ___ were ridiculous because no one can be completely original. He wrote, "We mortals can't create—we can only copy."

NOTE: Now check your answers to these items by turning to page 178. Going over the answers carefully will help you prepare for the next two practices, for which answers are not given.

Sentence Check 2

Using the answer lines provided, complete each item below with **two** words from the box. Use each word once.

_____
_____ 1–2. The living room looked ___ except for a lump under the carpet, a(n) ___ sign that my son had taken a shortcut in cleaning up.

_____
_____ 3–4. After the bully struck him, Jules wanted to ___ by throwing a rock, but he had ___s about doing anything so dangerous.

_____
_____ 5–6. The little girl was so ___ after her illness that her parents carefully ___(e)d fattening meals that were sure to arouse her appetite.

_____   7–8. "At least I know you aren't guilty of ___," said my teacher. "Nobody else
_____   would have ___(e)d the report so badly that it's impossible to follow."

_____   9–10. Willie is a ___ on our school. Not only does he start fights with opposing
_____   players on the basketball court, but he also ___s after he's benched, as if
he's proud of causing such turmoil°. In fact, although he's a great player, the
coach is pondering° kicking him off the team.

Final Check: *A Cruel Teacher*

Here is a final opportunity for you to strengthen your knowledge of the ten words. First read the following
selection carefully. Then fill in each blank with a word from the box at the top of the previous page.
(Context clues will help you figure out which word goes in which blank.) Use each word once.

It has been twenty years since I was in Mr. Brill's
tenth-grade biology class, but I still get nervous thinking
about it. Mr. Brill was a tall, (1)_____ man
who resembled the skeleton at the back of the room.
His meanness was (2)_____. For his
most difficult questions, he would call on the shyest kids,
those most vulnerable° to the pain of embarrassment. And
when they nervously (3)_____(e)d
their answers, he would (4)_____,
as if their poor performance were a personal victory for
him. The discomfort of some of his victims was almost
tangible°, nearly as solid as the wooden pointer which he
sometimes loudly slammed across his desk just to shock
us. He seemed to (5)_____ situations
just to make us miserable. For example, if our fingernails
were not (6)_____, we were sent out of class. As if we needed clean hands
to dissect a frog! One time I worked extremely hard on a paper for class, but he accused me of
(7)_____. He said I must have copied it because I was too dumb to write anything
that good. Without a (8)_____, he gave me an F, which ruined my average and
demoralized° me for the rest of the year. All of us students would imagine ways to get even with him,
but we were too afraid to (9)_____. Why a teacher like that was allowed to
continue teaching was an enigma° to us, one I still have not figured out. In all the years since, I've never met
a person who was such a (10)_____ on the teaching profession.

| Scores | Sentence Check 2 _____% | Final Check _____% |

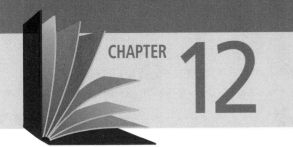

-ate	forc, fort
bio-	hum
claim, clam	pater, patri-
fin	semi-
flex, flect	-ward

Ten Word Parts in Context

Figure out the meanings of the following ten word parts by looking *closely* and *carefully* at the context in which they appear. Then, in the space provided, write the letter of the meaning closest to that of each word part.

1 -ate

- Teachers often find it difficult to **motivate** students to want to learn.
- The TV history series **fascinated** viewers with such details as a seventeenth-century English children's hospital that gave each child two gallons of beer per week.

___ The word part *-ate* means   A. cause to become.   B. call.   C. end.

2 bio-

- Helen Keller wrote a touching **autobiography** titled *The Story of My Life*.
- **Biology** is the science of living things, both plant and animal.

___ The word part *bio-* means   A. bend.   B. life.   C. partly.

3 claim, clam

- In 2008, American theater critics **acclaimed** *In the Heights*, which won four Tony awards, as the best musical of the year.
- The **exclamation** point emphasizes passionate, sudden, and surprised outcries, such as "Aha!" and "That hurts!"

___ The word part *claim* or *clam* means   A. cry out.   B. father.   C. partly.

4 fin

- The **final** word in many prayers is *amen*, which means "May it be so."
- "Ooooooooh! Aaaaaaaah!" the crowd exclaimed, enjoying the spectacular five-minute **finale** that closed the Fourth of July fireworks display.

___ The word part *fin* means   A. strong.   B. toward.   C. end.

5 flex, flect

- Gymnasts must be extremely **flexible** so that they can bend their bodies into many positions.
- When they enter church, Catholics **genuflect**—that is, they bend one knee, as a sign of reverence.

___ The word part *flex* or *flect* means   A. bend.   B. father.   C. person.

6 forc, fort

- The burglar **forcibly** entered the home by breaking the kitchen window.
- The children made a high wall of pressed snow to **fortify** themselves against a snowball attack by the kids across the street.

___ The word part *forc* or *fort* means   A. person.   B. direction of.   C. strong.

7 hum

- "We have done all that is **humanly** possible to save your grandmother's life," said the doctor.
- A resident of the shelter for the homeless complained, "The treatment here is not **humane**. We want to be treated like people, not objects."

___ The word part *hum* means   A. in the direction of.   B. having to do with people.   C. call.

8 pater, patri-

- Mike just became a father, so he is taking six months' **paternity** leave to help care for the baby.
- The soldiers' **patriotism** was so strong that they risked their lives to defend their fatherland.

___ The word part *pater* or *patri-* means   A. partly.   B. toward.   C. father.

9 semi-

- My grandfather is only **semiretired**—he works part-time as a plumber.
- I use **semisweet** chocolate in my frosting to keep it from being too bitter or too sweet.

___ The word part *semi-* means   A. partly.   B. of living things.   C. toward.

10 -ward

- Everyone at the fair looked **skyward** in horror as the colorful hot-air balloon exploded.
- The children tried walking to school **backward** but gave up before even reaching the end of their block.

___ The word part *-ward* means   A. call.   B. in the direction of.   C. of living things.

Matching Word Parts with Definitions

Following are definitions of the ten word parts. Clearly write or print each word part next to its definition. The sentences above and on the previous page will help you decide on the meaning of each word part.

1. _____ Bend

2. _____ Partly; half

3. _____ Life; of living things

4. _____ Father

5. _____ Cause to become

6. _____ In the direction of; toward

7. _____ Call; cry out

8. _____ Strong

9. _____ Person; having to do with people

10. _____ End

CAUTION: Do not go any further until you are sure the above answers are correct. Then you can use the definitions to help you in the following practices. Your goal is eventually to know the word parts well enough so that you don't need to check the definitions at all.

Sentence Check 1

Using the answer line provided, complete each *italicized* word below with the correct word part from the box. Use each word part once.

A. -ate	B. bio-	C. claim, clam	D. fin	E. flex
F. forc, fort	G. hum	H. pater, patri-	I. semi-	J. -ward

_____   1. Little Jesse loudly (*ex . . . ed*) ___ that his father was the smartest man on the block.

_____   2. A (*. . . rhythm*) ___ is any cycle of periodic changes in life, such as daily changes in body temperature.

_____   3. The jury found the disturbed young man, who had shot his father, guilty of (*. . . cide*) ___.

_____   4. After a cold, rainy weekend of camping, the Boy Scouts were relieved to head (*home . . .*) ___.

_____   5. My mother was so (*in . . . ible*) ___ that she never once bent the rule and let me stay out past curfew.

_____   6. The candidate's (*. . . eful*) ___ speech in favor of reduced military spending made a powerful impression on me.

_____   7. Uncle Carlos was in a (*. . . private*) ___ room in the hospital. The other man in the room had also suffered a heart attack.

_____   8. There are only two (*. . . alists*) ___ in the last episode of *American Idol*.

_____   9. Bishop Desmond Tutu of South Africa received the Nobel Peace Prize for his (*. . . anitarian*) ___ efforts to bring justice to his country's people.

_____ 10. In 1961, administrators of New York's Museum of Modern Art were (*humili . . . d*) ___ to learn that for weeks a painting had been displayed upside down.

NOTE: Now check your answers to these items by turning to page 178. Going over the answers carefully will help you prepare for the next two practices, for which answers are not given.

Sentence Check 2

Using the answer line provided, complete each *italicized* word in the sentences below with the correct word part from the box. Use each word part once.

_____
_____   1–2. I looked (*down . . .*) ___ and watched the doctor tap my knee to see if its (*re . . .*) ___ was normal.

_____
_____   3–4. My supervisor, Mr. Kane, is (*. . . nal*) ___. He (*en . . . es*) ___ the rules in a fatherly way—firmly but kindly. In addition, my coworkers are all very amiable°, making for an extremely friendly atmosphere.

_____
_____   5–6. After the accident, my brother was (*. . . conscious*) ___ for several hours. (*. . . ally*)___, around midnight, he became fully alert and mobile° enough to walk out of the hospital on his own.

_____   7–8. When the teacher asked students to write a (. . . *graphy*) ___, she meant the
_____   life story of a (. . . *an*) ___. But Harry wrote the life story of Tarzan, his pet
                         snake.

_____   9–10. In 1863, Abraham Lincoln issued a (*pro . . . ation*) ___ freeing the slaves.
_____   But it would be almost one hundred years after his announcement before
                         real efforts were made to (*integr . . .*) ___ black people into society's
                         mainstream.

Final Check: *It's Never Too Late*

Here is a final opportunity for you to strengthen your knowledge of the ten word parts. First read the
following selection carefully. Then complete each *italicized* word in the parentheses below with a word
part from the box at the top of the previous page. (Context clues will help you figure out which word part
goes in which blank.) Use each word part once.

I almost fell out of my chair last night when my father
(*pro . . . ed*) (1)_____, "I quit my job
today. I'm going to college." He realizes that people may
think him eccentric° to start school at his age, but he's
willing to appear odd because he's tired of (. . . *skilled*)
(2)_____ work in a factory. He wants
a job that requires more skill and training. Both of my
(. . . *nal*) (3)_____ grandparents died
when Dad was a child, so he and his brothers were forced
to quit school early to work. Dad finished high school at
night. Now he will venture° working only part-time in order
to (*educ . . .*) (4)_____ himself
further. He still isn't sure what his major will be, but he
has always liked science. He definitely wants to take a
(. . . *logy*) (5)_____ course because all living things interest him. He'd like to focus
his (*ef . . . s*) (6)_____ in a field that benefits (. . . *anity*) (7)_____,
such as physical therapy, where he could help rehabilitate° people with certain infirmities°. He's also
thinking about nursing. Most men of his generation think of nursing as women's work, so Dad's interest in
this field shows me he is more (. . . *ible*) (8)_____ in his thinking than I ever realized.
Whatever his choice, he is looking (*for . . .*) (9)_____ to classes with great zeal°. I
know that when he (. . . *ishes*) (10)_____ his schooling, no one will be prouder of him
than I already am.

Scores	Sentence Check 2 _____%	Final Check _____%

Enter your scores above and in the **Vocabulary Performance Chart** on the inside back cover of the book.

The box at the right lists twenty-five words from Unit Two. Using the clues at the bottom of the page, fill in these words to complete the puzzle that follows.

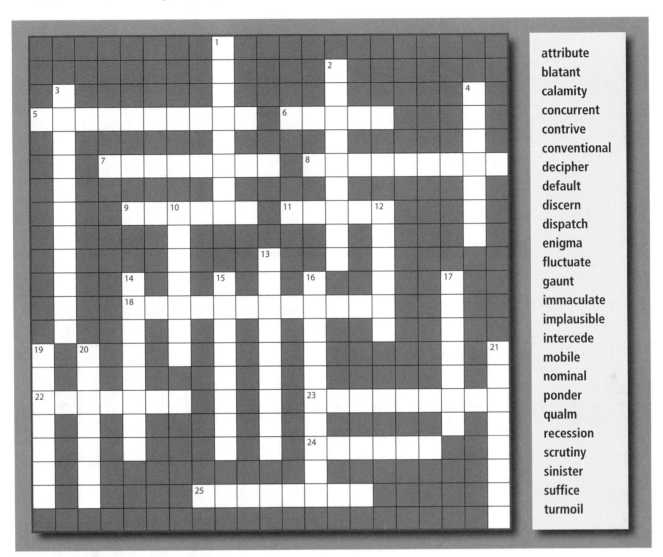

attribute
blatant
calamity
concurrent
contrive
conventional
decipher
default
discern
dispatch
enigma
fluctuate
gaunt
immaculate
implausible
intercede
mobile
nominal
ponder
qualm
recession
scrutiny
sinister
suffice
turmoil

ACROSS

5. Perfectly clean
6. Thin and bony
7. An event bringing great loss and misery
8. A quality or feature of a person or thing
9. To consider carefully
11. An uneasy feeling about how right or proper a particular action is
18. Customary; ordinary
22. To be good enough
23. A temporary decline in business
24. A mystery or puzzle
25. To send to a specific place or a specific business

DOWN

1. To plan cleverly; think up
2. To vary irregularly; to go up and down or back and forth
3. Difficult to believe; unlikely
4. Very obvious, often offensively so
10. Slight; very small compared to what might be expected
12. Moving or able to move from place to place
13. To make a request or plead on behalf of someone else
14. Close inspection; careful examination
15. To interpret or read (something confusing or hard to make out)
16. Happening or existing at the same time; simultaneous
17. Complete confusion; uproar
19. To recognize; detect
20. To fail to do something required
21. Evil; wicked

66

PART A

Choose the word that best completes each item and write it in the space provided.

_____ 1. According to legend, vampires are ___ creatures who cannot survive in daylight.

      A. incoherent   B. immaculate   C. nocturnal   D. conventional

_____ 2. The counseling program to ___ addicts includes job training.

      A. rehabilitate   B. contrive   C. ponder   D. exemplify

_____ 3. Unless figure skaters practice regularly, their skills will ___.

      A. retaliate   B. degenerate   C. confiscate   D. decipher

_____ 4. It may sound ___, but a camel can drink twenty-five gallons of water at a time.

      A. implausible   B. gaunt   C. mobile   D. nominal

_____ 5. Movie subtitles should be ___ with the spoken words they are translating.

      A. flagrant   B. hypothetical   C. incoherent   D. concurrent

_____ 6. Even the most ___ people have microscopic creatures clinging to their hair.

      A. sinister   B. immaculate   C. incoherent   D. intricate

_____ 7. Measles remains a serious ___ worldwide, killing over a million people each year.

      A. blight   B. plagiarism   C. qualm   D. prerequisite

_____ 8. The Peace Corps continues to ___ American volunteers to live and work in developing nations.

      A. discern   B. garble   C. dispatch   D. default

_____ 9. The government student loan program is in serious trouble because many students ___ on their payments.

      A. suffice   B. attest   C. intercede   D. default

_____ 10. In a race across New Jersey in 1901, drivers traveling up to thirty miles an hour were arrested for their ___ disregard of the speed limit, which was eight miles an hour.

      A. flagrant   B. hypothetical   C. conventional   D. immaculate

(Continues on next page)

PART B

On the answer line, write the letter of the choice that best completes each item.

_____ 11. **Conventional** business clothing for a man includes
  A. Bermuda shorts and a Hawaiian shirt.
  B. jeans and a sleeveless tank top.
  C. a suit and tie.
  D. swimming trunks.

_____ 12. In order to **attest** to what it feels like to walk on the moon's surface, a person must
  A. have read about an astronaut who did it.
  B. have walked there himself or herself.
  C. be a scientist who has studied the moon.
  D. have a good imagination.

_____ 13. A person who has lost his or her eyesight can become more **mobile** by
  A. learning to read Braille.
  B. becoming depressed and refusing to go out.
  C. learning to get around with a Seeing Eye dog.
  D. listening to the radio.

_____ 14. A usual **prerequisite** to getting a driver's license is
  A. purchasing a car.
  B. committing many traffic offenses.
  C. passing a driving test.
  D. refusing to have one's photograph taken.

_____ 15. When her brother and sister argue, Rachel often **intercedes** by
  A. leaving the house.
  B. covering her ears.
  C. ignoring them both.
  D. helping each see the other's point of view.

_____ 16. College students who don't eat properly and don't get much sleep are **vulnerable** to
  A. good health.
  B. their doctors.
  C. driving places.
  D. illness.

_____ 17. The parrot **garbled** its words,
  A. making us all laugh at its mixed-up speech.
  B. amazing us by speaking so clearly.
  C. embarrassing us with its dirty words.
  D. boring us by repeating the same few words.

_____ 18. Which of the following **constitutes** a good breakfast?
  A. A neighborhood diner
  B. Orange juice and bran flakes with milk and bananas
  C. Spaghetti with anchovy sauce
  D. Customers at a pancake house

_____ 19. The tennis player's performance **fluctuated** during the tournament. It
  A. was magnificent one day, awful the next, and average the following day.
  B. was consistently excellent.
  C. began well but went steadily downhill all week.
  D. started badly but became better every day.

_____ 20. Since she wanted to **gloat** about her promotion at work, Kris
  A. didn't mention it to anyone.
  B. worked harder than ever to show that she deserved it.
  C. said to a coworker, "Sorry, loser. I got it."
  D. became very nervous about her new responsibilities.

Score   (Number correct) _____ x 5 = _____%

Enter your score above and in the **Vocabulary Performance Chart** on the inside back cover of the book.

PART A

Complete each item with a word from the box. Use each word once.

A. **attribute**	B. **calamity**	C. **decipher**	D. **enigma**	E. **exemplify**
F. **nominal**	G. **orient**	H. **qualm**	I. **recession**	J. **retaliate**
K. **scrutiny**	L. **sinister**	M. **suffice**		

_____ 1. The sinking of the ship *Titanic*, which struck an iceberg, was a(n) ___ in which nearly 1,600 people died.

_____ 2. People who can't read must ___ themselves in a city by relating to familiar places, not signs.

_____ 3. "A hint to my daughter to take out the garbage won't ___," Alonso insisted. "She needs to be told to do it."

_____ 4. I don't know who sent me the birthday card because I couldn't ___ the signature.

_____ 5. A shortage of a single product, such as sugar, could cause a(n) ___ in several industries.

_____ 6. Don't buy a used car unless you examine it closely and also have a mechanic give it careful ___.

_____ 7. Although our library charges only a ___ fee to use a computer, I don't think it should charge students any fee at all.

_____ 8. In some religions, gods and goddesses represent various human ___s, such as strength, beauty, and wisdom.

_____ 9. Through the years, people with ___s about having cheated on their income taxes have sent gifts of money to the IRS.

_____ 10. The citizens in that small country ___(e)d against their communist dictator, who had ordered mass murders, by executing him.

_____ 11. One of the oddest ___ plots of all time was thought up by a wealthy Frenchman. He fed his victims rich foods until they died of overeating.

_____ 12. The thousands of oak leaves that covered the ground in a Scottish town in 1889 were a(n) ___. The nearest oak trees were eight miles away.

_____ 13. Lightning bolts, which travel at millions of miles an hour and produce five times the heat of the sun's surface, ___ nature's tremendous energy.

(Continues on next page)

PART B

Write **C** if the italicized word is used **correctly**. Write **I** if the word is used **incorrectly**.

_____ 14. The *turmoil* of a smooth, clear lake always makes me feel at peace.

_____ 15. A wonderfully *incoherent* speaker, Abraham Lincoln was widely admired for his powerful speeches.

_____ 16. James Bond was about to step into his enemy's trap when a beautiful woman, a former enemy who had fallen in love with him, *pondered* him to escape.

_____ 17. The Democratic and Republican parties are *predominant* in the United States, but other parties are also represented on the ballots.

_____ 18. Shortly before his birthday, Hollis *contrived* to get his parents to walk past the toy store so that he could point out the PlayStation 3 games displayed in the window.

_____ 19. Each year, thousands of Americans who think themselves too *gaunt* have some fat surgically removed.

PART C

On the answer line, write the letter of the word that is the **synonym** of the boldfaced word.

Example: __C__ **nominal**   A. personal   B. enormous   C. slight

_____ 20. **confiscate**   A. give back   B. seize   C. combine

_____ 21. **enhance**   A. improve   B. lead   C. weaken

_____ 22. **comprehensive**   A. limited   B. broad   C. irregular

PART D

On the answer line, write the letter of the word that is the **antonym** of the boldfaced word.

Example: __B__ **nominal**   A. personal   B. enormous   C. slight

_____ 23. **intricate**   A. complicated   B. musical   C. simple

_____ 24. **persevere**   A. look   B. give up   C. persist

_____ 25. **blatant**   A. strange   B. obvious   C. hidden

Score   (Number correct) _____ x 4 = _____%

Enter your score above and in the **Vocabulary Performance Chart** on the inside back cover of the book.

Each item below starts with a pair of words in CAPITAL LETTERS. For each item, figure out the relationship between these two words. Then decide which of the choices (A, B, C, or D) expresses a similar relationship. Write the letter of your choice on the answer line.

_____ 1. CALAMITY : SUFFERING ::
    A. magnet : repels   C. tragedy : sadness
    B. tragedy : joy   D. table : chair

_____ 2. PERSEVERE : QUIT ::
    A. open : shut   C. drink : thirsty
    B. perspire : sweat   D. continue : persist

_____ 3. VENTURE : EXPLORER ::
    A. see : blind person   C. cow : milk
    B. teach : professor   D. ocean : ship

_____ 4. CONVENTIONAL : UNCOMMON ::
    A. conduct : experiment   C. owner : possesses
    B. thoughtful : considerate   D. quiet : noisy

_____ 5. MOBILE : UNMOVING ::
    A. rapid : slow   C. excited : lively
    B. write : words   D. wet : water

_____ 6. ENIGMA : MYSTERIOUS ::
    A. baseball : bat   C. funny : serious
    B. joke : funny   D. clue : detective

_____ 7. OWL : NOCTURNAL ::
    A. tiger : cat   C. day : night
    B. tiger : fierce   D. child : adult

_____ 8. DISCERN : LOOK ::
    A. hear : listen   C. cold : touch
    B. smell : taste   D. ignore : see

_____ 9. DECIPHER : CODE ::
    A. surgeon : doctor   C. puzzle : piece
    B. untangle : knot   D. evident : clear

_____ 10. CONFISCATE : SEIZE ::
    A. confuse : clarify   C. take : give
    B. cry : funeral   D. contribute : give

(Continues on next page)

____   11. HYPOTHETICAL : ACTUAL ::
        A. brave : cowardly   C. old : ancient
        B. scary : frightening   D. problem : solve

____   12. DEFAULT : LOAN ::
        A. pass : course   C. break : promise
        B. pay : salary   D. tax : income

____   13. INTRICATE : COMPLEX ::
        A. difficult : simple   C. circular : round
        B. headlight : car   D. scold : soothe

____   14. DEGENERATE : IMPROVE ::
        A. solve : equation   C. ride : train
        B. generous : giving   D. grow : shrink

____   15. IMPLAUSIBLE : UNLIKELY ::
        A. straight : crooked   C. furniture : house
        B. unfortunate : unlucky   D. unfortunate : lucky

____   16. SANCTUARY : SAFETY ::
        A. hideout : secrecy   C. wheel : steer
        B. enclosed : exposed   D. dinner : breakfast

____   17. GAUNT : PLUMP ::
        A. tall : short   C. precious : jewelry
        B. thin : skinny   D. fruit : nutrition

____   18. BLIGHT : DESTROYS ::
        A. flood : dries   C. pianist : piano
        B. medicine : heals   D. agreement : disagree

____   19. QUALM : CONSCIENCE ::
        A. love : hatred   C. cramp : muscle
        B. room : fireplace   D. pain : health

____   20. PLAGIARISM : IDEAS ::
        A. criminal : crime   C. writing : paper
        B. host : party   D. shoplifting : merchandise

Score   (Number correct) _____ x 5 = _____ %

UNIT TWO: Test 4 (Word Parts)

PART A

Listed in the left-hand column below are ten common word parts, followed by words in which the parts are used. In each blank, write in the letter of the correct definition on the right.

Word Parts	**Examples**	**Definitions**
____ 1. **-ate**	motivate, fascinate	A. Father
____ 2. **bio-**	autobiography, biology	B. Call; cry out
____ 3. **claim, clam**	acclaim, exclamation	C. Partly
____ 4. **fin**	final, finale	D. End
____ 5. **flex, flect**	flexible, genuflect	E. Cause to become
____ 6. **forc, fort**	forcibly, fortify	F. In the direction of; toward
____ 7. **hum**	humanly, humane	G. Person; having to do with people
____ 8. **pater, patri-**	paternity, patriotism	H. Strong
____ 9. **semi-**	semiretired, semisweet	I. Bend
____ 10. **-ward**	skyward, backward	J. Life; of living things

PART B

Using the answer line provided, complete each *italicized* word in the sentences below with the correct word part from the box. Not every word part will be used.

A. **-ate**	B. **bio-**	C. **clam**	D. **fin**	E. **flex**
F. **fort**	G. **hum**	H. **patri-**	I. **semi-**	J. **-ward**

_____ 11. To (*activ . . .*) ___ yeast, put it in a warm liquid.

_____ 12. When I meditate, I focus (*in . . . ly*) ___ by mentally repeating a nonsense word.

_____ 13. In the seventeenth century, England (*. . . ified*) ___ its weakening wool trade by passing a law that all corpses must be buried in wool.

_____ 14. The French king Louis XIV's (*. . . al*) ___ words before his death were to his servants: "Why do you weep? Did you think I was immortal?"

_____ 15. Why are robots often given a (*. . . anoid*) ___ appearance? Are we more comfortable with "smart" machines that resemble us?

(Continues on next page)

PART C

Use your knowledge of word parts to determine the meaning of the **boldfaced** words. On the answer line, write the letter of each meaning.

_____ 16. The dining club is **semipublic**.

    A. fully public   B. partly public   C. private

_____ 17. A **patriarchy** is a form of social organization in which families are headed by

    A. the strongest.   B. the oldest.   C. the father.

_____ 18. My chemistry teacher also teaches **biochemistry**, which is the chemistry of

    A. life processes.   B. lakes.   C. weather.

_____ 19. Albert Einstein **claimed** that his brain was his laboratory.

    A. realized   B. made known   C. silently wished

_____ 20. The company I work for has decided to experiment with **flextime** for employees.

    A. longer work hours   B. shorter work hours   C. adjustable work hours

Score   (Number correct) _____ x 5 = _____%

Enter your score above and in the **Vocabulary Performance Chart** on the inside back cover of the book.

Unit Three

Chapter 13

curtail	indispensable
devastate	intermittent
digress	rigor
incentive	squander
incorporate	succumb

Chapter 14

alleviate	infamous
benefactor	intrinsic
covert	revulsion
cynic	speculate
demise	virile

Chapter 15

abstain	deficit
affiliate	dissent
agnostic	diversion
aspire	lucrative
benevolent	mandatory

Chapter 16

charisma	poignant
contemporary	prevalent
contend	proponent
conversely	quest
extrovert	traumatic

Chapter 17

congenial	prone
flippant	rapport
impasse	rationale
perception	relentless
prompt	reprisal

Chapter 18

cor, cour	-ish
di-, du-	magni-, magn-
-dom	phob
-fy	pro-
il-, im-	psych-, psycho-

CHAPTER 13

curtail	indispensable
devastate	intermittent
digress	rigor
incentive	squander
incorporate	succumb

Ten Words in Context

In the space provided, write the letter of the meaning closest to that of each **boldfaced** word. Use the context of the sentences to help you figure out each word's meaning.

1 curtail
(kər-tāl′)
-verb

● Upon hearing reports of a huge snowstorm, the principal **curtailed** the school day so students could go home early.

● I need to **curtail** my volunteer activities so that I can spend more time earning money to pay back a loan.

___ *Curtail* means   A. to combine.   B. to shorten.   C. to extend.

2 devastate
(dĕv′əs-tāt′)
-verb

● Learning that their son had been arrested for armed robbery **devastated** the Huttons. They couldn't believe he'd do such a terrible thing.

● Vera is so fond of Andy. She'll be **devastated** to hear he has cancer.

___ *Devastate* means   A. to thrill.   B. to annoy.   C. to upset greatly.

3 digress
(dī-grĕs′)
-verb

● Professor Rubin never **digresses** during a lecture. Even his jokes relate to the day's topic.

● I tried to teach my three-year-old niece our phone number, but we **digressed** to a discussion of whether Winnie the Pooh has a telephone.

___ *Digress* means   A. to listen carefully.   B. to go off the subject.   C. to get up.

4 incentive
(ĭn-sĕn′tĭv)
-noun

● The insurance company offers an **incentive**—a free vacation—to encourage its representatives to make more sales.

● The thought of myself in a bathing suit next summer provides me with an adequate **incentive** to exercise.

___ *Incentive* means   A. encouragement.   B. liberty.   C. change.

5 incorporate
(ĭn-kôr′pər-āt′)
-verb

● Jerry **incorporated** all of his favorite desserts into one: a chocolate-covered banana-cream pecan pie.

● Since the number of young children has gone down in my neighborhood, the two elementary schools have been **incorporated** into one.

___ *Incorporate* means   A. to give up.   B. to join together.   C. to raise.

6 indispensable
(ĭn-dĭ-spĕn′sə-bəl)
-adjective

● Because there's no bus or train service nearby, a car is **indispensable** in my neighborhood.

● When you're broke, you find that many things you thought were **indispensable** aren't actually necessary after all.

___ *Indispensable* means   A. free.   B. needed.   C. expensive.

7 intermittent
(ĭn′tər-mĭt′ənt)
-adjective

- You have to work steadily with your dog to train him well. **Intermittent** practice won't work.
- Dora realized that her weight loss on a diet would be **intermittent**, so she didn't give up when the losses stopped. She knew they would start again.

___ *Intermittent* means   A. irregular.   B. too much.   C. steady.

8 rigor
(rĭg′ər)
-noun

- New Marines must go through the **rigors** of boot camp, such as completing an obstacle course and running several miles a day.
- The **rigor** of working at two part-time jobs while going to school proved too much for Jamal. Exhausted, he quit both jobs.

___ *Rigor* means   A. a gamble.   B. an expense.   C. a hardship.

9 squander
(skwŏn′dər)
-verb

- It's sad to see such a wonderful artist **squander** her talent designing labels for baked-bean cans.
- The company lunchroom now closes promptly at one o'clock so that workers can't **squander** time on long lunch breaks.

___ *Squander* means   A. to share.   B. to misuse.   C. to upset.

10 succumb
(sə-kŭm′)
-verb

- Leah **succumbed** to her daughter's begging and bought her a pet lizard for her birthday.
- Once the suspect was arrested, he quickly **succumbed** and confessed to stealing the car stereo.

___ *Succumb* means   A. to yield.   B. to delay.   C. to anger.

Matching Words with Definitions

Following are definitions of the ten words. Clearly write or print each word next to its definition. The sentences above and on the previous page will help you decide on the meaning of each word.

1. _____ To waste; spend or use foolishly

2. _____ To cut short or reduce

3. _____ Something that moves one to take action or work harder; a motivation

4. _____ To turn aside, or stray, especially from the main topic in speaking or writing

5. _____ Great hardship or difficulty; harshness; severity

6. _____ To upset deeply; overwhelm

7. _____ To give in; stop resisting

8. _____ Necessary

9. _____ To unite into a single whole; combine

10. _____ Starting and stopping from time to time; off-and-on

CAUTION: Do not go any further until you are sure the above answers are correct. Then you can use the definitions to help you in the following practices. Your goal is eventually to know the words well enough so that you don't need to check the definitions at all.

Sentence Check 1

Using the answer line provided, complete each item below with the correct word from the box. Use each word once.

A. curtail	B. devastate	C. digress	D. incentive	E. incorporate
F. indispensable	G. intermittent	H. rigor	I. squander	J. succumb

_____ 1. ___ rain kept interrupting the ballgame.

_____ 2. The sight of her bandaged husband in an oxygen tent ___(e)d Claire.

_____ 3. Someone has managed to ___ a tomato and a potato into one plant.

_____ 4. A home computer, a telephone, and a fax machine are ___ tools for many self-employed people.

_____ 5. Airlines offer "frequent flier miles" toward free trips as a(n) ___ to get people to fly often.

_____ 6. Many teenagers don't foresee the ___s of parenthood, such as staying up all night with a sick child.

_____ 7. By examining her last two months of spending, Coretta discovered that she had ___(e)d money on too many expensive meals.

_____ 8. The man on the street corner offered to sell me a watch, but he quickly ___(e)d his sales pitch when he saw a police officer approaching.

_____ 9. Because our history teacher loved to talk, we often could get him to ___ from the lesson by asking him a question about sports or politics.

_____ 10. Carl tried hard to ignore the double-fudge chocolate cake on the menu, but he finally ___(e)d and ordered a slice.

NOTE: Now check your answers to these items by turning to page 178. Going over the answers carefully will help you prepare for the next two practices, for which answers are not given.

Sentence Check 2

Using the answer lines provided, complete each item below with **two** words from the box. Use each word once.

_____
_____ 1–2. Duane feels he ___(e)d too many years in inactivity, so now he welcomes the ___s of an exercise program.

_____
_____ 3–4. The company decided to ___ the construction of its new plant until the architects could decide on how to ___ an employee gym into the new building.

_____
_____ 5–6. My aunt has only ___ success in quitting smoking. Every few months she ___s to temptation, and then she has to quit all over again.

_____   7–8. As Leo explained a failed business deal that had once ___(e)d him,
_____   he ___(e)d into the even more interesting tale of his romance with Molly, his
                            business partner.

_____   9–10. The infomercial offered free samples, ninety-day trials, and every other ___
_____   possible to get me to buy the "miracle medicine that would change my life."
                            However, I found the sales pitch highly implausible°. I simply could not
                            believe that this product was ___ to my well-being.

Final Check: *Learning to Study*

Here is a final opportunity for you to strengthen your knowledge of the ten words. First read the following selection carefully. Then fill in each blank with a word from the box at the top of the previous page. (Context clues will help you figure out which word goes in which blank.) Use each word once.

Linda never had to work very hard to make good grades in high school. But in college, where the (1)_____s of course work were greater, she soon learned that her casual high-school study habits would no longer suffice°. Linda was also learning how easy it was to (2)_____ time on surfing the Web and partying. She didn't realize how badly she was doing until she saw her midterm grades, which (3)_____(e)d her. She knew she had to make some changes right away and began to ponder° what they should be. As a(n) (4)_____ to work harder, she tried studying with her friend Denise. But that didn't work; their conversation would (5)_____ from European history to personal topics, such as dates or favorite songs.

Linda decided she'd have to go it alone. She began to skip parties during the week and also to (6)_____ the time she spent text-messaging or exchanging e-mails with friends. She discovered that a good place to study was (7)_____ to her new study habits. She found the library's silent third floor a sanctuary°, a place with no temptations to which she could (8)_____. She also became more methodical° in her study habits, keeping an assignment book, writing due dates on a calendar, and setting up a study schedule. At first, Linda's performance fluctuated°, and so the improvement in her grades was (9)_____—A's and B's alternated with C's and D's. But little by little, she learned to (10)_____ a social life with serious study and earn grades she was proud of.

Scores   Sentence Check 2 _____%   Final Check _____%

Enter your scores above and in the **Vocabulary Performance Chart** on the inside back cover of the book.

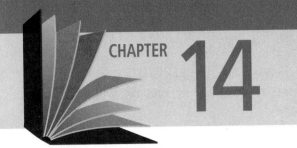

alleviate	infamous
benefactor	intrinsic
covert	revulsion
cynic	speculate
demise	virile

Ten Words in Context

In the space provided, write the letter of the meaning closest to that of each **boldfaced** word. Use the context of the sentences to help you figure out each word's meaning.

1 alleviate
(ə-lē′vē-āt′)
-verb

● To **alleviate** his loneliness, the widower moved closer to his daughter and her family.

● After a long game in the August heat, the young baseball players **alleviated** their thirst with ice-cold lemonade.

___ *Alleviate* means   A. to consider.   B. to hide.   C. to ease.

2 benefactor
(běn′ə-făk′tər)
-noun

● The Second Street Bank is a long-time **benefactor** of the arts. This year it will sponsor a series of free jazz concerts in the parks.

● The wealthy **benefactor** who paid for the child's operation prefers to remain anonymous.

___ *Benefactor* means   A. a financial supporter.   B. a social critic.   C. a cooperative person.

3 covert
(kŭv′ərt, kōv′ərt)
-adjective

● Miriam and David's relationship is so **covert** that they never eat out. Even their best friends don't know they are seeing each other.

● If you enjoy **covert** activities, you should become a secret agent.

___ *Covert* means   A. obvious.   B. concealed.   C. easy to bear.

4 cynic
(sĭn′ĭk)
-noun

● Her parents' nasty divorce has made Libby a **cynic** about marriage.

● Mr. Bryant was a **cynic** about people until he fell down on a street corner and several strangers rushed to his aid.

___ *Cynic* means   A. someone who believes the worst.   B. someone who gives help.   C. someone with a bad reputation.

5 demise
(dĭ-mīz′)
-noun

● During my years in grade school and high school, the untimely **demise** of several of my classmates made me very aware of my mortality.

● In 1567, a beard caused a man's **demise**. Hans Steininger's beard was so long that he stepped on it while climbing stairs, lost his balance, fell down the steps, and died.

___ *Demise* means   A. popularity.   B. a secret.   C. dying.

6 infamous
(ĭn′fə-məs)
-adjective

● King Henry VIII of England was **infamous** throughout Europe for executing two of his six wives.

● Visitors to the dungeons of ancient castles always want to see the instruments of torture, including the **infamous** Iron Maiden—a body-shaped box with spikes inside.

___ *Infamous* means   A. known unfavorably.   B. thought to be annoying.   C. giving hope.

7 intrinsic
(ĭn-trĭn′sĭk)
-*adjective*

- Trust is **intrinsic** to any good friendship.
- Because Lian has an **intrinsic** desire to learn, she doesn't need the reward of good grades to motivate her studies.

___ *Intrinsic* means   A. secret.   B. fundamental.   C. unnecessary.

8 revulsion
(rĭ-vŭl′shən)
-*noun*

- Whenever I read about child abuse in the newspaper, I am filled with such **revulsion** that I often cannot finish the article.
- When Sharon met the man who had cheated her father, she was overcome with **revulsion**.

___ *Revulsion* means   A. interest.   B. hatred.   C. understanding.

9 speculate
(spĕk′yə-lāt′)
-*verb*

- It's interesting to **speculate** how history might have been different if Abraham Lincoln had lived a few years longer.
- The therapist asked Cassie to **speculate** about what might happen if she told Leon her true feelings.

___ *Speculate* means   A. to remember.   B. to announce.   C. to guess.

10 virile
(vîr′əl)
-*adjective*

- Men who are unsure about their masculinity sometimes try to "prove" they are **virile** by being overly aggressive.
- When a male heron stamps his feet and sticks his neck out, and then drops his head and says "plop-buzz," the female finds him very **virile**. In fact, that behavior is how the male attracts a mate.

___ *Virile* means   A. having attractive male qualities.   B. lacking in confidence.   C. unselfish.

Matching Words with Definitions

Following are definitions of the ten words. Clearly write or print each word next to its definition. The sentences above and on the previous page will help you decide on the meaning of each word.

1. _____ Secret; hidden

2. _____ A person who believes the worst of people's behavior and motives; someone who believes people are motivated only by selfishness

3. _____ Belonging to a person or thing by its very nature (and thus not dependent on circumstances); built-in

4. _____ Having a very bad reputation; widely known for being vicious, criminal, or deserving of contempt

5. _____ A person or organization that gives help, especially financial aid

6. _____ Manly; masculine

7. _____ Death

8. _____ To come up with ideas or theories about a subject; theorize

9. _____ To relieve; make easier to endure

10. _____ Great disgust or distaste

CAUTION: Do not go any further until you are sure the above answers are correct. Then you can use the definitions to help you in the following practices. Your goal is eventually to know the words well enough so that you don't need to check the definitions at all.

Sentence Check 1

Using the answer line provided, complete each item below with the correct word from the box. Use each word once.

A. alleviate	B. benefactor	C. covert	D. cynic	E. demise
F. infamous	G. intrinsic	H. revulsion	I. speculate	J. virile

_____ 1. Problems are ___ to life; they're unavoidable.

_____ 2. My hunger isn't fully satisfied, but the apple ___(e)d it somewhat.

_____ 3. Teenage guys usually welcome a deepening voice and a thickening beard as signs that they are becoming more ___.

_____ 4. The selfless work of the nuns in the slums of India is enough to touch the hearts of most hardened ___s.

_____ 5. Though she was tried and found not guilty, Lizzie Borden is still ___ for killing her parents with a hatchet.

_____ 6. The children loved the ___ activities involved in preparing their mother's surprise party.

_____ 7. The mass murderer's neighbors were overcome with ___ when they learned what their "friend" had been doing in his basement.

_____ 8. "As no group has claimed responsibility, we can only ___ on the motives for the bombing," said the newscaster.

_____ 9. Roger Novak had been a well-known ___ of AIDS research, so it was no surprise that he left a lot of money for the research in his will.

_____ 10. It's a good idea for married couples to discuss their funeral plans in case of each other's ___. For example, do they wish to be buried or cremated?

NOTE: Now check your answers to these items by turning to page 178. Going over the answers carefully will help you prepare for the next two practices, for which answers are not given.

Sentence Check 2

Using the answer lines provided, complete each item below with **two** words from the box. Use each word once.

_____
_____ 1–2. Nursing is a good career for Dee because it's a(n) ___ part of her personality to try to ___ people's pain. In addition, her physical and mental strength will help her handle the rigors° of nursing, such as intense stress and long hours.

_____
_____ 3–4. Although everything about the Nazis filled the Dutch spy with ___, his ___ assignment was to make friends with top Nazi scientists. He had few qualms° about faking such friendships—he would have felt more guilty if he hadn't done everything in his power to fight the Nazis.

_____   5–6. The ___s in town said that Joyce's sorrow over her husband's ___ was much
_____   less than her joy in getting the money from his insurance policy.

_____   7–8. Young men who are bullies usually think of themselves as ___, but a ___ of
_____   the weak is far more manly than someone who takes advantage of weakness.

_____   9–10. With all the stories told about Jesse James, the Dalton Gang, and other ___
_____   figures of the Wild West, we can only ___ as to how much is fact and how
                                   much is fiction.

Final Check: *The Mad Monk*

Here is a final opportunity for you to strengthen your knowledge of the ten words. First read the following selection carefully. Then fill in each blank with a word from the box at the top of the previous page. (Context clues will help you figure out which word goes in which blank.) Use each word once.

Shortly before the Russian Revolution, an eccentric° man named Rasputin became (1)_____ as the "mad monk." Because he dressed like a peasant, drank heavily, and rarely bathed, the nobility often felt (2)_____ during their encounters° with him at the palace.

Yet despite his outward appearance, Rasputin possessed a(n) (3)_____ charm that drew many to him, including the Russian empress. She thought him a great man of God and a special (4)_____ of her seriously ill son, whose condition she felt Rasputin (5)_____(e)d.

Many (6)_____s believed otherwise. To them, Rasputin was no healer; instead, he was a man who exploited° his relationship with the empress for his own benefit. Rather than praise Rasputin, his enemies preferred to malign° him. In a pamphlet titled *The Holy Devil*, one of his critics described him as a sinister° man. This author even dared to (7)_____ that the monk and the empress were romantically involved. This theory was strengthened by the fact that the empress's "holy man" pursued many women and boasted about how (8)_____ he was.

Finally, a group of Russian noblemen made (9)_____ plans to kill Rasputin. Somehow, the secret must have gotten out, for a Russian official warned Rasputin of a plot against him. He nevertheless accepted the noblemen's invitation to a dinner party, where they served him poisoned wine and cake. When Rasputin did not appear to succumb° to the poison, his enemies hastened his (10)_____ by shooting and stabbing him and then dumping him into an icy river. An autopsy revealed that he had died by drowning.

Scores   Sentence Check 2 _____%   Final Check _____%

Enter your scores above and in the **Vocabulary Performance Chart** on the inside back cover of the book.

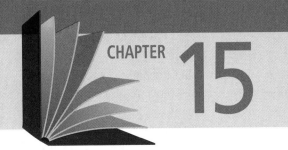

abstain	deficit
affiliate	dissent
agnostic	diversion
aspire	lucrative
benevolent	mandatory

Ten Words in Context

In the space provided, write the letter of the meaning closest to that of each **boldfaced** word. Use the context of the sentences to help you figure out each word's meaning.

1 abstain
(ăb-stān′)
-verb

● Although Luis has given up high-calorie desserts, he doesn't **abstain** completely from chocolate. He allows himself one small square of a Hershey bar a day.

● My sister called off her engagement to Clayton because he wouldn't **abstain** from dating other women.

___ *Abstain from* means   A. to desire.   B. to believe in.   C. to deny oneself.

2 affiliate
(ə-fĭl′ē-āt′)
-verb

● Diane is neither a Democrat nor a Republican. She isn't **affiliated** with any political party.

● The young singer could have earned more if she had been **affiliated** with the musicians' union, but she couldn't afford the membership dues.

___ *Affiliate* means   A. to join.   B. to study.   C. to hold back.

3 agnostic
(ăg-nŏs′tĭk)
-noun

● Iris believes there is a God, and Marcia feels sure there isn't. Jean, an **agnostic**, feels that we can't be certain one way or the other.

● My uncle, who was an **agnostic**, used to say, "Humans cannot understand a flower, let alone whether or not there's a God."

___ *Agnostic* means   A. one who denies God's existence.   B. one who feels we can't know if God exists.   C. one who is sure there is a God.

4 aspire
(ə-spīr′)
-verb

● Twelve-year-old Derek, who loves drawing buildings, **aspires** to be an architect.

● Millions of young people **aspire** to be professional athletes, but only a few will succeed.

___ *Aspire* means   A. to fear.   B. to wish.   C. to volunteer.

5 benevolent
(bə-nĕv′ə-lənt)
-adjective

● People are more **benevolent** at Christmas, the "season for giving."

● In 1878, William Booth founded a **benevolent** association to help the poor of London. He called it the Salvation Army.

___ *Benevolent* means   A. recreational.   B. profitable.   C. charitable.

6 deficit
(dĕf′ə-sĭt)
-noun

● Our club has spent much more money than it has taken in, so it now has a huge budget **deficit**.

● Residents are asked not to water their lawns because a **deficit** of rain has dangerously lowered the water supply.

___ *Deficit* means   A. a lack.   B. an overflow.   C. a collection.

7 dissent
(dĭ-sĕnt′)
-noun

- The committee was so torn by **dissent** that its members could not even agree on whether or not to schedule another meeting.
- The dictator permitted people to agree with his policies or keep silent about them, but not to express **dissent**.

___ *Dissent* means   A. plans.   B. opposition.   C. relief.

8 diversion
(də-vûr′zhən)
-noun

- My history teacher says that one of her favorite **diversions** during summer vacation is reading mystery novels.
- Skip likes his job, but he also enjoys such **diversions** as playing video games, watching baseball, and reading humorous stories.

___ *Diversion* means   A. a way to relax.   B. something easy.   C. an assignment.

9 lucrative
(lōō′krə-tĭv)
-adjective

- Investments in the stock market can be **lucrative**. However, they can also result in great financial loss.
- "Teaching at a small college isn't **lucrative**," Professor Baum admitted, "but I've never felt the need to make lots of money."

___ *Lucrative* means   A. required.   B. financially rewarding.   C. risky.

10 mandatory
(măn′də-tôr′ē)
-adjective

- Members of the basketball team have to follow strict rules. For example, it's **mandatory** that each player attend at least 80 percent of the practices.
- "A research paper isn't **mandatory**," the instructor said, "but if you write one, you'll get extra credit."

___ *Mandatory* means   A. unimportant.   B. helpful.   C. essential.

Matching Words with Definitions

Following are definitions of the ten words. Clearly write or print each word next to its definition. The sentences above and on the previous page will help you decide on the meaning of each word.

1. _____ To strongly desire; to be ambitious (to do something or to get something)

2. _____ Profitable; well-paying

3. _____ A shortage; a lack (in amount)

4. _____ To hold oneself back from something; refrain

5. _____ Showing kindness; charitable

6. _____ A person who believes we cannot know whether or not there is a God

7. _____ Required

8. _____ An amusement or pastime; anything that relaxes or amuses

9. _____ To associate; join

10. _____ Disagreement

CAUTION: Do not go any further until you are sure the above answers are correct. Then you can use the definitions to help you in the following practices. Your goal is eventually to know the words well enough so that you don't need to check the definitions at all.

Sentence Check 1

Using the answer line provided, complete each item below with the correct word from the box. Use each word once.

A. **abstain**	B. **affiliate**	C. **agnostic**	D. **aspire**	E. **benevolent**
F. **deficit**	G. **dissent**	H. **diversion**	I. **lucrative**	J. **mandatory**

_____ 1. My kid brother ___s to become the video-game champion of the world.

_____ 2. The ___ fund at my church collects money to help poor families in our parish.

_____ 3. My parents enjoy card games, but my sister and I prefer such ___s as computer games and music videos.

_____ 4. An entrance fee wasn't ___, but a sign at the museum entrance suggested that visitors make a donation.

_____ 5. Because Hank needs to lose weight, his doctor recommended that he ___ from all sweets and fatty foods.

_____ 6. We could overcome a(n) ___ of organs for transplants if more people would agree to have their organs donated after they die.

_____ 7. There was no ___ in the family on whether or not to start a vegetable garden this year. We all agreed it was a great idea.

_____ 8. Yong could have joined the all-male club, but he prefers to ___ with organizations that welcome both men and women.

_____ 9. "When someone who believes in God marries someone who does not," the comic asked, "do they give birth to a(n) ___?"

_____ 10. Acting is ___ for only a small percentage of performers. The rest need additional sources of income, such as waiting on tables or parking cars.

NOTE: Now check your answers to these items by turning to page 178. Going over the answers carefully will help you prepare for the next two practices, for which answers are not given.

Sentence Check 2

Using the answer lines provided, complete each item below with **two** words from the box. Use each word once.

_____
_____ 1–2. My uncle decided to splurge and ___ with a country club because golf is his favorite ___.

_____
_____ 3–4. Gail didn't ___ from smoking cigarettes until her employer made not smoking ___. Keeping her job was a very good incentive° to get her to quit.

_____
_____ 5–6. Some people think that since Stan is a(n) ___, he must be amoral°. It's true he's not sure if God exists, but that doesn't mean he lacks a moral sense. In fact, he recently founded a ___ society at work to raise money for disabled children in the area.

_____   7–8. The ___ in the township treasury is causing a lot of ___ over whether or not
_____   taxes should be raised.

_____   9–10. Because my father ___s to make enough money to send his children to
_____   college, he's working hard to make his auto repair business as ___ as
                                   possible.

Final Check: *Conflict Over Holidays*

Here is a final opportunity for you to strengthen your knowledge of the ten words. First read the following selection carefully. Then fill in each blank with a word from the box at the top of the previous page. (Context clues will help you figure out which word goes in which blank.) Use each word once.

While Jeanne and Paul are generally a happily married couple, they do struggle over one point of (1)_____. They disagree as to how their family should observe religious holidays.

"The emphasis on presents," says Jeanne, "has made the season (2)_____ for all those mercenary° retailers who overcharge at holiday time. Also, people who should be watching their expenses create unnecessary (3)_____s in their budgets by squandering° money on unimportant gifts." She complains that exchanging presents at Christmas is practically

(4)_____, whether or not one believes in the holiday's religious significance. Jeanne (5)_____s to keep her home free of all such nonreligious customs and thus wants her children to (6)_____ from traditions such as gift-giving and dyeing Easter eggs. She feels the family's money would be better spent if it were donated to a (7)_____ organization for helping the poor. Some of Jeanne's neighbors assume that she is a(n) (8)_____ because of her lack of holiday spirit. They are wrong, however. Jeanne believes deeply in God and is (9)_____(e)d with a church.

While Paul understands Jeanne's concerns, he prefers the conventional° way of celebrating holidays. "Children enjoy the customary (10)_____s that are connected with the holidays," he says. "What would Christmas be without a visit to Santa and gifts under the tree? What would Easter be without colorful eggs and an Easter egg hunt? These are pleasant practices that enhance° the joy of the season."

| Scores | Sentence Check 2 _____ % | Final Check _____ % |

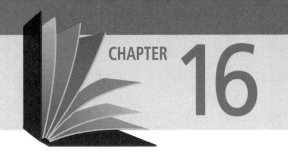

CHAPTER 16

charisma	poignant
contemporary	prevalent
contend	proponent
conversely	quest
extrovert	traumatic

Ten Words in Context

In the space provided, write the letter of the meaning closest to that of each **boldfaced** word. Use the context of the sentences to help you figure out each word's meaning.

1 charisma
(kə-rĭz′mə)
-noun

● Kamal has such **charisma** that when he ran for class president, almost every person in the tenth grade voted for him. His classmates couldn't resist Kamal's magnetic personality.

● Great Britain's Princess Diana obviously had great **charisma**. She continues to have numerous loyal fans—long after her death.

___ *Charisma* means   A. feelings.   B. personal appeal.   C. luck.

2 contemporary
(kən-tĕm′pə-rĕr′ē)
-adjective

● Beth likes **contemporary** furniture, but her husband prefers antiques.

● My grandfather says that compared to kids in his day, **contemporary** youngsters are soft and lazy.

___ *Contemporary* means   A. common.   B. old-fashioned.   C. today's.

3 contend
(kən-tĕnd′)
-verb

● The defense attorney **contended** that his client was insane and therefore could not be held responsible for the murder.

● Scientists **contend** that no two snowflakes are identical, but how could they possibly prove it?

___ *Contend* means   A. to wish.   B. to deny.   C. to declare.

4 conversely
(kən-vûrs′lē)
-adverb

● Ron, who is basically bored by food, eats in order to live. **Conversely**, Nate loves food so much that he seems to live in order to eat.

● Mary drives her children to school whenever it rains. **Conversely**, Thea makes her kids walk because she thinks a little rain never hurt anyone.

___ *Conversely* means   A. in contrast.   B. in a modern way.   C. similarly.

5 extrovert
(ĕk′strə-vûrt′)
-noun

● Surprisingly, not all performers are **extroverts**. Offstage, many are quiet and shy.

● Ms. Stein hired Roberto to greet and chat with her clients because he's such an **extrovert**.

___ *Extrovert* means   A. a supporter of causes.   B. a timid person.   C. a sociable person.

6 poignant
(poin′yənt)
-adjective

● The service honoring American soldiers missing in action was touching. A speech by a friend of one of the soldiers was particularly **poignant**.

● I cried when I read a **poignant** story about a dying girl who gave away all of her dolls to "poor children."

___ *Poignant* means   A. affecting the emotions.   B. correct.   C. lively.

7 prevalent
(prĕv′ə-lənt)
-*adjective*

● Unemployment was **prevalent** during America's Great Depression. By 1932, over twelve million people were out of work.

● Television sets are more **prevalent** in the United States than bathtubs. Over half of American homes have three or more TVs. Far fewer homes have more than one bathtub.

___ *Prevalent* means   A. favorable.   B. found frequently.   C. unlikely.

8 proponent
(prō-pō′nənt)
-*noun*

● I voted for Senator Williams, a **proponent** of improved services for the elderly, because I feel that many older people need greater assistance.

● Although Elaine quit work to take care of her children, she is a **proponent** of employer-supported day care.

___ *Proponent* means   A. a recipient.   B. an opponent.   C. a supporter.

9 quest
(kwĕst)
-*noun*

● During Carlo's **quest** for the perfect pizza, he sampled the cheese pizza at twenty-seven different restaurants.

● Ponce de Leon's **quest** was for the Fountain of Youth; what he found instead was Florida.

___ *Quest* means   A. a hunt.   B. a question.   C. a design.

10 traumatic
(trô-măt′ĭk)
-*adjective*

● Divorce can be less **traumatic** for children if their fears and feelings are taken into account as the divorce takes place.

● My cousin has had nightmares ever since his **traumatic** experience of being trapped in a coal mine.

___ *Traumatic* means   A. familiar.   B. reasonable.   C. extremely upsetting.

Matching Words with Definitions

Following are definitions of the ten words. Clearly write or print each word next to its definition. The sentences above and on the previous page will help you decide on the meaning of each word.

1. _____ In an opposite manner; in an altogether different way

2. _____ The quality of a leader which captures great popular devotion; personal magnetism; charm

3. _____ A search; pursuit

4. _____ Widespread; common

5. _____ To state to be so; claim; affirm

6. _____ Modern; up-to-date

7. _____ Someone who supports a cause

8. _____ Emotionally moving; touching

9. _____ Causing painful emotions, with possible long-lasting psychological effects

10. _____ An outgoing, sociable person

CAUTION: Do not go any further until you are sure the above answers are correct. Then you can use the definitions to help you in the following practices. Your goal is eventually to know the words well enough so that you don't need to check the definitions at all.

Sentence Check 1

Using the answer line provided, complete each item below with the correct word from the box. Use each word once.

A. **charisma**	B. **contemporary**	C. **contend**	D. **conversely**	E. **extrovert**
F. **poignant**	G. **prevalent**	H. **proponent**	I. **quest**	J. **traumatic**

_____ 1. I study best in the morning. ___, my sister concentrates better at night.

_____ 2. Nancy is a(n) ___ by nature, but since she's become depressed, she has avoided other people.

_____ 3. At the airport, I was very moved by the ___ reunion of family members who had been separated for years.

_____ 4. Underage drinking was so ___ in the fraternity house that college officials ordered the house closed for a year.

_____ 5. "This woman ___s that she was here before you," said the supermarket checkout clerk. "Is it her turn now?"

_____ 6. Felipe is a(n) ___ of exercising for good health. He even encourages his young children to swim or cycle every day.

_____ 7. Certain movie stars may not be great actors, but they have a(n) ___ that makes people want to see their films.

_____ 8. Abby didn't like the apartment with the old-fashioned bathtub and radiators. She preferred a more ___ place.

_____ 9. Repeating third grade was ___ for my brother. It still pains him to think about it, even though he's a successful businessman now.

_____ 10. During the past three hundred years, several people have gone on a(n) ___ for Noah's ark. Some have looked for it in northeastern Turkey, on Mount Ararat, sixteen thousand feet above sea level.

NOTE: Now check your answers to these items by turning to page 178. Going over the answers carefully will help you prepare for the next two practices, for which answers are not given.

Sentence Check 2

Using the answer lines provided, complete each item below with **two** words from the box. Use each word once.

_____
_____ 1–2. Many people are surprised to learn how ___ poverty is in ___ America. Today, millions live below the poverty line, and the number seems to escalate° daily.

_____
_____ 3–4. Judy and Martin Reed exemplify° the old saying "Opposites attract." A(n) ___, Judy chooses work that brings her into constant contact with others. ___, Martin prefers jobs in which he mainly works alone.

_____ 5–6. Ever since the ___ experience of finding her twelve-year-old son dead from
_____   a drug overdose, Sophie has been a strong ___ of mandatory° drug education
                                       in the public schools. If drug education isn't required, she says, schools may
                                       cut corners and omit it.

_____ 7–8. My mother ___s that *Romeo and Juliet* is the most ___ story ever written, but
_____   my sister claims Erich Segal's *Love Story* is more moving.

_____ 9–10. Mahatma Gandhi's ___ and vision inspired millions of fellow Indians to join
_____   him enthusiastically in the ___ for peaceful solutions to national problems.
                                        Gandhi incorporated° nonviolence and political activism into a highly
                                        effective method for social change: passive resistance.

Final Check: *Dr. Martin Luther King, Jr.*

Here is a final opportunity for you to strengthen your knowledge of the ten words. First read the following selection carefully. Then fill in each blank with a word from the box at the top of the previous page. (Context clues will help you figure out which word goes in which blank.) Use each word once.

(1)_____ young people may be able to list the many accomplishments of the Reverend Dr. Martin Luther King, Jr. They may know that he was a civil rights leader who aspired° to achieve racial harmony and was a(n) (2)_____ of peaceful but direct action. They may know that he fought the discrimination against blacks that was so (3)_____ in our country in the 1950s and 1960s. They may also know that he received a great deal of acclaim° for his work. For example, in 1964 he won the Nobel Peace Prize. They may even (4)_____ that he is the most important social reformer in the history of our nation.

But can the young really know the (5)_____, the powerful personal magnetism of this man? He was a perfect blend of quiet, considerate thinker and bold, outspoken (6)_____. When Dr. King spoke, people listened. He had such a forceful yet (7)_____ way of speaking that those who heard him felt his message deep within. For most, this meant a stronger belief in and respect for the man and his ideals. (8)_____, for bigots, it meant hatred and fear of what he stood for.

Dr. King's (9)_____ for equal rights for all was clear when he said, "I have a dream that this nation will rise up and live out the true meaning of its creed: 'We hold these truths to be self-evident; that all men are created equal.'" He gave his time, his leadership, and, in the end, his life. His murder was a (10)_____ event in the lives of many Americans, who never fully recovered from that awful day. But because of Martin Luther King, Americans live with greater dignity. And many have taken up his fight against the inequities° of racism.

Scores   Sentence Check 2 _____%   Final Check _____%

congenial	prone
flippant	rapport
impasse	rationale
perception	relentless
prompt	reprisal

Ten Words in Context

In the space provided, write the letter of the meaning closest to that of each **boldfaced** word. Use the context of the sentences to help you figure out each word's meaning.

1 congenial
(kən-jēn′yəl)
-*adjective*

● I was nervous being at a party where I didn't know anyone, but the other guests were so **congenial** that I soon felt at ease.

● Beware of friendships that begin in Internet chat rooms. People who seem **congenial** online may be anything but pleasant in real life.

___ *Congenial* means   A. persistent.   B. intelligent.   C. friendly.

2 flippant
(flĭp′ənt)
-*adjective*

● "Don't give me a **flippant** answer," George's father told him. "Your financial situation is a serious matter."

● When a teenage boy is asked to clean his room, he's likely to give a **flippant** response such as "Why should I? I just cleaned it last month."

___ *Flippant* means   A. rude.   B. serious.   C. incorrect.

3 impasse
(ĭm′păs)
-*noun*

● The jurors had reached an **impasse**. They couldn't agree on a verdict—some thought the defendant was the murderer, but others were sure he was innocent.

● If you think you've reached an **impasse** when trying to solve a problem, take a break. The solution may occur to you while you're doing something else.

___ *Impasse* means   A. a deadlock.   B. a relationship.   C. an opportunity.

4 perception
(pər-sĕp′shən)
-*noun*

● Brenda's **perceptions** of others are usually accurate. She is a good judge of character.

● "Our **perceptions** of our problem differ," Tonya explained. "Sam thinks money is the main issue, but I believe it's a question of who controls the purse strings."

___ *Perception* means   A. a memory.   B. a view.   C. a desire.

5 prompt
(prŏmpt)
-*verb*

● To **prompt** her son Byron to get a job, Mrs. Davis pinned the want ads to his pillow.

● Fast-food clerks **prompt** customers to spend more money by asking such questions as "Would you like cookies or apple pie with that?"

___ *Prompt* means   A. to allow.   B. to agree with.   C. to encourage.

6 prone
(prōn)
-*adjective*

● Mr. Walker is **prone** to sleep problems, so he limits his intake of caffeine.

● **Prone** to fits of laughter during class, Chris controls himself by chewing on his pen.

___ *Prone* means   A. tending.   B. immune.   C. attracted.

7 rapport
(ră-pŏr')
-noun

- In high school, I had such good **rapport** with my gym teacher that our close relationship continues to this day.
- If no **rapport** develops between you and your therapist after a month or two, start looking for a counselor who makes you feel comfortable.

___ *Rapport* means   A. a report.   B. a personal connection.   C. a financial situation.

8 rationale
(răsh'ə-năl')
-noun

- Danielle's **rationale** for majoring in business was simple. She said, "I want to make a lot of money."
- The **rationale** for not lowering the drinking age to 18 is that self-control and good judgment are still being developed at that age.

___ *Rationale* means   A. a situation.   B. an explanation.   C. a question.

9 relentless
(rĭ-lĕnt'lĭs)
-adjective

- The dog's **relentless** barking got on my nerves. He barked the entire two hours his owners were out.
- In a large city, the noise of crowds and heavy traffic is so **relentless** that it can be difficult to find peace and quiet.

___ *Relentless* means   A. occasional.   B. exciting.   C. nonstop.

10 reprisal
(rĭ-prī'zəl)
-noun

- In **reprisal** for being fired, a troubled man shot several people at the factory where he used to work.
- Fear of **reprisal** may keep children from telling parents or teachers about a bully who has threatened them.

___ *Reprisal* means   A. disrespect.   B. revenge.   C. delay.

Matching Words with Definitions

Following are definitions of the ten words. Clearly write or print each word next to its definition. The sentences above and on the previous page will help you decide on the meaning of each word.

1. _____ Insight or understanding gained through observation; impression

2. _____ Having a tendency; inclined (to do something)

3. _____ Persistent; continuous

4. _____ The underlying reasons for something; logical basis

5. _____ Disrespectful and not serious enough

6. _____ Agreeable or pleasant in character; friendly; sociable

7. _____ To urge into action; motivate

8. _____ The paying back of one injury or bad deed with another

9. _____ A situation with no way out; dead end

10. _____ Relationship, especially one that is close, trusting, or sympathetic

CAUTION: Do not go any further until you are sure the above answers are correct. Then you can use the definitions to help you in the following practices. Your goal is eventually to know the words well enough so that you don't need to check the definitions at all.

Sentence Check 1

Using the answer line provided, complete each item below with the correct word from the box. Use each word once.

A. congenial	B. flippant	C. impasse	D. perception	E. prompt
F. prone	G. rapport	H. rationale	I. relentless	J. reprisal

_____ 1. Raquel is ___ to accidents, so her car insurance rates are quite high.

_____ 2. You will get along better in life if you are ___ to other people, rather than unpleasant.

_____ 3. My brother hides his lack of confidence by being ___. He rarely treats anything seriously.

_____ 4. It took his best friend's heart attack to ___ my dad to start exercising and eating right.

_____ 5. There was instant ___ between Duke and Otis. They talked as if they'd known each other for years.

_____ 6. At the movie's turning point, the bad guys reached a(n) ___. On one side of them was the police; on the other was a steep cliff.

_____ 7. During April and May, the rain was so ___ that we thought we might have to start building an ark.

_____ 8. Floyd's ___ of human nature is strongly colored by some bad experiences. He thinks everyone is basically selfish.

_____ 9. When Lacey and John divorced, she tried to get over half his income. In ___, he tried not to give her any of his income at all.

_____ 10. The ___ behind encouraging pregnant women to gain about twenty-five pounds is that low weight gain can lead to dangerously low birth weights.

NOTE: Now check your answers to these items by turning to page 178. Going over the answers carefully will help you prepare for the next two practices, for which answers are not given.

Sentence Check 2

Using the answer lines provided, complete each item below with **two** words from the box. Use each word once.

_____
_____ 1–2. Because Wade is so ___ and easy to talk to, we established a warm ___ the first day we met.

_____
_____ 3–4. Although the company president explained the ___ behind the pay cuts, his announcement ___(e)d an employee protest. However, once it was learned that the president was also taking a big pay cut, the employees' dissent° died down.

_____   5–6. The waitresses in our local diner are ___ to be funny and not always polite. If
_____   a customer says, "I'm ready to order now," he may get a ___ response such
                                      as, "And I'm ready to retire, but you don't hear me making a big deal about
                                      it."

_____   7–8. My ___ of the situation is that talks between the factory management and
_____   union officials reached a(n) ___ because neither side would compromise
                                      on salary increases and health benefits. In such situations, flexibility is a
                                      prerequisite° to progress.

_____   9–10. Alma could put up with occasional kidding, but her brother's teasing was
_____   often ___, going on for weeks at a time. Sick of it all, she finally planned a(n)
                                      ___ that would embarrass him in front of his friends.

Final Check: *Relating to Parents*

Here is a final opportunity for you to strengthen your knowledge of the ten words. First read the following
selection carefully. Then fill in each blank with a word from the box at the top of the previous page.
(Context clues will help you figure out which word goes in which blank.) Use each word once.

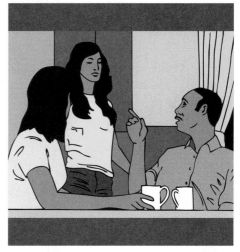

How do you respond when your parents deny you
permission to do something? For example, if you want to
travel and work around the country for the summer, but
your parents say you're too young, do you become irate° and
angrily demand that they stop curtailing° your rights? Do you
plan a(n) (1)_____, vowing to sabotage°
their summer plans because they've ruined yours? Or do
you explain the (2)_____ behind your
request, so that your parents will understand your reasoning?

The way you behave when you and your parents reach
a(n) (3)_____ on an issue can have a big
effect on how they view you. Sure, you could retort°, "Fine. I'll
go buy a leash so you can really run my life." But if you are consistently (4)_____ like
that, you'll just strengthen their (5)_____ of you as being too immature to be on your
own. Also, if you are (6)_____ in your begging, asking them three hundred times a day,
"But *why* won't you let me travel alone?" you might elicit° this response: "You may do some traveling alone
right now—go directly to your room."

Instead, approach your parents in a (7)_____ way and try to develop
a strong, friendly (8)_____ with them. An amiable°, respectful relationship
will make them more (9)_____ to see things your way. Even if you can't
(10)_____ them to change their minds about this summer's plans, your chances of
getting their support will be better the next time you want to try something new.

Scores   Sentence Check 2 _____%   Final Check _____%

cor, cour	-ish
di-, du-	magni-, magn-
-dom	phob
-fy	pro-
il-, im-	psych-, psycho-

Ten Word Parts in Context

Figure out the meanings of the following ten word parts by looking *closely* and *carefully* at the context in which they appear. Then, in the space provided, write the letter of the meaning closest to that of each word part.

1 cor, cour

● I felt truly welcomed by my **cordial** hosts. Their kindness and generosity were heartfelt.

● Emmy was **courageous** enough to face the bully without backing down. I would have been too scared to do the same.

___ The word part *cor* or *cour* means   A. resembling.   B. double.   C. heart.

2 di-, du-

● When Tyrone and Verna got **divorced**, they had to spend a difficult day dividing their household possessions into two groups.

● One of the three band members didn't show up, so only a **duo** played at the dance.

___ The word part *di-* or *du-* means   A. make.   B. two.   C. great.

3 -dom

● A few actors achieve overnight success, but for most, the road to **stardom** is long and difficult.

● "One sure way to put my husband into a deep state of **boredom**," Jasmin said, "is to take him with me when I shop for shoes."

___ The word part *-dom* means   A. like.   B. state of being.   C. fear.

4 -fy

● Would it **simplify** matters if I held your baby while you go into the dressing room to try on the slacks?

● First **liquefy** the ice cream over heat. Then mix in the strawberry jam.

___ The word part *-fy* means   A. cause to become.   B. again.   C. dislike.

5 il-, im-

● Nita doesn't seem to care that it's **illegal** to park next to a fire hydrant.

● My brother-in-law is so **immature** that he often acts as if he is 16 instead of a married man of 26.

___ The word part *il-* or *im-* means   A. not.   B. double.   C. like.

6 -ish

● My **devilish** brother once videotaped me huffing and puffing my way through aerobics, and now he shows the tape to every new friend I bring home.

● Of all the girls at school, Jessie was the most **stylish**, wearing only the latest clothing featured in the fashion magazines.

___ The word part *-ish* means   A. forth.   B. characteristic of.   C. mind.

7 magni-, magn-

● My grandmother uses a **magnifying** glass to make the small print in the newspaper appear larger.

● Eight years after starting Standard Oil in 1870, oil **magnate** John D. Rockefeller controlled about 85 percent of the country's oil industry.

__ The word part *magni-* or *magn-* means

    A. forward.   B. fear.   C. large.

8 phob

● One of the most unusual **phobias** is the fear of peanut butter sticking to the roof of one's mouth.

● Marilyn's mother has developed **agoraphobia** to the point that she is afraid even of going to the mailbox at the end of the driveway.

__ The word part *phob* means

    A. forth.   B. quality.   C. fear.

9 pro-

● **Proceed** down to the end of this hallway, make a left, and you will see the x-ray department.

● One scientist **propels** his car with a fuel he gets by burning garbage.

__ The word part *pro-* means

    A. forward.   B. resembling.   C. dislike.

10 psych-, psycho-

● To treat her depression, Lee takes medication and also sees a **psychiatrist** once a week.

● A **psychoactive** drug is one that affects mental processes.

__ The word part *psych-* or *psycho-* means

    A. mind.   B. make.   C. again.

Matching Word Parts with Definitions

Following are definitions of the ten word parts. Clearly write or print each word part next to its definition. The sentences above and on the previous page will help you decide on the meaning of each word part.

1. _____ Great; large

2. _____ Cause to be or become; make

3. _____ Forward; forth

4. _____ Fear

5. _____ Two; double

6. _____ Resembling; like; characteristic of

7. _____ Heart

8. _____ Mental processes; mind

9. _____ State of being; condition

10. _____ Not

CAUTION: Do not go any further until you are sure the above answers are correct. Then you can use the definitions to help you in the following practices. Your goal is eventually to know the word parts well enough so that you don't need to check the definitions at all.

Sentence Check 1

Using the answer line provided, complete each *italicized* word below with the correct word part from the box. Use each word part once.

A. **cour**	B. **di-, du-**	C. **-dom**	D. **-fy**	E. **il-, im-**
F. **-ish**	G. **magni-**	H. **phob**	I. **pro-**	J. **psycho-**

_____ 1. Despite her (*boy . . .*) ___ hairstyle, Paula looks very feminine.

_____ 2. (*Wis . . .*) ___ is what we gain when we learn from our mistakes.

_____ 3. The parents were greatly (*dis . . . aged*) ___ when every attempt to find their son failed.

_____ 4. To keep the accident victim (*. . . mobile*) ___, the paramedics tied her to a stretcher.

_____ 5. The reason these life-size dolls are so expensive is that only one hundred are (*. . . duced*) ___ each year.

_____ 6. The funhouse mirror (*. . . fied*) ___ my reflection so that I looked fifty pounds heavier.

_____ 7. I always (*. . . plicate*) ___ important papers and letters so that if the original gets lost, I still have the copy.

_____ 8. Barb's (*. . . analyst*) ___ asked her to write down her dreams, as they might be helpful in understanding her problems.

_____ 9. If you want to find a job before all the graduates start looking for employment next month, you'd better (*intensi . . .*) ___ your search.

_____ 10. It's lucky Santa Claus doesn't have (*claustro . . . ia*) ___. Otherwise, he would be too frightened of confined spaces to come down the chimney.

NOTE: Now check your answers to these items by turning to page 178. Going over the answers carefully will help you prepare for the next two practices, for which answers are not given.

Sentence Check 2

Using the answer line provided, complete each *italicized* word in the sentences below with the correct word part from the box. Use each word part once.

_____
_____ 1–2. The apartment the realtor showed us was (*. . . ficent*) ___, but it was (*. . . practical*) ___ for us. Not only was it too large, but it would also make an uncomfortable dent in our budget.

_____
_____ 3–4. Everyone has fears, but (*. . . ic*) ___ people need to gain (*free . . .*) __ from the extreme fears that devastate° them and their families.

_____
_____ 5–6. The purpose of (*. . . therapy*) ___ is to (*. . . mote*) ___ mental health.

_____   7–8. Florence and I felt (*fool* . . .) ___ when we sang "The Star-Spangled Banner"
_____   as a (. . . *et*) ___ and forgot the words halfway through.

_____   9–10. The mayor didn't allow racial tensions to (*dis* . . . *age*) ___ him. He just made
_____   more of an effort to (*uni* . . .) ___ the city.

Final Check: *Held Back by Fears*

Here is a final opportunity for you to strengthen your knowledge of the ten word parts. First read the following selection carefully. Then complete each *italicized* word in the parentheses below with a word part from the box at the top of the previous page. (Context clues will help you figure out which word part goes in which blank.) Use each word part once.

At age 24, Gina is facing a major (. . . *lemma*°)
(1)_____. She desperately wants
to live and work outside her hometown, but she
is prevented from traveling by her (. . . *ias*)
(2)_____. She suffers from
(. . . *logical*) (3)_____ but intense
fears of bridges and airplanes that are so traumatic°
that they cause nightmares and breathing problems.
Gina is convinced that if she doesn't fall off a bridge
or crash in an airplane, the mere possibility of such a
calamity° will so (*terri* . . .) (4)_____ her that she'll succumb° to a heart attack.

For some time now, Gina's friends have tried to persuade her to start seeing a (. . . *logist*)
(5)_____. They believe her problem will only increase in (. . . *tude*)
(6)_____ if she doesn't get help. But her relatives often make flippant° remarks
about Gina's condition, saying that she is just too cheap to travel. Accusing her of being (*child* . . .)
(7)_____, her brothers call her "baby" and "chicken." They say if she only had a little
more (. . . *age*) (8)_____, she would be able to go places. They don't realize that if
she could have controlled her fears by now, she would have.

Gina is seriously considering her friends' advice because she feels she has squandered° too much
of her time and energy on her fears. She hopes she will make rapid (. . . *gress*) (9)_____
in gaining (*free* . . .) (10)_____ from her fears so that she can start to live a full life.

Scores	Sentence Check 2 _____ %	Final Check _____ %

Enter your scores above and in the **Vocabulary Performance Chart** on the inside back cover of the book.

The box at the right lists twenty-five words from Unit Three. Using the clues at the bottom of the page, fill in these words to complete the puzzle that follows.

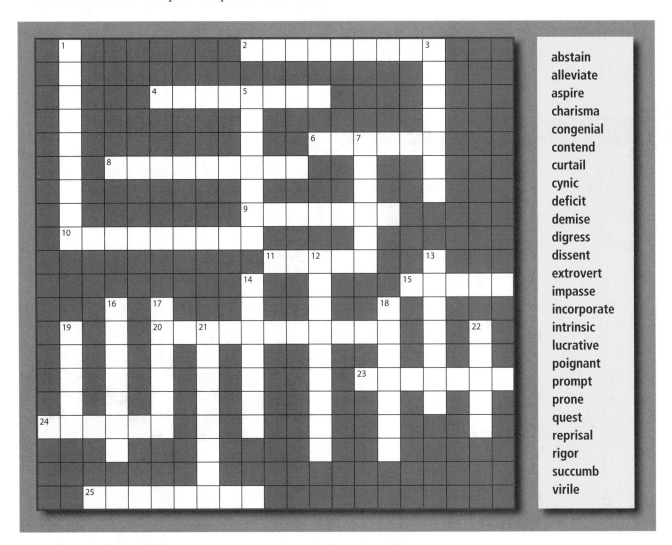

abstain
alleviate
aspire
charisma
congenial
contend
curtail
cynic
deficit
demise
digress
dissent
extrovert
impasse
incorporate
intrinsic
lucrative
poignant
prompt
prone
quest
reprisal
rigor
succumb
virile

ACROSS

2. Belonging to a person or thing by its very nature (and thus not dependent on circumstances)

4. The paying back of one injury or bad deed with another

6. To strongly desire; to be ambitious (to do something or to get something)

8. To relieve; make easier to endure

9. To give in; stop resisting

10. Profitable; well paying

11. A search; pursuit

15. Great hardship or difficulty

20. To unite into a single whole; combine

23. Disagreement

24. Death

25. Emotionally moving; touching

DOWN

1. Agreeable or pleasant in character; friendly

3. To state to be so; claim

5. A situation with no way out; dead end

7. To urge into action

12. An outgoing, sociable person

13. To turn aside, or stray, especially from the main topic in speaking or writing

14. To cut short or reduce

16. To hold oneself back from something; refrain

17. Manly; masculine

18. A shortage; a lack (in amount)

19. Having a tendency; inclined

21. The quality of a leader which captures great popular devotion; personal magnetism

22. A person who believes the worst of people's behavior and motives

PART A

Choose the word that best completes each item and write it in the space provided.

_____ 1. In irregular bursts of energy, dying stars give off ___ radio signals.

    A. virile   B. intermittent   C. congenial   D. flippant

_____ 2. Scientists ___ that the average life span of a dinosaur was probably 100 to 120 years.

    A. speculate   B. digress   C. detract   D. squander

_____ 3. The ___ of a Connecticut man was strange indeed. He died when his five-hundred-pound wife sat on him.

    A. diversion   B. charisma   C. perception   D. demise

_____ 4. A power failure ___ our viewing of the TV mystery, so we never found out who had committed the murder.

    A. prompted   B. curtailed   C. contended   D. dissented

_____ 5. The CIA's ___ activities often include "bugging" people's telephone lines with tiny hidden microphones.

    A. covert   B. traumatic   C. virile   D. congenial

_____ 6. ___ of gun control point out that gun accidents in American homes result in over a thousand deaths each year.

    A. Quests   B. Incentives   C. Proponents   D. Rigors

_____ 7. The talks between the two countries reached a(n) ___ when each side claimed the oil-rich border area as its own.

    A. benefactor   B. rapport   C. diversion   D. impasse

_____ 8. ___ to oversleeping, Rashid keeps his alarm clock across the room so he has to get out of bed to turn it off.

    A. Intrinsic   B. Lucrative   C. Prone   D. Covert

_____ 9. Alcohol is involved in nearly half of all traffic deaths in the United States, so people should ___ from drinking and driving.

    A. affiliate   B. abstain   C. contend   D. aspire

_____ 10. When I realized that I didn't have enough money for holiday gifts, I decided to overcome the ___ by taking an extra part-time job in December.

    A. charisma   B. perception   C. dissent   D. deficit

(Continues on next page)

PART B

On the answer line, write the letter of the choice that best completes each item.

_____ 11. If you **aspire** to be an Olympic swimmer,
A. then find a sport you prefer.   C. become a coach instead.
B. you must be ready to practice continually. D. you may have a fear of water.

_____ 12. A child with **relentless** questions is probably
A. ill.   C. curious.
B. angry.   D. too shy to ask.

_____ 13. The enormously successful movie *Titanic* **incorporated**
A. many millions of dollars.   C. elements of romance, adventure, and tragedy.
B. an ocean liner which struck an iceberg. D. Leonardo DiCaprio.

_____ 14. Many men try to make themselves look more **virile** by
A. eating more fruits and vegetables.   C. making quilts.
B. learning to play a musical instrument. D. lifting weights.

_____ 15. The boss's **perception** of Cory was
A. the comment "Good morning."   C. the afternoon shift.
B. that Cory was a hard worker. D. eight dollars an hour.

_____ 16. Joel seems to believe that his friends exist in order to serve him. **Conversely**, Julie
A. believes she exists to serve her friends. C. has far fewer friends than Joel.
B. agrees with Joel's point of view.   D. is not a friend of Joel's.

_____ 17. In his lecture about television, the speaker **digressed** by
A. mentioning a game-show series.
B. saying, "Good morning. My topic today is television."
C. discussing a soccer game he had seen the night before.
D. examining television ads aimed at children.

_____ 18. Carmen's face showed **revulsion** as she listened to the speaker talk about
A. exactly what happens to a person's body as he is electrocuted.
B. the gourmet appetizers, meals, and desserts served on the cruise ship.
C. advances in spinal-cord research that hold great promise for accident victims.
D. financial-aid packages available to incoming college freshmen.

_____ 19. Elaine works hard at her job as a lawyer. For **diversion**, she
A. reads all the latest law journals to keep up with recent developments.
B. gardens and plays field hockey.
C. writes briefs, attends hearings, and meets with clients.
D. attended college and law school.

_____ 20. Knowing that her auto accident had been a **traumatic** experience, Beverly's friends
A. expected her to heal soon.
B. were hesitant to make her talk about the horrible event.
C. wondered why she was making such a big deal of it.
D. knew she would be joking about it soon.

Score   (Number correct) _____ x 5 = _____%

Enter your score above and in the **Vocabulary Performance Chart** on the inside back cover of the book.

PART A

Complete each item with a word from the box. Use each word once.

A. benefactor	B. contend	C. devastate	D. extrovert	E. flippant
F. lucrative	G. poignant	H. quest	I. rapport	J. rationale
K. reprisal	L. rigor	M. succumb		

_____ 1. Jill was ____(e)d when she lost her job and, with it, her hopes of affording a house.

_____ 2. I have excellent ___ with my brother, but I haven't spoken to my older sister for years.

_____ 3. Rudy is such a(n) ___ that he makes friends with most of the customers at his beauty salon.

_____ 4. Before the turn of the century, the ___s of prizefighting included boxing without gloves.

_____ 5. City Council ___(e)d to public pressure and passed a law that made smoking in restaurants illegal.

_____ 6. My ___ for using cloth napkins is that they result in fewer trees being cut down to make paper napkins.

_____ 7. It was ___ to see the bear immediately adopt the orphaned cub.

_____ 8. Halloween is ___ for candy manufacturers. The holiday earns them about a billion dollars a year.

_____ 9. In some fairy tales, the hero searches far and wide, on a(n) ___ for some precious object or missing person.

_____ 10. The high school's chief ___ has offered to pay all college costs for any low-income student who graduates from the school.

_____ 11. When her brother kept taking her bike without asking, Meg's ___ was simply not to warn him that one of the tires was going flat.

_____ 12. The street's residents ___ that they complained for months about the huge pothole before the city government did anything about it.

_____ 13. When the principal asked Randy why he had spilled milk on some girls in the lunchroom, his ___ response was "Because they were thirsty."

(Continues on next page)

PART B

Write **C** if the italicized word is used **correctly**. Write **I** if the word is used **incorrectly**.

____ 14. For two weeks, the newspapers reported on the crimes of the *infamous* serial killer.

____ 15. Fran often *squanders* her money by walking through rain or snow instead of paying for a cab.

____ 16. Priests, rabbis, and other *agnostics* signed the petition asking for aid to the homeless.

____ 17. The comedian Groucho Marx once joked that he wouldn't want to *affiliate* himself with any club that would accept him as a member.

____ 18. The desire to aid others seems *intrinsic* to many animals. Baboons, for example, will try to free other baboons that are caged.

____ 19. Halloween has *contemporary* roots. Each year, the ancient Irish would dress as demons and witches to frighten away ghosts who might otherwise claim their bodies.

PART C

On the answer line, write the letter of the word that is the **synonym** of the boldfaced word.

Example: __A__ **traumatic**   A. upsetting   B. surprising   C. comforting

____ 20. **benevolent**   A. cruel   B. gifted   C. kind

____ 21. **alleviate**   A. relieve   B. worsen   C. raise

____ 22. **indispensable**   A. essential   B. expensive   C. unnecessary

PART D

On the answer line, write the letter of the word that is the **antonym** of the boldfaced word.

Example: __C__ **traumatic**   A. upsetting   B. surprising   C. comforting

____ 23. **prevalent**   A. heavy   B. rare   C. common

____ 24. **congenial**   A. disagreeable   B. clever   C. pleasant

____ 25. **mandatory**   A. required   B. optional   C. noisy

Score   (Number correct) _____   x 4 = _____%

Enter your score above and in the **Vocabulary Performance Chart** on the inside back cover of the book.

Each item below starts with a pair of words in CAPITAL LETTERS. For each item, figure out the relationship between these two words. Then decide which of the choices (A, B, C, or D) expresses a similar relationship. Write the letter of your choice on the answer line.

_____ 1. CURTAIL : SHORTEN ::
    A. seek : find   C. silence : conversation
    B. depart : arrive   D. ask : inquire

_____ 2. DEVASTATE : DISASTER ::
    A. harm : nurse   C. bore : surprise
    B. amaze : miracle   D. cold : snow

_____ 3. INCENTIVE : MONEY ::
    A. youth : adulthood   C. vehicle : motorcycle
    B. cash : poverty   D. sanitation worker : garbage

_____ 4. BENEFACTOR : SUPPORTS ::
    A. surgeon : operates   C. soldier : helmet
    B. leader : follows   D. waiter : waitress

_____ 5. CYNIC : OPTIMISTIC ::
    A. cucumber : vegetable   C. outcast : excluded
    B. criminal : law-abiding   D. ballerina : graceful

_____ 6. VIRILE : FEMININE ::
    A. manly : macho   C. popular : celebrity
    B. apartment : dwelling   D. fashionable : outmoded

_____ 7. AGNOSTIC : RELIGIOUS ::
    A. salesperson : persuasive C. hermit : sociable
    B. secretary : telephone   D. corn : crop

_____ 8. DISSENT : DISAGREEMENT ::
    A. remedy : solution   C. discord : harmony
    B. chemist : scientist   D. rival : helpful

_____ 9. DEFICIT : SURPLUS ::
    A. debt : poverty   C. clouds : rain
    B. border : interior   D. race car : speedy

_____ 10. CONTEMPORARY : OLD-FASHIONED ::
    A. outdated : old   C. thoughtful : gift
    B. copy : original   D. handlebar : bicycle

(Continues on next page)

____ 11. EXTROVERT : FRIENDLINESS ::
      A. performer : shyness   C. artist : creativity
      B. victor : defeated   D. clown : circus

____ 12. POIGNANT : TRAGEDY ::
      A. mobile : motionless   C. giggle : baby
      B. depressing : comedy   D. noisy : riot

____ 13. PROMPT : DISCOURAGE ::
      A. careful : careless   C. fragrant : flower
      B. book : library   D. late : tardy

____ 14. FLIPPANT : REMARK ::
      A. runner : sprint   C. modest : humble
      B. insulting : gesture   D. singer : chorus

____ 15. REPRISAL : ENEMY ::
      A. tears : joke   C. revenge : ally
      B. cooperation : teammate   D. terror : fear

____ 16. INTERMITTENT : STEADY ::
      A. fortunate : unlucky   C. wise : advice
      B. treacherous : dishonest D. instrument : violin

____ 17. SPECULATE : THEORY ::
      A. speak : silent   C. draw : picture
      B. primary : secondary   D. manual : electronic

____ 18. DIVERSION : FISHING ::
      A. work : play   C. guitar : drum
      B. fun : exciting   D. dessert : apple pie

____ 19. CHARISMA : BLAND ::
      A. honest : trustworthy   C. premature : early
      B. modesty : boastful   D. emergency : rush

____ 20. IMPASSE : PROBLEMATIC ::
      A. round : corners   C. alien : native
      B. success : satisfying   D. traitor : betrayal

Score   (Number correct) _____ x 5 = _____ %

PART A

Listed in the left-hand column below are ten common word parts, followed by words in which the parts are used. In each blank, write in the letter of the correct definition on the right.

Word Parts	Examples	Definitions
_____ 1. **cor, cour**	cordial, courageous	A. Two; double
_____ 2. **di-, du-**	divorced, duo	B. Mental processes; mind
_____ 3. **-dom**	stardom, boredom	C. Not
_____ 4. **-fy**	simplify, liquefy	D. Fear
_____ 5. **il-, im-**	illegal, immature	E. Heart
_____ 6. **-ish**	devilish, stylish	F. Forward; forth
_____ 7. **magni-, magn-**	magnifying, magnate	G. Great; large
_____ 8. **phob**	phobia, agoraphobia	H. State of being; condition
_____ 9. **pro-**	proceed, propel	I. Cause to be or become; make
_____ 10. **psych-, psycho-**	psychiatrist, psychologist	J. Resembling; like; characteristic of

PART B

Using the answer line provided, complete each *italicized* word in the sentences below with the correct word part from the box. Not every word part will be used.

A. **-cour**	B. **-dom**	C. **du-**	D. **-fy**	E. **il-**
F. **-ish**	G. **magni-**	H. **phob**	I. **pro-**	J. **psycho-**

_____ 11. Considering all the books, movies, and TV programs in everyday life, there's no reason for (*bore . . .*) ___.

_____ 12. The car that is used for driving instruction has (*. . . al*) ___ controls, one set for the student and one for the teacher.

_____ 13. A filter added to the kitchen faucet will remove chemicals, thereby (*puri . . . ing*) ___ the water and making it taste better.

_____ 14. The (*nightmar . . .*) ___ experience of constantly hiccuping can be stopped with drugs.

_____ 15. A victim of (*acro . . . ia*) ___, a fear of heights, Diane refused any job that required working higher than the second floor.

(Continues on next page)

PART C

Use your knowledge of word parts to determine the meaning of the **boldfaced** words. On the answer line, write the letter of each meaning.

_____ 16. "Go through the red double doors," said the secretary, "and then **proceed** down the hallway."

      A. go quickly   B. go fearfully   C. go forward

_____ 17. A blue moon is **improbable**.

      A. shocking   B. unlikely   C. beautiful

_____ 18. Our parents received a **magnum** of champagne as an anniversary gift.

      A. a large bottle   B. a medium-sized bottle   C. a small bottle

_____ 19. Ken's report emphasized the **core** of the plan.

      A. the details   B. the background   C. the central part

_____ 20. Belle suffered from a **psychosis**.

      A. a physical disease   B. a mental disorder   C. a heart problem

Score   (Number correct) _____ x 5 = _____%

Unit Four

Chapter 19

benign	glib
blasé	haughty
comprise	libel
condescend	pseudonym
facade	redundant

Chapter 20

averse	endow
detract	expulsion
disdain	mortify
divulge	nullify
elation	ominous

Chapter 21

credible	interim
cursory	latent
designate	secular
deviate	shun
improvise	simulate

Chapter 22

commemorate	empathy
complacent	menial
consensus	niche
deplete	transcend
diligent	waive

Chapter 23

bizarre	gist
conducive	hamper
falter	paradox
flaunt	repertoire
frenzy	viable

Chapter 24

aster-, astro-	mis-
contra-	omni-
-er, -or	pop
-gamy	rect
geo-	the, theo-

benign	glib
blasé	haughty
comprise	libel
condescend	pseudonym
facade	redundant

Ten Words in Context

In the space provided, write the letter of the meaning closest to that of each **boldfaced** word. Use the context of the sentences to help you figure out each word's meaning.

1 benign
(bĭ-nīn′)
-adjective

● Finding a stranger on our doorstep startled me, but the **benign** expression on his face told me not to worry.

● Gorilla mothers, usually loving and **benign**, have been known to attack their babies if they are put in the same cage.

__ *Benign* means   A. realistic.   B. kindhearted.   C. bored.

2 blasé
(blă-zā′)
-adjective

● The new staff members were enthusiastic at the weekly meetings, but the old-timers were pretty **blasé**.

● No matter how many games I see, I will never become **blasé** about baseball. Each game is new and exciting to me.

__ *Blasé* means   A. unexcited.   B. obvious.   C. repetitive.

3 comprise
(kŏm-prīz′)
-verb

● The United Kingdom **comprises** England, Scotland, Wales, and Northern Ireland.

● Saliva **comprises** about sixty ingredients, including minerals that help repair tooth enamel.

__ *Comprise* means   A. to cause.   B. to reveal.   C. to be made up of.

4 condescend
(kŏn′dĭ-sĕnd′)
-verb

● The snobby millionaire wouldn't **condescend** to associate with anyone who wasn't also rich.

● Although everyone else in the office took turns making coffee, Bill would not **condescend** to perform "such a lowly task."

__ *Condescend* means   A. to lower oneself.   B. to dare something frightening.   C. to remember.

5 facade
(fə-sŏd′)
-noun

● The **facade** of the old department store was cleaned this summer. Now the store's brick front is an inviting bright orange-red.

● The **facade** of the hotel—facing Main Street—was marble, but the sides and back were made of steel.

__ *Facade* means   A. an inside.   B. a top.   C. a front.

6 glib
(glĭb)
-adjective

● Always ready with a slick promise, the **glib** politician smoothly talked his way into being re-elected.

● Jerome thought his conversation would impress Sofia, but she found it **glib** and insincere.

__ *Glib* means   A. bored.   B. strict.   C. smooth.

110

7 haughty
(hô′tē)
-adjective

● The Smiths acted as though they were better than anybody else. Not surprisingly, their **haughty** manner made them unpopular with their neighbors.
● After being promoted to manager, Gil was **haughty** with his old office buddies, saying he now had more important things to do than waste time with them.

___ *Haughty* means   A. snobbish.   B. angry.   C. wordy.

8 libel
(lī′bəl)
-noun

● When Nick saw his name listed in the article as a gang member, he was furious. "That's **libel**!" he yelled. "How dare they print such a lie about me?"
● Many magazine editors double-check the facts they publish about a person. Then, if they are accused of **libel**, they can prove that they stated the truth.

___ *Libel* means   A. a false name.   B. a printed falsehood.   C. a repeated expression.

9 pseudonym
(sōō′də-nǐm′)
-noun

● When writing a personal story for a family magazine, Bev used a **pseudonym**. She didn't want everyone in town to know about her problems.
● The author Stephen King uses a **pseudonym** on some of his books so readers won't be aware that so many of the horror novels on the market are his.

___ *Pseudonym* means   A. a weak vocabulary.   B. a personal experience.   C. a false name.

10 redundant
(rǐ-dǔn′dənt)
-adjective

● The TV ad for a headache medicine was so **redundant** that it gave me a headache! The name of the product was repeated at least a dozen times.
● The teacher wrote "**redundant**" in several spots in the essay where Eric had repeated a point or used extra, unneeded words.

___ *Redundant* means   A. grammatical.   B. proud.   C. repetitious.

Matching Words with Definitions

Following are definitions of the ten words. Clearly write or print each word next to its definition. The sentences above and on the previous page will help you decide on the meaning of each word.

1. _____ A false name used by an author; a pen name

2. _____ To do something one feels is beneath oneself

3. _____ Unexcited or bored about something already experienced repeatedly

4. _____ The front of a building

5. _____ Wordy or needlessly repetitive

6. _____ Kindly; gentle

7. _____ The publishing of false information that harms a person's reputation

8. _____ Proud of one's appearance or accomplishments to the point of looking down on others; arrogant

9. _____ To consist of; include

10. _____ Characterized by a smooth, easy manner of speaking that often suggests insincerity or thoughtlessness

CAUTION: Do not go any further until you are sure the above answers are correct. Then you can use the definitions to help you in the following practices. Your goal is eventually to know the words well enough so that you don't need to check the definitions at all.

Sentence Check 1

Using the answer line provided, complete each item below with the correct word from the box. Use each word once.

A. benign	B. blasé	C. comprise	D. condescend	E. facade
F. glib	G. haughty	H. libel	I. pseudonym	J. redundant

_____ 1. A receptionist's job ___s answering the phone, greeting customers, opening the mail, dealing with messengers, and smiling.

_____ 2. My aunt's e-mails are annoyingly ___, repeating "news" she has already given us by telephone.

_____ 3. Since becoming a fashion model, Nora has been very ___, even snubbing some of her old, unglamorous friends.

_____ 4. One actress sued a magazine for ___ because it printed a false and damaging story about her being drunk in public.

_____ 5. Harry, always ready with some made-up excuse, is ___ enough to talk himself out of any difficulty at the snap of a finger.

_____ 6. In his usual ___ manner, my neighbor carefully picked up the ant in his kitchen, brought it outside, and gently put it down on the sidewalk.

_____ 7. When my sister first got her job at the recording studio, she was thrilled to go to work each day. Now, after ten years, she's ___ about her work and wants to change jobs.

_____ 8. Lidia's grandfather made her a dollhouse with a ___ just like the front of her family's house: black shutters, a red front door, and even the same address.

_____ 9. The conceited young baseball player wouldn't ___ to talk to his fans until an old-timer reminded him that the fans were the ones who had made him a star.

_____ 10. Samuel Langhorne Clemens wasn't the first author to use the ___ Mark Twain. A newspaper writer of the time used the same pen name.

NOTE: Now check your answers to these items by turning to page 178. Going over the answers carefully will help you prepare for the next two practices, for which answers are not given.

Sentence Check 2

Using the answer lines provided, complete each item below with **two** words from the box. Use each word once.

_____
_____ 1–2. Believing he was better than everyone else at the supermarket, Dan was so ___ that he would rarely ___ to speak to the other cashiers.

_____
_____ 3–4. One author was accused of ___ when he wrote a damaging article about the governor's wife. Subsequently°, he used a ___ so people wouldn't know he was the author whose facts were in doubt.

_____ 5–6. At first Joanne thought Barry was too ___, that his smooth talk was all show.

_____   As she got to know him better, however, her perception° of him changed. She found that his easy manner reflected a friendly and ___ nature.

_____ 7–8. The scenery crew for the summer theatre ___(e)d three artists and a set

_____   designer. They created an intricate° ___ of a medieval castle, complete with a carved door, a drawbridge, and a moat.

_____ 9–10. The writing teacher had become ___ from repeatedly seeing the same

_____   problems: careless organization, lack of focus, and writing so ___ that many sentences said the same thing. In addition, students often turned to plagiarism° rather than use their own words.

Final Check: *Interview with a Rude Star*

Here is a final opportunity for you to strengthen your knowledge of the ten words. First read the following selection carefully. Then fill in each blank with a word from the box at the top of the previous page. (Context clues will help you figure out which word goes in which blank.) Use each word once.

When a famous actress arrived in town to work on a movie, an editor asked me to interview her. Because this was my first interview assignment, I felt far from (1)_____ about it. Instead, I was both excited and scared. Would a star (2)_____ to see me, an unknown, inexperienced reporter?

When I arrived at the movie set, I saw the actress standing in front of the painted (3)_____ of a mansion. During a break in the filming, I approached her and introduced myself. Trying to be as congenial° as possible, I smiled and told her I was pleased to meet her. "Well, let's get this over with," she said, clearly annoyed.

The interview went terribly. My dream of establishing a comfortable rapport° with the star soon vanished as the interview degenerated° into an awkward, demoralizing° situation that I just wanted to end. Although it (4)_____(e)d carefully thought-out questions, she sighed or rolled her eyes at every one of them. And no matter how (5)_____ my manner, she seemed to view me as some sort of threat. At one point, she became irate° and yelled, "That's (6)_____! I don't have time to answer the same question twice." When I asked her about serious issues, her answers were totally (7)_____—insincere and shallow.

Now I have to write about her. Here's my dilemma°: Should I hide my revulsion° and say good things about her? Or should I tell the truth—that she's a (8)_____, rude woman who thinks only of herself and expects others to do the same? If I do, she might accuse me of maligning° her and sue me for (9)_____. Maybe the editor will let me use a (10)_____, so my real name won't appear on an article about this miserable woman.

Scores	Sentence Check 2 _____%	Final Check _____%

averse	endow
detract	expulsion
disdain	mortify
divulge	nullify
elation	ominous

Ten Words in Context

In the space provided, write the letter of the meaning closest to that of each **boldfaced** word. Use the context of the sentences to help you figure out each word's meaning.

1 averse
(ə-vûrs′)
-*adjective*

- That little boy was once so **averse** to tomatoes that the very sight of them made him gag.
- Being **averse** to screaming crowds, I'd rather just listen to my iPod than go to a rock concert.

___ *Averse* means   A. opposed.   B. accustomed.   C. open.

2 detract
(dĭ-trăkt′)
-*verb*

- Julius thinks the scar on his cheek **detracts** from his good looks, but it's barely noticeable.
- All of the litter in the park certainly **detracts** from the beauty of the trees and flowers.

___ *Detract* means   A. to result.   B. to benefit.   C. to take away.

3 disdain
(dĭs-dān′)
-*noun*

- The snobby server in the French restaurant viewed Tanya with **disdain** because she couldn't pronounce anything on the menu.
- I was afraid my request to see the state senator would be treated with **disdain**. Instead, the senator's secretary politely made an appointment for me.

___ *Disdain* means   A. pride.   B. disrespect.   C. sorrow.

4 divulge
(dĭ-vŭlj′)
-*verb*

- My father wouldn't **divulge** the type of car he had bought, saying only, "It's a surprise."
- It's against the law to ask people to **divulge** their age at a job interview.

___ *Divulge* means   A. to hide.   B. to recall.   C. to tell.

5 elation
(ĭ-lā′shən)
-*noun*

- The principal shouted with **elation** when the football team scored the winning touchdown.
- Roy had expected to feel **elation** at his graduation. Instead, he felt sadness at the thought of not seeing his high-school friends every day.

___ *Elation* means   A. anger.   B. confusion.   C. happiness.

6 endow
(ĕn-dou′)
-*verb*

- Nature has **endowed** hummingbirds with the ability to fly backward.
- The author Oscar Wilde was **endowed** with the ability to find humor in any situation. While dying, he said of the ugly wallpaper in his hotel room, "One of us had to go."

___ *Endow* means   A. to equip.   B. to curse.   C. to threaten.

7 expulsion
(ĕks-pŭl′shən)
-noun

- The manager told us we risked **expulsion** from the theater if we continued to talk on our cell phones during the movie.
- **Expulsion** from school is supposed to be a punishment, but some students may consider not being allowed to attend classes a reward.

___ *Expulsion* means   A. being canceled.   B. being forced out.   C. being embarrassed.

8 mortify
(môr′tə-fī′)
-verb

- It would **mortify** me if my voice cracked during my choir solo.
- I doubt anything will ever **mortify** me more than the streamer of toilet paper that clung to my shoe as I returned from the ladies' room to rejoin my date in a fancy restaurant.

___ *Mortify* means   A. to shame.   B. to insult.   C. to delay.

9 nullify
(nŭl′ə-fī′)
-verb

- The college will **nullify** my student ID at the end of the term unless I update it with a new sticker.
- A soft-drink company decided to **nullify** its contract with a well-known athlete because he was convicted of drunken driving.

___ *Nullify* means   A. to renew.   B. to reveal.   C. to cancel.

10 ominous
(ŏm′ə-nəs)
-adjective

- To many, cemeteries have an **ominous** quality, particularly at night or on Halloween, when the threat of ghosts can seem very real.
- The sore's failure to heal was **ominous**, a possible sign of cancer.

___ *Ominous* means   A. embarrassing.   B. threatening.   C. unworthy.

Matching Words with Definitions

Following are definitions of the ten words. Clearly write or print each word next to its definition. The sentences above and on the previous page will help you decide on the meaning of each word.

1. _____ To provide with a talent or quality

2. _____ An attitude or feeling of contempt; scorn

3. _____ The act or condition of being forced to leave

4. _____ Threatening harm or evil; menacing

5. _____ To reveal; make known

6. _____ Having a feeling of dislike or distaste for something

7. _____ To humiliate or embarrass

8. _____ To lessen what is admirable or worthwhile about something

9. _____ A feeling of great joy or pride

10. _____ To make legally ineffective; cancel

CAUTION: Do not go any further until you are sure the above answers are correct. Then you can use the definitions to help you in the following practices. Your goal is eventually to know the words well enough so that you don't need to check the definitions at all.

Sentence Check 1

Using the answer line provided, complete each item below with the correct word from the box. Use each word once.

A. averse	B. detract	C. disdain	D. divulge	E. elation
F. endow	G. expulsion	H. mortified	I. nullified	J. ominous

_____ 1. People talking in a movie theater greatly ___ from the enjoyment of watching a film.

_____ 2. Because of the dark, ___ storm clouds, we canceled the softball game.

_____ 3. I'm ___ to speaking in public because I don't enjoy making a fool of myself.

_____ 4. When he received the college scholarship, my brother felt such ___ that he wept with joy.

_____ 5. The results of the mayoral election were ___ after the townspeople found evidence of voting fraud.

_____ 6. The American water shrew is ___(e)d with feet that have air pockets, enabling the small animal to walk on water.

_____ 7. Some people want a law calling for the ___ of illegal immigrants. Others want them to be forgiven and allowed to stay in the United States permanently.

_____ 8. Vinnie's repeated boasts about his muscle-building backfired. They caused his date to look at him with ___, not admiration.

_____ 9. Never trust Esta with a secret. She'll ___ it the minute you turn your back.

_____ 10. The reporter was ___ when he learned that he had delivered much of his news story facing away from the TV camera.

NOTE: Now check your answers to these items by turning to page 178. Going over the answers carefully will help you prepare for the next two practices, for which answers are not given.

Sentence Check 2

Using the answer lines provided, complete each item below with **two** words from the box. Use each word once.

_____
_____ 1–2. Some people are so ___ to living near a nuclear plant that they want the plant's license to be ___. They say the plant infringes° on every homeowner's right to safety.

_____
_____ 3–4. Shannon is ___(e)d with beautiful curly red hair, but her self-image is so low that she feels her hair ___s from her looks. However, others find her hair to be one of her many attractive physical attributes°.

_____
_____ 5–6. When someone ___(e)d to a counselor that a certain student was selling drugs, an investigation began that led to that student's ___ from school.

_____   7–8. Amy was ___ by the low grade she received for her speech, a grade she
_____   considered a sign of the teacher's ___ for her. However, the teacher's
                                     rationale° for the grade was that the speech was incoherent°.

_____   9–10. Marty had believed his headaches and blurred vision were ___ signs of some
_____   terrible syndrome°, so he felt ___ when he learned that he simply needed
                                     glasses.

Final Check: *The Nightmare of Gym*

Here is a final opportunity for you to strengthen your knowledge of the ten words. First read the following selection carefully. Then fill in each blank with a word from the box at the top of the previous page. (Context clues will help you figure out which word goes in which blank.) Use each word once.

I was not (1)_____(e)d with athletic ability. In a frequent nightmare, I'm still trying to pass my mandatory° gym class so that I can graduate from high school. The situation always looks grim. For one thing, the teacher has threatened me with (2)_____ from school if I don't pass. Also appearing in my dream is the terrifying vault horse, the very sight of which (3)_____s from my mental health. I run toward the horse, leap, and nose-dive into the mat. Ignoring my despair, the rest of the gym class laughs. Once again, I am (4)_____ by my athletic performance.

Next, a single (5)_____ rope threatens overhead, where it hangs from the ceiling. I try to contrive° some excuse to get out of climbing it. However, my excuses are so incoherent° that my teacher says, "I don't understand anything you're saying. Get started." Wondering if anyone has ever died from rope burn, I struggle to climb it. Almost to the top, I sweat so much that I slide back to the floor, landing at the gym teacher's feet. "What a loser," the teacher mutters with an expression of total (6)_____.

Because I've always been (7)_____ to square-dancing, that too appears in the nightmare. Having forgotten my sneakers, I'm forced to dance in my socks. I slip, rather than dance, around the polished floor. During one high-speed turn, I go sliding—right into the men's locker room, where the smell causes me to pass out.

The only pleasant part of the dream comes near the end. With amazement and (8)_____, I learn that I will graduate after all. I smile, thinking I'll never have to face the rigors° of gym class again.

But then, the principal (9)_____s the terrible truth. I haven't managed to pass gym. My graduation depends on my agreeing to take four more years of gym when I get to college. If I don't, my high school diploma will be (10)_____.

Scores   Sentence Check 2 _____%   Final Check _____%

credible	interim
cursory	latent
designate	secular
deviate	shun
improvise	simulate

Ten Words in Context

In the space provided, write the letter of the meaning closest to that of each **boldfaced** word. Use the context of the sentences to help you figure out each word's meaning.

1 credible
(krĕd′ə-bəl)
-adjective

- Some jurors doubted the witness's testimony, but most of them found it **credible**.
- As **credible** as Mr. Bower's resumé may seem, I don't think you should hire him without checking his references.

___ *Credible* means   A. long.   B. boring.   C. believable.

2 cursory
(kûr′sə-rē)
-adjective

- Most people do only a **cursory** job of brushing their teeth. To avoid cavities, however, you must brush for at least two minutes.
- Because James had to work late, he had only enough time to give his apartment a **cursory** cleaning before his parents arrived.

___ *Cursory* means   A. careful.   B. consistent.   C. quick.

3 designate
(dĕz′ĭg-nāt′)
-verb

- At the party, Isabel drank soda rather than beer because her friends had **designated** her as the driver for the trip home.
- A coworker was **designated** to present Vonnie with the "Employee of the Year" award at the company banquet.

___ *Designate* means   A. to forbid.   B. to assign.   C. to hire.

4 deviate
(dē′vē-āt′)
-verb

- Having taken the wrong exit off the highway, we had to **deviate** somewhat from the route marked on the map.
- If you **deviate** even a little from the directions when you write your paper, you might hurt your grade.

___ *Deviate* means   A. to follow.   B. to depart.   C. to gain.

5 improvise
(ĭm′prə-vīz′)
-verb

- Nadia can **improvise** accompaniments on the piano to songs she's never heard before. How can she play so well without any preparation or sheet music?
- When I rang the doorbell, I wasn't expecting Ellen's father to come to the door, so I had to quickly **improvise** an explanation for my visit.

___ *Improvise* means   A. to remember.   B. to keep away from.   C. to make up.

6 interim
(ĭn′tər-ĭm)
-noun

- Cassie hadn't seen her nephews for years. In the **interim**, they had grown from troubled boys into serious young men.
- After the secretary left, it took two weeks for her replacement to arrive at the real-estate office. In the **interim**, the agents had to do their own typing.

___ *Interim* means   A. the time between.   B. the future.   C. the place.

7 latent
(lāt′ənt)
-adjective

● Certain viruses, such as the one for AIDS, can be **latent** in the body for years before symptoms appear.

● After he retired, my father discovered his **latent** artistic talent. He took up oil painting and now sells much of his work.

___ *Latent* means   A. partial.   B. inactive.   C. absent.

8 secular
(sĕk′yə-lər)
-adjective

● While our government is **secular**, some countries are governed according to religious laws.

● Devoting himself to a deeply religious life, the Hindu holy man denied himself most **secular** pleasures.

___ *Secular* means   A. spiritual.   B. reliable.   C. nonreligious.

9 shun
(shŭn)
-verb

● I used to see a lot of Tracy, but since our argument, she **shuns** me whenever possible.

● The Amish live without many modern conveniences. For example, they **shun** automobiles and electric lights.

___ *Shun* means   A. to keep away from.   B. to recognize.   C. to observe.

10 simulate
(sĭm′yōō-lāt′)
-verb

● The tan plastic of our kitchen table, with its wood-grain design, **simulates** oak.

● Equipment that **simulates** a human heart can keep someone alive only for a short time, until an actual heart can be substituted.

___ *Simulate* means   A. to contrast with.   B. to imitate.   C. to be made of.

Matching Words with Definitions

Following are definitions of the ten words. Clearly write or print each word next to its definition. The sentences above and on the previous page will help you decide on the meaning of each word.

1. _____ To compose, perform, or provide without preparation; invent

2. _____ Believable

3. _____ The period of time in between; meantime

4. _____ To name to an office or duty; appoint

5. _____ To act or look like; imitate

6. _____ Not directly related to religion; not spiritual; worldly

7. _____ Done quickly and without attention to detail

8. _____ To keep away from; avoid consistently

9. _____ Present but hidden or inactive

10. _____ To turn aside or stray, as from a path, direction, or standard

CAUTION: Do not go any further until you are sure the above answers are correct. Then you can use the definitions to help you in the following practices. Your goal is eventually to know the words well enough so that you don't need to check the definitions at all.

Sentence Check 1

Using the answer line provided, complete each item below with the correct word from the box. Use each word once.

A. credible	B. cursory	C. designate	D. deviate	E. improvise
F. interim	G. latent	H. secular	I. shun	J. simulate

_____ 1. Nikki's ___ ability in basketball became apparent when she turned 12. Her movements had once been clumsy, but now they were smooth and controlled.

_____ 2. Presidents ___ as Supreme Court justices people who share their political views.

_____ 3. I hear Andy dropped out of college. What caused him to ___ from his plan of getting his degree?

_____ 4. Because his story about a flat tire sounded ___, my parents allowed the stranger to use our telephone.

_____ 5. In the ___ between applying to college and getting the letter of acceptance, I spent a lot of time worrying.

_____ 6. Margo couldn't identify the driver of the car that had hit her. She'd given him only a(n) ___ glance at the time of the accident.

_____ 7. The chorus is known for its gospel music, but it also performs ___ compositions, including show tunes.

_____ 8. When the actor forgot his lines, he was forced to ___ some dialog until the stage manager whispered to him from offstage.

_____ 9. Tony found the hardest part of overcoming his addiction was learning to ___ people and places that would tempt him to use drugs again.

_____ 10. The zoo's exhibits ___ the natural environments of animals. The orangutans, for example, live in a space that looks much like an Asian rain forest.

NOTE: Now check your answers to these items by turning to page 179. Going over the answers carefully will help you prepare for the next two practices, for which answers are not given.

Sentence Check 2

Using the answer lines provided, complete each item below with **two** words from the box. Use each word once.

_____
_____ 1–2. In seventh grade, Jack looked upon girls with great disdain°. Then, in the ___ between seventh and eighth grades, his ___ interest in them suddenly surfaced.

_____
_____ 3–4. In looking for a college, Luke gave only ___ attention to ___ schools. He was quite sure he wanted to attend a Catholic school.

_____   5–6. Matt told his mother he was late because he had fallen while running home.
_____   To make his story more ___, he had scratched his knee with a rock to ___ an
                                   injury from a fall.

_____   7–8. Della wanted to be a cheerleader, but she willingly ___(e)d from that goal
_____   when she was ___(e)d class mascot and got to wear a polar bear costume to
                                   all the games.

_____   9–10. Proud of his ability to create new dishes, Franco tended to ___ cookbooks.
_____   He preferred to ___ meals, using whatever ingredients happened to be on
                                    hand. In fact, cooking was one of his favorite diversions°.

Final Check: *Skipping Church*

Here is a final opportunity for you to strengthen your knowledge of the ten words. First read the following selection carefully. Then fill in each blank with a word from the box at the top of the previous page. (Context clues will help you figure out which word goes in which blank.) Use each word once.

I remember so well the time my mother's back injury prevented her from going to church with my brother and me. For five weeks, we were supposed to go by ourselves. Zack and I back then preferred (1)_____ activities to religious ones, so we decided to (2)_____ church while Mom was recovering. We (3)_____(e)d the churchgoers she wanted us to be by getting dressed every Sunday in our good clothes and leaving home and returning at the right times. We spent the (4)_____ at a restaurant or at the movies. Of course, we knew Mom would question us about the service. Each week one of us was (5)_____(e)d to invent a sermon. I thought Zack's sermons sounded not only (6)_____, but also inspiring. I, conversely°, tended to (7)_____ on the spot and didn't sound so believable. But Mom never seemed to notice how weak my sermons were or how (8)_____ our answers were when she asked whom we'd seen and what news we'd heard.

Finally, she was ready to attend church again. Over dinner Saturday evening, she began what seemed to be an innocent conversation. Gently, but showing a previously (9)_____ talent for cross-examination that could have made her a star attorney, she questioned us in a quiet but relentless° manner about our "church-going." The more she persisted, the more Zack and I stumbled and (10)_____(e)d from our official story. We eventually concluded we were caught, and the realization mortified° us. Looking downward in shame, we divulged° all the details of our "secret" scheme. We felt pretty foolish when we learned she'd known all along that we had never set foot in church.

Scores   Sentence Check 2 _____%   Final Check _____%

Enter your scores above and in the **Vocabulary Performance Chart** on the inside back cover of the book.

commemorate	empathy
complacent	menial
consensus	niche
deplete	transcend
diligent	waive

Ten Words in Context

In the space provided, write the letter of the meaning closest to that of each **boldfaced** word. Use the context of the sentences to help you figure out each word's meaning.

1 commemorate
(kə-mĕm′ə-rāt′)
-verb

● Thomas devoted himself to feeding the hungry. So on the anniversary of his death, it seems wrong to **commemorate** his life with a fancy dinner party that only the rich can attend.

● Each year, my parents **commemorate** their first date by having dinner at McDonalds, the place where they first met.

__ *Commemorate* means   A. to share.   B. to celebrate.   C. to believe.

2 complacent
(kəm-plā′sənt)
-adjective

● Elected officials cannot afford to be **complacent** about winning an election. Before long, they'll have to campaign again for the voters' support.

● Getting all A's hasn't made Ivy **complacent**. She continues to work hard at school.

__ *Complacent* means   A. very eager.   B. reasonable.   C. too much at ease.

3 consensus
(kən-sĕn′səs)
-noun

● A vote revealed strong agreement among the teachers. The **consensus** was that they would strike if the school board did not act quickly to raise their pay.

● The family **consensus** was that we should go camping again this summer. Ray was the only one who wanted to do something else for a change.

__ *Consensus* means   A. a majority view.   B. an unusual idea.   C. a question.

4 deplete
(dĭ-plēt′)
-verb

● I'd like to help you out with a loan, but unexpected car repairs have managed to **deplete** my bank account.

● In order not to **deplete** their small supply of canned food, the shipwreck survivors searched the island for plants they could eat.

__ *Deplete* means   A. to use up.   B. to forget.   C. to find.

5 diligent
(dĭl′ə-jənt)
-adjective

● I wish I had been more **diligent** about practicing piano when I was younger. It would be nice to be able to play well now.

● Diane was lazy when she first joined the family business, but she soon became so **diligent** that she inspired others to work harder.

__ *Diligent* means   A. self-satisfied.   B. lucky.   C. hard-working.

6 empathy
(ĕm′pə-thē)
-noun

● Families who lost loved ones in the attacks on the World Trade Center and the Pentagon have **empathy** for one another because of their shared grief.

● Ms. Allan is an excellent career counselor partly because of her great **empathy**. She understands each student's feelings and point of view.

__ *Empathy* means   A. a common opinion.   B. a sympathetic understanding.   C. an efficiency.

7 menial
(mē′nē-əl)
-adjective

- Julio seems to think my summer job delivering pizza is **menial** work, but I've found that it requires some skills.
- Every job can be done with pride. Even **menial** jobs such as washing windows or scrubbing floors can be performed with care.

___ *Menial* means   A. unskilled.   B. steady.   C. satisfying.

8 niche
(nĭch)
-noun

- Although her degree was in accounting, Kendra decided her **niche** was really in business management, so she went back to school for more training.
- Dom spent the years after college moving restlessly from job to job, never finding a comfortable **niche** for himself.

___ *Niche* means   A. a shared opinion.   B. a suitable place.   C. an education.

9 transcend
(trăn-sĕnd′)
-verb

- The psychic convinced her clients that she could **transcend** time and space and talk directly with the dead.
- Yoga can help one **transcend** the cares of the world and reach a state of relaxation.

___ *Transcend* means   A. to participate in.   B. to go past.   C. to use up.

10 waive
(wāv)
-verb

- The defendant decided to **waive** his right to an attorney and, instead, speak for himself in court.
- Since Lin had studied so much math on her own, the school **waived** the requirement that she take high school algebra.

___ *Waive* means   A. to lose.   B. to honor.   C. to give up.

Matching Words with Definitions

Following are definitions of the ten words. Clearly write or print each word next to its definition. The sentences above and on the previous page will help you decide on the meaning of each word.

1. _____ Not requiring special skills or higher intellectual abilities

2. _____ The ability to share in someone else's feelings or thoughts

3. _____ To rise above or go beyond the limits of; exceed

4. _____ To honor the memory of someone or something, as with a ceremony; celebrate; observe

5. _____ To willingly give up (as a claim, privilege, or right); do without

6. _____ An opinion held by everyone (or almost everyone) involved

7. _____ Self-satisfied; feeling too much satisfaction with oneself or one's accomplishments

8. _____ Steady, determined, and careful in work

9. _____ An activity or situation especially suited to a person

10. _____ To use up

CAUTION: Do not go any further until you are sure the above answers are correct. Then you can use the definitions to help you in the following practices. Your goal is eventually to know the words well enough so that you don't need to check the definitions at all.

Sentence Check 1

Using the answer line provided, complete each item below with the correct word from the box. Use each word once.

| A. commemorate | B. complacent | C. consensus | D. deplete | E. diligent |
| F. empathy | G. menial | H. niche | I. transcend | J. waive |

_____ 1. The old man decided to ___ any claim he had to the family fortune, preferring to see the money go to the younger generation.

_____ 2. The American Inventors' Association gathered at a banquet to ___ Thomas Edison.

_____ 3. My grandfather, who's recovering from heart surgery, is weak, so it doesn't take much effort for him to ___ the little energy he has.

_____ 4. Many people believe that Shakespeare's works ___ those of all other authors.

_____ 5. The hair salon got off to a good start, but then the owners became ___ about their success and stopped trying to attract new customers.

_____ 6. Several sessions with a career counselor helped Suzanne consider what her ___ in the working world might be.

_____ 7. The children like to help out at the family restaurant, but they are able to perform only ___ tasks, such as mopping floors and cleaning tables.

_____ 8. Arnie has been ___ in his study of German because he hopes to speak the language with his relatives from Germany when they visit next summer.

_____ 9. I had hoped the restaurant would be good, but our group's ___ was that the food was only so-so, and the service was even worse.

_____ 10. Dr. Grange is a brilliant mathematician, but she lacks ___ for her students. She doesn't understand how they can find some problems so difficult.

NOTE: Now check your answers to these items by turning to page 179. Going over the answers carefully will help you prepare for the next two practices, for which answers are not given.

Sentence Check 2

Using the answer lines provided, complete each item below with **two** words from the box. Use each word once.

_____
_____ 1–2. Lynn begged the bank to ___ the overdraft charge of thirty dollars, telling them that it would entirely ___ her savings.

_____
_____ 3–4. In high school, Julio was voted "Most Likely to Become a Psychologist." It was the ___ of his classmates that he was the student endowed° with the most ___ for other people.

_____
_____ 5–6. My mother could have stayed in her comfortable ___ as part of the secretarial pool, but she was averse° to remaining there. She wanted to ___ the limits of that job and become an executive herself.

_____

_____

7–8. "On this, our hundredth anniversary celebration," said the company president, "I'd like to ___ our founder with a toast. He ran the company from top to bottom, doing even such ___ jobs as emptying garbage cans. He truly exemplified° the values of dedication and hard work."

_____

_____

9–10. Dr. Roberts and Dr. Krill practice medicine very differently. Dr. Roberts is ___ about reading journals and learning new techniques. Conversely°, Dr. Krill is more ___ and never tries anything new.

Final Check: *A Model Teacher*

Here is a final opportunity for you to strengthen your knowledge of the ten words. First read the following selection carefully. Then fill in each blank with a word from the box at the top of the previous page. (Context clues will help you figure out which word goes in which blank.) Use each word once.

At Eastman High School reunions, the conversation usually gets around to the question "Who was our best teacher?" And year after year, the (1)_____ of the graduates has been that Mr. MacDonald was the best. Many remember Joe MacDonald as the epitome° of teaching—the teacher against whom they measured all others.

He had started his professional life as a highly paid attorney. However, never at home with the law, he left his lucrative° practice and found his (2)_____ as an English teacher in the shabby classrooms at Eastman. Mr. MacDonald somehow helped his students (3)_____ their broken-down surroundings and experience the magic in the words of Shakespeare, Dickinson, or Frost. Even those who tended to shun° reading began to think there might be something to this literature stuff after all.

Mr. MacDonald's enthusiasm for his work was never (4)_____(e)d. In fact, instead of being used up, his zeal° actually increased through the years. Other teachers became (5)_____ about their work and did only cursory° lesson preparation. But Mr. MacDonald never became blasé°; he was as (6)_____ as an eager first-year teacher. He could often be found talking with students after school, as his great (7)_____ for students—he had good rapport° with them and understood their problems—was well known. He was fun, too. On the first really beautiful spring day of each year, he'd (8)_____ his lesson plan and take the class outdoors to sit in the sunshine and talk about literature. And no task was too (9)_____ for him. He was often seen picking up trash from the grounds—something other teachers would never condescend° to do.

After Mr. MacDonald's retirement, his former students wanted to honor him in some way. They thought about a statue, but decided to (10)_____ his teaching in the way that he'd like best, with a college scholarship for an Eastman student, which was established in his name.

Scores   Sentence Check 2 _____%   Final Check _____%

Enter your scores above and in the **Vocabulary Performance Chart** on the inside back cover of the book.

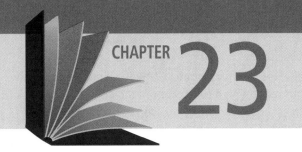

bizarre	gist
conducive	hamper
falter	paradox
flaunt	repertoire
frenzy	viable

Ten Words in Context

In the space provided, write the letter of the meaning closest to that of each **boldfaced** word. Use the context of the sentences to help you figure out each word's meaning.

1 bizarre
(bĭ-zär′)
-adjective

- Some mentally ill people have **bizarre** ideas. For example, they may think that the TV is talking to them or that others can steal their thoughts.
- Wally's outfits may seem **bizarre**, but when you see him with his even stranger-looking friends, his clothing looks quite ordinary.

___ *Bizarre* means   A. limited.   B. ordinary.   C. odd.

2 conducive
(kən-dōō′sĭv)
-adjective

- A deliciously warm and sunny April day is **conducive** to a bad case of spring fever.
- Learning to budget an allowance at a young age is **conducive** to good spending habits later in life.

___ *Conducive* means   A. favorable.   B. similar.   C. damaging.

3 falter
(fôl′tər)
-verb

- Vince **faltered** on the first few notes of his piano piece but then played the rest without pausing.
- Even public speakers who now sound smooth and confident must have **faltered** when giving their first speeches.

___ *Falter* means   A. to show off.   B. to hesitate.   C. to succeed.

4 flaunt
(flônt)
-verb

- Instead of enjoying their wealth quietly, the Stewarts **flaunt** every new thing they buy in front of their poor relatives.
- Tamika never **flaunted** her high grades. In fact, I didn't know that she was first in her class until she received the highest academic award at graduation.

___ *Flaunt* means   A. to interfere with.   B. to approve of.   C. to exhibit.

5 frenzy
(frĕn′zē)
-noun

- When Grace couldn't find her little son in the department store, she went into a **frenzy** and didn't calm down until she knew he was safe.
- The holiday season always includes a **frenzy** of last-minute shopping.

___ *Frenzy* means   A. a calm condition.   B. an angry condition.   C. an excited condition.

6 gist
(jĭst)
-noun

- We asked Alex to skip the details and get right to the **gist** of the argument.
- The **gist** of Joan Didion's book *The Year of Magical Thinking* is that life as you know it can change in a second.

___ *Gist* means   A. the small parts.   B. the main idea.   C. the benefit.

7 hamper
(hăm′pər)
-verb

● "We never meant to **hamper** your struggle for independence," Tom's parents said. "From now on, we'll let you handle your own life, including your laundry and meals."

● A series of major computer crashes **hampered** business all along the West Coast today.

__ *Hamper* means   A. to restrict.   B. to show off.   C. to promote.

8 paradox
(păr′ə-dŏx′)
-noun

● When Della kept postponing her decision about whether or not to go back to school, I reminded her of the **paradox** "No decision is also a decision."

● The story of King Midas illustrates a famous **paradox**: "When the gods wish to punish us, they answer our prayers." The king gets what he thinks will be the best thing in the world—the golden touch—and then discovers that it is the worst thing when he accidentally turns his daughter into a golden statue.

__ *Paradox* means   A. an outburst.   B. a simple statement.   C. a seeming contradiction.

9 repertoire
(rĕp′ər-twŏr′)
-noun

● The actor's **repertoire** includes drama, storytelling, song, and dance.

● In order to be successful in school, it's important to have a **repertoire** of study strategies from which to choose.

__ *Repertoire* means   A. a variety of skills.   B. a reason to do something.   C. a statement of intent.

10 viable
(vī′ə-bəl)
-adjective

● The parties in the labor dispute can reach a **viable** agreement only if both sides benefit equally.

● The little boy quickly learned that using plastic tape is not a **viable** solution to mending a broken vase.

__ *Viable* means   A. practical.   B. attractive.   C. expensive.

Matching Words with Definitions

Following are definitions of the ten words. Clearly write or print each word next to its definition. The sentences above and on the previous page will help you decide on the meaning of each word.

1. _____ The main point or essential part of a matter; central idea

2. _____ To act or speak with uncertainty; hesitate

3. _____ To limit, interfere with, or restrict

4. _____ A wild outburst of excited feelings or actions

5. _____ Workable; capable of being successful or effective

6. _____ A statement that seems contradictory yet may be true

7. _____ A range or collection of skills or accomplishments

8. _____ Dramatically unusual, as in manner or appearance; strange

9. _____ Tending to promote or bring about

10. _____ To show off (something)

CAUTION: Do not go any further until you are sure the above answers are correct. Then you can use the definitions to help you in the following practices. Your goal is eventually to know the words well enough so that you don't need to check the definitions at all.

Sentence Check 1

Using the answer line provided, complete each item below with the correct word from the box. Use each word once.

A. **bizarre**	B. **conducive**	C. **falter**	D. **flaunt**	E. **frenzy**
F. **gist**	G. **hamper**	H. **paradox**	I. **repertoire**	J. **viable**

_____ 1. Halloween offers everyone the chance to look as ___ as possible.

_____ 2. Al Pacino's ___ includes both modern dramas and Shakespearean plays.

_____ 3. When a reporter asked Senator Drake a difficult question, the senator ___(e)d for a moment before answering.

_____ 4. For snails, heat is ___ to sleep. In fact, desert snails may sleep three or four years at a time.

_____ 5. The ___ of Kelly's essay was that school should be open only four days a week, from 8 a.m. to 6 p.m.

_____ 6. Since ordinary clothes may ___ movement, sweatpants and loose T-shirts are recommended for the exercise class.

_____ 7. This morning, the staff could not come up with a ___ plan to improve business. Every suggestion had a drawback.

_____ 8. When Chun's parents said they worried when he didn't call home, he said, "Remember that well-known ___—no news is good news."

_____ 9. Delia was in a ___ because she had locked her keys in the car and she was already twenty minutes late for work.

_____ 10. Lucas believed the only way he could get a date was to ___ his wealth by wearing a gold watch and driving an expensive sports car.

NOTE: Now check your answers to these items by turning to page 179. Going over the answers carefully will help you prepare for the next two practices, for which answers are not given.

Sentence Check 2

Using the answer lines provided, complete each item below with **two** words from the box. Use each word once.

_____
_____ 1–2. Although Jenny chose the songs from her ___ that she knew best, she wasn't complacent° about being prepared. Afraid she would ___ the night of the concert, she practiced the songs over and over.

_____
_____ 3–4. The ___ of the lecture was that although the United States encourages free trade, some other countries ___ it.

_____ 5–6. Unfortunately, forming a committee wasn't ___ to alleviating° the company's parking problem. No one could think of a ___ plan to increase the number of parking spaces.
_____

_____ 7–8. Bruno is so prone° to changing his mind that his rapid shifts of opinion sometimes make me irate°. Once, in a ___ of anger, I shouted this ___: "You're always the same—always changing your mind!"
_____

_____ 9–10. My mother took me aside at the party and said, "That looks more like a strange costume than a dress. It's bad enough your clothing looks so ___, but do you have to mortify° me and ___ it in front of all my friends?"

Final Check: *My Talented Roommate*

Here is a final opportunity for you to strengthen your knowledge of the ten words. First read the following selection carefully. Then fill in each blank with a word from the box at the top of the previous page. (Context clues will help you figure out which word goes in which blank.) Use each word once.

"If you've got it, (1)_____ it!" That's the (2)_____ of Georgia's philosophy. Georgia is my dorm roommate. A dance and theater major, she is a true extrovert°—always showing off, always "onstage." It seems she is in constant motion, going from graceful leaps down the hall to such (3)_____ acrobatics as swinging by her knees from the clothes rod in her closet. Some days Georgia performs her entire (4)_____ right in our room. The (5)_____ "less is more" doesn't apply to her on those occasions, when she delights by acting, singing, and dancing everything she's ever learned. Attracted by her talent and charisma°, an audience always gathers to watch. The lack of space in our room never seems to (6)_____ her movements. Since Georgia's shows are not very (7)_____ to good studying on my part, I join the crowd drawn by her magnetism. She is so smooth and confident—I have never seen her (8)_____. She moves easily from ballet to tap to jazz. She'll tell jokes, sing part of an opera, and perform a scene from *A Chorus Line*. Not knowing all the words never stops her—she simply improvises° lines as she goes along. When she finishes, her audience breaks into a (9)_____ of applause. It's difficult to break into show business, which is why most drama students give up on this quest° and settle for a more conventional° career. But I contend° Georgia is talented enough to build a (10)_____ career in show business.

| Scores | Sentence Check 2 _____% | Final Check _____% |

Enter your scores above and in the **Vocabulary Performance Chart** on the inside back cover of the book.

aster-, astro-	mis-
contra-	omni-
-er, -or	pop
-gamy	rect
geo-	the, theo-

Ten Word Parts in Context

Figure out the meanings of the following ten word parts by looking *closely* and *carefully* at the context in which they appear. Then, in the space provided, write the letter of the meaning closest to that of each word part.

1 aster-, astro-

● The **aster** is a lovely flower named for its starlike shape: its petals point outward from a yellow disk.

● **Astrologers** claim to interpret the influence of the stars and planets on our lives.

___ The word part *aster-* or *astro-* means

A. someone who does something.   B. star.   C. marriage.

2 contra-

● **Contrary** to his campaign promise, the governor is going to raise gasoline taxes.

● The warning label on the bottle of arthritis medicine contained this **contraindication**: "We recommend against taking this product if you are already using aspirin or similar painkillers."

___ The word part *contra-* means

A. all.   B. straight.   C. against.

3 -er, -or

● When the young **singer** at an NBA game forgot the words to the National Anthem, the coach came over and sang along with her.

● American **visitors** to Canadian cities are often amazed by how clean the streets are.

___ The word part *-er* or *-or* means

A. god.   B. wrong.   C. someone who does something.

4 -gamy

● Jackson brought charges of **bigamy** against his wife after he learned that she was still legally married to her first husband.

● King Mongut of Siam, whose story was told in the musical *The King and I*, practiced **polygamy**. He was reported to have had 9,000 wives.

___ The word part *-gamy* means

A. marriage.   B. opposite.   C. god.

5 geo-

● Pierce County, North Dakota, has the distinction of being the **geographic** center of North America.

● **Geophysics** is the science of the matter and forces of the Earth, including oceans, volcanoes, and earthquakes.

___ The word part *geo-* means

A. earth.   B. people.   C. outer space.

6 mis-

● I think there is something wrong with a child who never **misbehaves**.

● The telephone caller **misrepresented** herself. She said she was doing a survey, but she really wanted to sell me life insurance.

___ The word part *mis-* means

A. for.   B. straight.   C. badly.

7 omni-

- Until they lost to the Giants in the Super Bowl, the 2007–2008 New England Patriots seemed **omnipotent**. They defeated all their opponents, completing the first 18–0 season in NFL history.
- Some dinosaurs ate only plants, and others ate only meat. Still others were **omnivorous**—they ate all kinds of food.

___ The word part *omni-* means   A. right.   B. all.   C. wrong.

8 pop

- In 1770, the United States was not very **populous**. Only about two million people lived here then.
- In order to **populate** the West, the government gave free land to people who would build on it.

___ The word part *pop* means   A. people.   B. everywhere.   C. opposite.

9 rect

- Every time I play Monopoly, I seem to pick the card that reads, "Go **directly** to jail. Do not pass Go. Do not collect $200."
- "Suck in those stomachs!" yelled the coach. "Pull back those shoulders, and stand **erect**!"

___ The word part *rect* means   A. opposite.   B. straight.   C. wrong.

10 the, theo-

- **Monotheism** is the belief that there is only one God.
- **Theology** is the study of the nature of God and religious truth.

___ The word part *the* or *theo-* means   A. god.   B. everywhere.   C. for.

Matching Word Parts with Definitions

Following are definitions of the ten word parts. Clearly write or print each word part next to its definition. The sentences above and on the previous page will help you decide on the meaning of each word part.

1. _____ Wrong; badly

2. _____ Straight

3. _____ Star, outer space

4. _____ People

5. _____ Someone who (does something)

6. _____ Earth; geography

7. _____ God or a god

8. _____ All; everywhere

9. _____ Marriage

10. _____ Against; contrasting; opposite

CAUTION: Do not go any further until you are sure the above answers are correct. Then you can use the definitions to help you in the following practices. Your goal is eventually to know the word parts well enough so that you don't need to check the definitions at all.

Sentence Check 1

Using the answer line provided, complete each *italicized* word below with the correct word part from the box. Use each word part once.

A. aster-, astro-	B. contra-	C. -er, -or	D. -gamy	E. geo-
F. mis-	G. omni-	H. pop	I. rect	J. the, theo-

_____ 1. Wade, a professional (*act . . .*) ___, seems to be playing a part even when he's offstage.

_____ 2. The study of the chemical makeup of the Earth's crust is called (. . . *chemistry*) ___.

_____ 3. Poverty is (. . . *present*) ___ in large cities in India, where people beg on every street.

_____ 4. A small starlike figure called an (. . . *isk*) ___ (*) is often used in books and magazines to indicate a footnote.

_____ 5. On a movie set, the (*di . . . or*) ___ is the person who keeps everyone and everything running on course.

_____ 6. John Wesley was the eighteenth-century British (. . . *logian*) ___ who founded Methodism.

_____ 7. If I don't hang my house key on a special hook in the kitchen as soon as I get home, I'll (. . . *place*) ___ it.

_____ 8. Young children go through a stage in which they (. . . *dict*) ___ everything a parent says. If the parent says yes, the child will usually say no.

_____ 9. (*Mono . . .*) ___ doesn't stop people from having more than one husband or wife. It only requires them to have one at a time.

_____ 10. The few places on Earth that have not yet been (. . . *ulated*) ___ by humans probably would not appeal to many. Who wants to live on the snowcapped peak of a mountain?

NOTE: Now check your answers to these items by turning to page 179. Going over the answers carefully will help you prepare for the next two practices, for which answers are not given.

Sentence Check 2

Using the answer line provided, complete each *italicized* word in the sentences below with the correct word part from the box. Use each word part once.

_____
_____ 1–2. The kindergartners were asked to draw a (. . . *angle*) ___, but several made a (. . . *take*) ___ and drew a circle instead.

_____
_____ 3–4. (*Pan . . . ists*) ___ believe that God is not a personality but an (. . . *present*) ___ force of nature, present throughout the universe.

_____ 5–6. (*Doct . . .*) ___ Fisher was very (*. . . ular*) ___ with the townspeople because
_____   she always took the time to answer their questions and had great empathy°
                        for her patients' suffering.

_____ 7–8. The two Mayfield brothers made (*. . . ry*) career decisions. One is an
_____   archaeologist who speculates° about what our past might have been like. The
                        other is an (*. . . naut*) who thinks about our future in space.

_____ 9–10. In (*. . . graphy*) ___ class, we learned not only about the location and climate
_____   of various countries but also about customs. For example, in some African
                         nations, (*exo . . .*) ___, or marrying outside the tribe, is customary; those who
                         refuse risk expulsion° from their native community.

Final Check: *Fascinating Courses*

Here is a final opportunity for you to strengthen your knowledge of the ten word parts. First read the
following selection carefully. Then complete each *italicized* word in the parentheses below with a word
part from the box at the top of the previous page. (Context clues will help you figure out which word part
goes in which blank.) Use each word part once.

Each semester, I like to choose one fascinating course unrelated to
my major. Last fall, for example, I took a(n) (*. . . logy*) (1) _____
course that focused on the remarkable changes in the Earth's surface
over time. Then in the spring, I took (*. . . nomy*) (2)_____.
When I looked at the stars through a telescope, I felt tiny and insignificant
in (*. . . st*) (3)_____ to the enormous sizes and
distances of outer space. This experience made me ponder° the nature
of God and prompted° me to look for a class on religion.

So this semester I'm taking a course in (*. . . logy*) (4)_____.
One day we spent three hours discussing this question: If God is
(*. . . potent*) (5)_____, then why hasn't He
or She alleviated° all of humanity's suffering? We've also talked about how much (*. . . understanding*)
(6)_____ arises when people do not know about each other's beliefs. This
confusion hampers° the pursuit of unity in the world. For example, I've long heard my (*minist . . .*)
(7)_____ preach that we should be true to one partner, but I never knew that
in some other religions, (*poly . . .*) (8)_____ is quite acceptable. Conversely°, in
Catholicism, priests and nuns have to abstain° from marrying. It seems there's no clear consensus° on
this subject.

If we were to take a survey of the world's (*. . . ulation*) (9)_____, many people
would probably say they look to their church for (*di . . . ion*) (10)_____ in their lives. I've
learned that there's a rationale° for understanding other religions as well.

Scores	Sentence Check 2 _____%	Final Check _____%

The box at the right lists twenty-five words from Unit Four. Using the clues at the bottom of the page, fill in these words to complete the puzzle that follows.

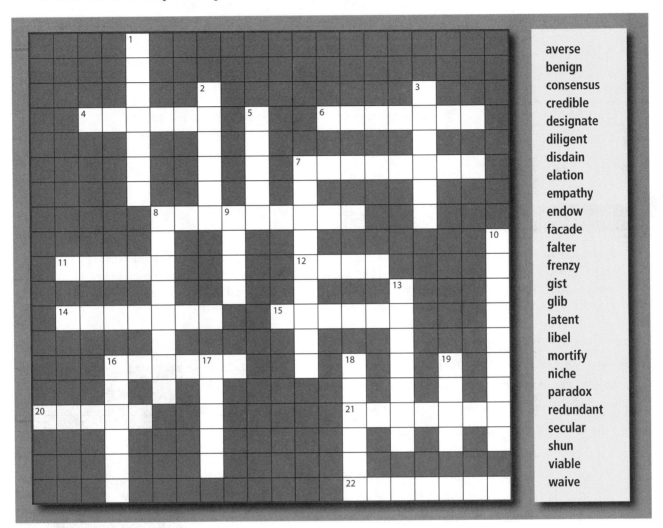

averse
benign
consensus
credible
designate
diligent
disdain
elation
empathy
endow
facade
falter
frenzy
gist
glib
latent
libel
mortify
niche
paradox
redundant
secular
shun
viable
waive

ACROSS

4. Workable; capable of being successful or effective

6. An attitude of contempt; scorn

7. Steady, determined, and careful in work

8. An opinion held by most or all involved

11. An activity or situation especially suited to a person

12. The main point or essential part of a matter; central idea

14. To humiliate or embarrass

15. The front of a building

16. To act or speak with uncertainty; hesitate

20. The publishing of false information that harms a person's reputation

21. A feeling of great joy or pride

22. The ability to share in another's feelings or thoughts

DOWN

1. A statement that seems contradictory yet may be true

2. Kindly; gentle

3. Present but hidden or inactive

5. To willingly give up; do without

7. To name to an office or duty; appoint

8. Believable

9. To keep away from; avoid consistently

10. Wordy or needlessly repetitive

13. Not directly related to religion; not spiritual; worldly

16. A wild outburst of excited feelings or actions

17. To provide with a talent or quality

18. Having a feeling of dislike or distaste for something

19. Characterized by a smooth, easy manner of speaking that often suggests insincerity

PART A

Choose the word that best completes each item and write it in the space provided.

_____ 1. The rain ___ the work of the road construction crew.

      A. hampered   B. improvised   C. flaunted   D. designated

_____ 2. Suddenly dizzy from the heat, the speaker ___ and covered his eyes.

      A. transcended   B. simulated   C. faltered   D. waived

_____ 3. It's hard to become ___ about great music. No matter how often you hear it, you never tire of it.

      A. viable   B. haughty   C. blasé   D. secular

_____ 4. When he decided to become a teacher, Brian certainly ___ from his plan to become a stockbroker.

      A. improvised   B. deviated   C. simulated   D. divulged

_____ 5. Though pleased with the A on her last English paper, Lee was careful not to become ___—she began work on the next assignment immediately.

      A. complacent   B. secular   C. ominous   D. menial

_____ 6. We were amazed to learn that gentle, soft-spoken Dr. Geyer writes horror novels under the ___ of Trent Paterson.

      A. interim   B. pseudonym   C. consensus   D. expulsion

_____ 7. When Scott won the gymnastics competition, his parents' ___ was as great as his own joy and pride.

      A. elation   B. facade   C. niche   D. libel

_____ 8. My nephew's ___ of tricks for getting his own way includes pouting, crying, and throwing tantrums.

      A. interim   B. empathy   C. consensus   D. repertoire

_____ 9. I'm not quick with home repairs, but I'm ___. I work steadily and carefully until I get the job done.

      A. diligent   B. glib   C. haughty   D. cursory

_____ 10. Because the article made unproven accusations against the mayor, the editors wouldn't print it for fear of being sued for ___.

      A. paradox   B. expulsion   C. empathy   D. libel

(Continues on next page)

PART B

On the answer line, write the letter of the choice that best completes each item.

_____ 11. Among Beverly's many pets, the most **bizarre** is her
    A. green parrot.   C. miniature poodle.
    B. hissing cockroach.   D. goldfish.

_____ 12. According to cartoons, situation comedies, and the like, which of the following job types is most likely to attract **glib** characters?
    A. Cowboy   C. Used-car salesperson
    B. Accountant   D. Plumber

_____ 13. A person **endowed** with an honest nature
    A. wishes he had an honest nature.   C. pretends to have an honest nature.
    B. is lacking an honest nature.   D. possesses an honest nature.

_____ 14. **Ominous** music in a movie score generally means that
    A. a love scene is about to happen.   C. an exciting action scene is about to happen.
    B. something scary or evil is about to happen.   D. the opening credits are about to be shown.

_____ 15. Napoleon Bonaparte was so **averse** to cats that he
    A. insisted one live in every room of his palace.   C. sneezed and itched whenever one was near.
    B. stroked one for luck every morning.   D. left the room in disgust if one entered.

_____ 16. Concerning fish, the term "feeding **frenzy**" refers to
    A. the period after eating when fish are relaxed.   C. a quiet, methodical search for food.
    B. a period of starvation when food is scarce.   D. a wild, excited period of feeding.

_____ 17. New England **comprises**
    A. the Atlantic Ocean.
    B. clam chowder, lobster, and lighthouses.
    C. Maine, New Hampshire, Massachusetts, Rhode Island, Connecticut, and Vermont.
    D. shipbuilding, fishing, and manufacturing.

_____ 18. Our cat has tested positive for the disease feline leukemia. But since the virus can be **latent**,
    A. we are having her put to sleep because she is suffering so much.
    B. she may not develop any symptoms for a long time.
    C. we know she will die very soon.
    D. we are sure she doesn't have the virus.

_____ 19. Marissa told her employer that she felt dizzy and feverish and needed to see a doctor. Her boss answered, with great **empathy**,
    A. "Well, don't let your personal problems interfere with your work."
    B. "Sorry to hear that. Can you work overtime tonight?"
    C. "You must be feeling terrible. Is there anything I can do?"
    D. "Do you think you have the flu? Don't give it to me!"

_____ 20. A frequent dream of mine always **mortifies** me. In it,
    A. I am in public and suddenly realize I'm naked.
    B. I can fly as easily as a bird.
    C. I am in my childhood home talking with my father, who is young and healthy again.
    D. I am in a furious argument with a coworker whom I dislike.

Score   (Number correct) _____ x 5 = _____%

Enter your score above and in the **Vocabulary Performance Chart** on the inside back cover of the book.

PART A

Complete each item with a word from the box. Use each word once.

A. commemorate	B. consensus	C. credible	D. designate	E. divulge
F. flaunt	G. gist	H. improvise	I. interim	J. paradox
K. secular	L. simulate	M. viable		

_____ 1. It's a(n) ___ that we can sometimes be more generous by giving less.

_____ 2. Authors often state the ___ of an article in the introductory paragraph.

_____ 3. Alonso ___s his good voice by singing louder than anyone else in the choir.

_____ 4. More and more nuns are wearing ___ clothes rather than traditional religious dress.

_____ 5. On Presidents' Day, the nation ___s George Washington and Abraham Lincoln.

_____ 6. I think it's selfish of Dolly not to ___ her secret recipe for poppyseed salad dressing.

_____ 7. Films that ___ the experience of riding on a roller coaster give me a genuine feeling of nausea.

_____ 8. I don't mind speaking before a group if I have time to prepare, but I'd be scared to death if I had to ___ a speech on the spot.

_____ 9. The only ___ plan for making enough money to keep up the payments on the house is to rent out some of its rooms.

_____ 10. Although the businessman at first seemed to be a ___ witness, the police started doubting him once he began to change the details of his story.

_____ 11. The ___ among the city's sportswriters is that Bridgewater High will win the basketball championship this year.

_____ 12. When the church's pastor resigned, a retired minister stepped in for the ___ until a permanent replacement was found.

_____ 13. The boys ___(e)d my little brother the treasurer of their tree-house club because he's the only one who receives a regular allowance.

(Continues on next page)

PART B

Write **C** if the italicized word is used **correctly**. Write **I** if the word is used **incorrectly**.

_____ 14. In a democracy, it's important for people to *waive* their right to vote.

_____ 15. "That bow tie *detracts* from Alan's appearance," said Paloma. "He looks strangled and gift-wrapped."

_____ 16. Wayne has *transcended* his usual good grades by failing three of his four classes this semester.

_____ 17. Because *menial* tasks require little thought, I was able to plan some of my essay while cleaning my apartment yesterday.

_____ 18. The host's famous sister remained in her room for most of the party, although she did *condescend* to come downstairs and say good night to the other guests before they left.

_____ 19. By careful saving, I managed to *deplete* my bank account from $80 to almost $1,200 by the summer's end.

PART C

On the answer line, write the letter of the word that is the **synonym** of the boldfaced word.

Example: __A__ bizarre   A. strange   B. ordinary   C. expensive

_____ 20. **haughty**   A. proud   B. humble   C. tall

_____ 21. **disdain**   A. loss   B. contempt   C. admiration

_____ 22. **benign**   A. cruel   B. broken   C. kindly

PART D

On the answer line, write the letter of the word that is the **antonym** of the boldfaced word.

Example: __B__ bizarre   A. strange   B. ordinary   C. expensive

_____ 23. **shun**   A. owe   B. seek   C. avoid

_____ 24. **facade**   A. back   B. light   C. front

_____ 25. **nullify**   A. ignore   B. approve   C. cancel

Score   (Number correct) _____ x 4 = _____%

Each item below starts with a pair of words in CAPITAL LETTERS. For each item, figure out the relationship between these two words. Then decide which of the choices (A, B, C, or D) expresses a similar relationship. Write the letter of your choice on the answer line.

_____ 1. PSEUDONYM : AUTHOR ::
    A. address : map   C. word : dictionary
    B. story : true   D. costume : actor

_____ 2. FACADE : BUILDING ::
    A. house : cellar   C. street : sign
    B. face : head   D. neighborhood : town

_____ 3. HAUGHTY : ARROGANCE ::
    A. thirsty : water   C. clever : intelligence
    B. brave : fear   D. muscle : strength

_____ 4. REDUNDANT : WORDY ::
    A. error : mistake   C. word : repeat
    B. paper : book   D. paper : read

_____ 5. DETRACT : IMPROVE ::
    A. blame : error   C. criticize : scold
    B. open : door   D. ascend : descend

_____ 6. ELATION : WONDERFUL NEWS ::
    A. pain : injury   C. satisfaction : failure
    B. wisdom : ignorance D. football : sport

_____ 7. OMINOUS : STORM CLOUDS ::
    A. bright : fog   C. flock : seagull
    B. fragrant : flowers D. sophomore : grade

_____ 8. CURSORY : CAREFUL ::
    A. sharp : blade   C. wild : untamed
    B. quick : rapid   D. plentiful : scarce

_____ 9. IMPROVISE : REHEARSE ::
    A. schedule : roster C. restore : destroy
    B. attempt : try   D. comedian : joke

_____ 10. SHUN : OUTCAST ::
    A. celebrate : hero   C. poem : poet
    B. triangle : shape   D. welcome : foe

(Continues on next page)

_____ 11. COMMEMORATE : ANNIVERSARY ::
      A. trophy : winner   C. break : diamond
      B. horn : bull   D. regret : mistake

_____ 12. DILIGENT : HARD-WORKING ::
      A. presence : absence   C. frightful : comforting
      B. dirty : unclean   D. silk : torn

_____ 13. EMPATHY : UNCARING ::
      A. liberty : free   C. reliability : irresponsible
      B. sympathy : compassionate   D. clarity : clear

_____ 14. CONDUCIVE : HELPFUL ::
      A. nervous : calm   C. lazy : idle
      B. actor : actress   D. prepared : unready

_____ 15. HAMPER : OBSTACLE ::
      A. forest : trees   C. gift : present
      B. assist : instruction   D. darken : bleach

_____ 16. VIABLE : IMPOSSIBLE ::
      A. sneaky : sly   C. applause : approval
      B. probable : likely   D. accidental : intentional

_____ 17. EXPULSION : SCHOOL ::
      A. eviction : apartment   C. celebration : funeral
      B. graduation : college   D. exercise : gym

_____ 18. COMPLACENT : SELF-DOUBT ::
      A. tired : exhaustion   C. transparent : clearness
      B. uninterested : indifference   D. rigid : flexibility

_____ 19. NICHE : SUITABLE ::
      A. kitchen cabinet : cereal   C. haunted house : scary
      B. high school : classroom   D. doctor's office : chilly

_____ 20. BIZARRE : ODDITY ::
      A. treacherous : traitor   C. unknown : celebrity
      B. strange : ordinary   D. landlord : tenant

Score   (Number correct) _____ x 5 = _____%

Enter your score above and in the **Vocabulary Performance Chart** on the inside back cover of the book.

PART A

Listed in the left-hand column below are ten common word parts, followed by words in which the parts are used. In each blank, write in the letter of the correct definition on the right.

Word Parts	Examples	Definitions
____ 1. **aster-, astro-**	aster, astrologer	A. Someone who (does something)
____ 2. **contra-**	contrary, contraindication	B. Star, outer space
____ 3. **-er, -or**	singer, visitor	C. All; everywhere
____ 4. **-gamy**	bigamy, polygamy	D. Straight
____ 5. **geo-**	geographic, geophysics	E. God or a god
____ 6. **mis-**	misbehave, misrepresent	F. Against; contrasting; opposite
____ 7. **omni-**	omnipotent, omnivorous	G. Marriage
____ 8. **pop**	populous, populate	H. Earth
____ 9. **rect**	directly, erect	I. People
____ 10. **the, theo-**	monotheism, theology	J. Wrong; badly

PART B

Using the answer line provided, complete each *italicized* word in the sentences below with the correct word part from the box. Not every word part will be used.

A. **aster-**	B. **contra-**	C. **-er**	D. **-gamy**	E. **geo-**
F. **mis-**	G. **omni-**	H. **pop**	I. **rect**	J. **theo-**

_____ 11. Vanilla ice cream is even more (. . . *ular*) ___ among Americans than chocolate is.

_____ 12. (. . . *ry*) ___ to what many suppose, Shakespeare made his living by acting as well as by writing.

_____ 13. Circling the sun between the paths of Mars and Jupiter are thousands of (. . . *oids*) ___, or small planets.

_____ 14. The movie was about a woman who, thinking her husband was dead, married again. Later, husband #1 showed up, making her guilty of (*bi* . . .) ___.

_____ 15. An interesting (. . . *graphic*) ___ fact is that Mount Everest, the highest mountain in the world, has grown a foot taller over the last century.

(Continues on next page)

PART C

Use your knowledge of word parts to determine the meaning of the **boldfaced** words. On the answer line, write the letter of each meaning.

____   16. Mr. Nolan is a man of many **misdeeds**.

      A. religious feelings   B. girlfriends   C. immoral acts

____   17. Houses are usually **rectilinear**; that is, they are characterized by

      A. opposing forces.   B. straight lines.   C. great cost.

____   18. There will be many **exhibitors** at the state fair this year.

      A. farm exhibits   B. people who exhibit   C. exhibit fees

____   19. Throughout history, a common form of government has been **theocracy**, in which the government is considered to be based on

      A. laws voted on by everyone.   B. immoral laws.   C. religious authority.

____   20. There's too much knowledge in the world today for any one person to claim **omniscience**.

      A. knowledge of biology   B. complete knowledge   C. partial knowledge

Score   (Number correct) _____ x 5 = _____%

Unit Five

Chapter 25

devoid	jeopardize
implore	sibling
infuriate	smug
intimidate	sneer
introvert	vivacious

Chapter 26

condone	furtive
contemplate	gape
feasible	pathetic
feign	precedent
fiscal	punitive

Chapter 27

cryptic	inhibition
deficient	ironic
depict	rupture
detrimental	saturate
implicit	vindictive

Chapter 28

constrict	habitat
exhaustive	pragmatic
fallible	pretentious
formulate	reconcile
genial	vile

Chapter 29

avid	mediate
dwindle	muted
esteem	nurture
evoke	pacify
legacy	transient

Chapter 30

aloof	longevity
ambivalent	magnitude
augment	mundane
dispel	obscure
explicit	render

devoid	jeopardize
implore	sibling
infuriate	smug
intimidate	sneer
introvert	vivacious

Ten Words in Context

In the space provided, write the letter of the meaning closest to that of each **boldfaced** word. Use the context of the sentences to help you figure out each word's meaning.

1 devoid
(dĭ-void′)
-adjective

● The French fries were so thin, dry, and **devoid** of taste that they seemed like toothpicks.

● Sometimes Carl is totally **devoid** of common sense. Once he went on vacation leaving his front door unlocked and the newspaper delivery service uncanceled.

___ *Devoid of* means   A. without.   B. equal to.   C. possessing.

2 implore
(ĭm-plôr′)
-verb

● Please hide all the candy bars, and don't tell me where they are no matter how much I **implore** you.

● The princess **implored** the evil magician to spare the handsome prince's life.

___ *Implore* means   A. to educate.   B. to deny.   C. to urge.

3 infuriate
(ĭn-fyŏŏr′ē-āt′)
-verb

● Peter so **infuriated** Sheila that she shut off her cell phone while he was still talking.

● At the grocery store, it **infuriates** me when people with a cartload of food get in the express line.

___ *Infuriate* means   A. to anger.   B. to encourage.   C. to frighten.

4 intimidate
(ĭn-tĭm′ə-dāt′)
-verb

● Will's huge size **intimidates** strangers, but anyone who knows him realizes that he's a very gentle man.

● Public speaking so **intimidates** Midori that she would rather write four term papers than give a single oral report.

___ *Intimidate* means   A. to calm.   B. to scare.   C. to annoy.

5 introvert
(ĭn′trə-vûrt′)
-noun

● Pearl is a very outgoing person, but her boyfriend Larry is such an **introvert** that he seldom socializes at all.

● It could be difficult for an **introvert** to succeed in a sales career, which involves a great deal of contact with the public.

___ *Introvert* means   A. a conceited person.   B. a shy person.   C. a busy person.

6 jeopardize
(jĕp′ər-dīz′)
-verb

● Molly is so clumsy that she **jeopardizes** every fragile item she touches. Whatever she picks up is liable to get broken.

● Pregnant women who take drugs **jeopardize** their babies' health.

___ *Jeopardize* means   A. to play with.   B. to take into account.   C. to put in danger.

7 sibling
(sĭb′lĭng)
-noun

- Do you think twins are more similar in personality than other **siblings**?
- It's hard enough for children to move to foster homes; it's even worse when **siblings** have to be separated.

___ *Sibling* means   A. a brother or sister.   B. a cousin.   C. a friend.

8 smug
(smŭg)
-adjective

- Self-confidence is a virtue, but being **smug** is carrying self-confidence too far.
- I avoid **smug** people. They are very generous in judging themselves while viewing others narrow-mindedly.

___ *Smug* means   A. full of life.   B. dishonest.   C. too self-satisfied.

9 sneer
(snēr)
-verb

- Sarita is terrific with little children. No matter how silly their questions are, she never **sneers** at them.
- Instead of encouraging us when we make a mistake, our biology teacher **sneers** at us with a scornful smile or a put-down.

___ *Sneer at* means   A. to leave.   B. to mock.   C. to ignore.

10 vivacious
(vĭ-vā′shəs)
-adjective

- My father is such a **vivacious** host that he makes his guests feel bright and lively too.
- Between scenes, the actors might appear tired and dull, but they become **vivacious** once the camera is running.

___ *Vivacious* means   A. good-looking.   B. peppy.   C. irritable.

Matching Words with Definitions

Following are definitions of the ten words. Clearly write or print each word next to its definition. The sentences above and on the previous page will help you decide on the meaning of each word.

1. _____ A shy or inwardly directed person

2. _____ Completely lacking

3. _____ A sister or brother

4. _____ To anger greatly

5. _____ Lively; full of life and enthusiasm

6. _____ To beg; plead

7. _____ To show or express contempt or ridicule

8. _____ To make timid or afraid; frighten

9. _____ Overly pleased with one's own cleverness, goodness, etc.; too self-satisfied

10. _____ To endanger; put at risk of loss or injury

CAUTION: Do not go any further until you are sure the above answers are correct. Then you can use the definitions to help you in the following practices. Your goal is eventually to know the words well enough so that you don't need to check the definitions at all.

Sentence Check 1

Using the answer line provided, complete each item below with the correct word from the box. Use each word once.

A. devoid	B. implore	C. infuriate	D. intimidate	E. introvert
F. jeopardize	G. sibling	H. smug	I. sneer	J. vivacious

_____ 1. You may call Linda charming and ___, but to me, she's just an irritating chatterbox.

_____ 2. I ___ you not to mention the DVD player to Hakim. I want to surprise him with it.

_____ 3. The genius who invents a chocolate ice cream that's ___ of calories should win a medal.

_____ 4. Working with computers all day suits my brother. He's too much of a(n) ___ to enjoy working much with other people.

_____ 5. I don't understand why Eileen enjoys activities that ___ her life, like skydiving and mountain climbing.

_____ 6. Christmas is the one time of year when my grandparents, parents, and three ___s are able to get together.

_____ 7. There used to be little that angered my father, but since he got laid off, it seems that everything we kids do ___s him.

_____ 8. When he found Art selling drugs near the elementary school, the arresting officer ___(e)d at him, snarling, "You scum."

_____ 9. It's better to get children's cooperation by setting shared goals than by trying to ___ them with threats of punishment.

_____ 10. Jenny would be more popular if she didn't get that ___ look on her face every time she answers the teacher's question correctly.

NOTE: Now check your answers to these items by turning to page 179. Going over the answers carefully will help you prepare for the next two practices, for which answers are not given.

Sentence Check 2

Using the answer lines provided, complete each item below with **two** words from the box. Use each word once.

_____
_____ 1–2. The people I love best can ___ me the most. No one can make me as angry as my parents and ___s can. I guess close relationships are conducive° to strong feelings, both positive and negative.

_____
_____ 3–4. Please don't ___ me to help you with your term paper. Since you delayed working on it for so long, I'm ___ of sympathy. I don't mean to gloat°, but why should I give up my evening when I was diligent° about getting the paper done and you were playing video games all week?

_____   5–6. I think Marvin only pretends to look down on the weightlifters in school. He
_____   ___s at them to hide the fact that they ___ him.

_____   7–8. Among her close friends, my sister is known as a really ___ woman,
_____   energetic and bubbly. But she often seems like a(n) ___ around people she
                            doesn't know well.

_____   9–10. I told Seth he would ___ his chances of getting a date for the dance if he
_____   waited until the last minute to ask someone. But he was ___ enough to think
                            that any girl he asked would be happy to break a date with someone else to
                            go to the dance with him.

Final Check: *Cal and His Sisters*

Here is a final opportunity for you to strengthen your knowledge of the ten words. First read the following selection carefully. Then fill in each blank with a word from the box at the top of the previous page. (Context clues will help you figure out which word goes in which blank.) Use each word once.

I've never met (1)_____s who are less alike than Cal and his sisters, Margo and Tina. First, they are different in their approach to school. All of them get good grades, but while Margo and Tina don't brag about their intelligence, Cal does. When he gets straight A's, he flaunts° his report card and (2)_____s at classmates who haven't done as well. Naturally, being so (3)_____ about his grades (4)_____s his chances of having many friends, and he's often by himself. Margo is a true extrovert°—she's completely (5)_____ of shyness. She's so (6)_____ that people naturally flock around her, and she's constantly busy with movie dates, study sessions with friends, and parties. Nothing seems to (7)_____ Margo. She will walk into a room full of strangers, boldly strike up a conversation, and leave an hour later with several new best friends. Conversely°, Tina is usually so quiet that people barely notice she is in the room. However, Tina is not a complete (8)_____. She's not shy; she just puts her energy into having a few close friends, rather than a crowd of acquaintances. I actually think Tina is the most interesting of the three. While Cal is devoted mostly to himself and his intelligence, and Margo is busy being popular, Tina is altruistic° and cares deeply about other people. It (9)_____s her to know that there are hungry, homeless people living in her own city, and she quietly volunteers some of her time to helping them. She once (10)_____(e)d Cal and Margo to get involved in the same kind of work, but neither of them had any interest in becoming affiliated° with her project.

Scores   Sentence Check 2 _____%   Final Check _____%

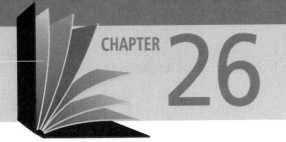

condone	furtive
contemplate	gape
feasible	pathetic
feign	precedent
fiscal	punitive

Ten Words in Context

In the space provided, write the letter of the meaning closest to that of each **boldfaced** word. Use the context of the sentences to help you figure out each word's meaning.

1 condone
(kən-dōn′)
-verb

● I cannot **condone** Elaine's smoking in public. It threatens other people's health.

● Teachers may overlook it when you're three minutes late. But they are not going to **condone** your walking into class a half hour late.

___ *Condone* means   A. to excuse.   B. to recall.   C. to punish.

2 contemplate
(kŏn′təm-plāt′)
-verb

● Because Ben hadn't studied for the test, he **contemplated** cheating. He quickly realized, however, that the eagle-eyed teacher would spot him.

● Whenever Anne's husband drank too much, she would **contemplate** separation, but then she would feel guilty for thinking about leaving a sick man.

___ *Contemplate* means   A. to consider.   B. to pretend.   C. to avoid.

3 feasible
(fē′zə-bəl)
-adjective

● It isn't **feasible** for me to work full time and keep the house clean unless someone helps me with the cleaning chores.

● Maya told her supervisor, "It just isn't **feasible** for this staff to do the work of the two people who were fired. You need to hire more people."

___ *Feasible* means   A. wrong.   B. legal.   C. possible.

4 feign
(fān)
-verb

● Since I had heard about my surprise party, I had to **feign** shock when everyone yelled, "Surprise!"

● You can **feign** a head cold by pretending you're too stuffed up to pronounce an *l, n,* or *m*. Try it by saying, "I have a code id by dose."

___ *Feign* means   A. to wish for.   B. to prove.   C. to fake.

5 fiscal
(fĭs′kəl)
-adjective

● The gift shop closed because of **fiscal** problems. It simply didn't make enough money to cover its expenses.

● Some states have passed laws allowing child-support payments to be taken directly from the paychecks of divorced parents who ignore their **fiscal** responsibility to their children.

___ *Fiscal* means   A. emotional.   B. financial.   C. unfair.

6 furtive
(fûr′tĭv)
-adjective

● At the football game, a guard in the stands noticed the **furtive** movement of a thief's hand toward a spectator's pocket.

● According to experts, teenagers who are **furtive** about where they are going and with whom may be involved with drugs.

___ *Furtive* means   A. sneaky.   B. dependable.   C. serious.

7 gape
(gāp)
-verb

- Everyone stopped to **gape** at the odd-looking sculpture in front of the library.
- Because drivers slowed down to **gape** at an accident in the southbound lanes, northbound traffic was backed up for miles.

___ *Gape* means   A. to yell.   B. to appreciate.   C. to stare.

8 pathetic
(pə-thĕt′ĭk)
-adjective

- That plumber's work was **pathetic**. Not only does the faucet still drip, but now the pipe is leaking.
- Health care in some areas of the world is **pathetic**. People are dying of diseases that are easily treatable with modern medicine.

___ *Pathetic* means   A. ordinary.   B. miserable.   C. expensive.

9 precedent
(prĕs′ĭ-dĕnt)
-noun

- When Jean's employer gave her three months off after her baby was born, a **precedent** was set for anyone else in the company who became a parent.
- To set a **precedent**, the teacher gave the student who stole the exam an F for the entire course. "Others will think twice before they do the same," he explained.

___ *Precedent* means   A. a question.   B. a delay.   C. a model.

10 punitive
(pyōō′nĭ-tĭv)
-adjective

- Judge Starn is especially **punitive** with drunken drivers, giving every one of them a jail term.
- Many parents find that reward is a better basis for teaching children than **punitive** action is.

___ *Punitive* means   A. punishing.   B. forgiving.   C. uneven.

Matching Words with Definitions

Following are definitions of the ten words. Clearly write or print each word next to its definition. The sentences above and on the previous page will help you decide on the meaning of each word.

1. _____ Possible; able to be done

2. _____ Done or behaving so as not to be noticed; secret

3. _____ To stare in wonder or amazement, often with one's mouth wide open

4. _____ Anything that may serve as an example in dealing with later similar circumstances

5. _____ To forgive or overlook

6. _____ Giving or involving punishment; punishing

7. _____ Financial

8. _____ To think about seriously

9. _____ Pitifully inadequate or unsuccessful

10. _____ To pretend; give a false show of

CAUTION: Do not go any further until you are sure the above answers are correct. Then you can use the definitions to help you in the following practices. Your goal is eventually to know the words well enough so that you don't need to check the definitions at all.

Sentence Check 1

Using the answer line provided, complete each item below with the correct word from the box. Use each word once.

A. condone	B. contemplate	C. feasible	D. feign	E. fiscal
F. furtive	G. gape	H. pathetic	I. precedent	J. punitive

_____ 1. Disabled people don't like others to ___ at them. Instead of a stare, a simple smile would be appreciated.

_____ 2. From time to time, I ___ attending business school, but so far I've made no firm decision.

_____ 3. Lawyers can strengthen a case by finding a useful ___ among previous similar cases.

_____ 4. It's not ___ for me to attend two weddings in the same afternoon, so I'll have to choose between them.

_____ 5. The principal does not ___ hitting students. He believes that every problem has a nonviolent solution.

_____ 6. At the low-cost clinic, Clayton had to give evidence of his ___ situation, such as a tax form or current pay stub, before he could receive treatment.

_____ 7. The people on the elevator didn't want to stare at the patch on my eye, but several took ___ glances.

_____ 8. Mr. Hall's living conditions were ___. There was no heat or electricity in his apartment, and the walls were crumbling.

_____ 9. When I gave my oral report in class, I tried to ___ confidence, but my shaking legs revealed my nervousness.

_____ 10. My mother wasn't usually ___, but one day I pushed her too far, and she said, "If you do that one more time, I will send you to your room for the rest of your adolescence."

NOTE: Now check your answers to these items by turning to page 179. Going over the answers carefully will help you prepare for the next two practices, for which answers are not given.

Sentence Check 2

Using the answer lines provided, complete each item below with **two** words from the box. Use each word once.

_____
_____ 1–2. "Would it be ___ for us to buy a new copy machine?" Hal asked at the office budget meeting. The boss replied, "Unfortunately, our ___ situation is too tight. That purchase would deplete° our funds and create a deficit° in our budget."

_____
_____ 3–4. Some parents take only ___ measures when children misbehave. They never take time to ___ the benefits of a gentler approach. However, benign° encouragement is often more effective than punishment.

_____ 5–6. Several passersby stopped to ___ at the homeless man and his ___ shelter,
_____   made of cardboard and a torn blanket. The poignant° sight moved one
                              woman to go to a restaurant and buy a meal for the man.

_____ 7–8. The fourth-grade teacher said, "I will not ___ any ___ behavior in my class.
_____   Rita, please stop passing notes under your desk to Ellen."

_____ 9–10. The ___ was set many years ago: When the winner of a beauty contest is
_____   announced, the runner-up ___s happiness for the winner, despite the fact that
                              she is quite devoid° of happiness at the moment.

Final Check: *Shoplifter*

Here is a final opportunity for you to strengthen your knowledge of the ten words. First read the following selection carefully. Then fill in each blank with a word from the box at the top of the previous page. (Context clues will help you figure out which word goes in which blank.) Use each word once.

Valerie took a (1)_____ glance around her. When it seemed that no one was watching, she stuffed a blue shirt into the bottom of her purse and darted out of the women's department. She walked slowly around the shoe department for a while and then left the store.

"Stop! You! Stop!" shouted a guard, who seemed to appear from nowhere. Then another man in street clothes grabbed her purse and pulled out the shirt.

"But . . . but . . . it's not mine. I don't know how it got there," Valerie cried.

The two men just looked at each other and laughed at the blatant° lie. The guard said, "That's what all shoplifters say. People steal without taking time to (2)_____ the possible results. Then when they're caught, they loudly (3)_____ innocence."

As the guard began to phone the police, Valerie implored° the men, "Please don't press charges. Please. This is the first time I've ever done anything like this, and I'll never do it again."

The men laughed again. "Your argument is (4)_____," the man in street clothes sneered°. "It's everyone's first time. Our store has a policy on shoplifters: It's mandatory° for us to press charges, even if it's the first offense. We can't set a bad (5)_____ by letting a shoplifter go, as if we (6)_____(e)d such crimes."

"That's right," said the guard. "Shoplifting is all too prevalent° in our store. This shirt costs only twenty dollars, but the twenties add up. Our (7)_____ officer reported a loss of about $150,000 worth of merchandise to shoplifters last year. So it simply isn't (8)_____ to let you walk away. Unfortunately, we have no choice but to take (9)_____ action."

Soon Valerie was led to the police car. She covered her face as other shoppers stopped to (10)_____ at the lovely young woman, an unlikely-looking criminal.

| Scores | Sentence Check 2 _____% | Final Check _____% |

cryptic	inhibition
deficient	ironic
depict	rupture
detrimental	saturate
implicit	vindictive

Ten Words in Context

In the space provided, write the letter of the meaning closest to that of each **boldfaced** word. Use the context of the sentences to help you figure out each word's meaning.

1 cryptic
(krĭp′tĭk)
-adjective

- Whenever I ask Tomas what's happening in his life, he always gives the same **cryptic** reply: "It's a green world, my friend."
- Next to the dead woman's body was a **cryptic** note that said, "Not now."

___ *Cryptic* means   A. cruel.   B. puzzling.   C. humorous.

2 deficient
(dĭ-fĭsh′ənt)
-adjective

- When people have too little iron in their blood, it sometimes means that their diet is also **deficient** in iron.
- Gil's manners are **deficient**. For example, I've never heard him thank anyone for anything.

___ *Deficient* means   A. lacking.   B. sensitive.   C. increasing.

3 depict
(dĭ-pĭkt′)
-verb

- The painting **depicts** a typical nineteenth-century summer day in the park.
- Harriet Beecher Stowe's novel *Uncle Tom's Cabin* **depicted** the cruelty of slavery so forcefully that the book helped to begin the Civil War.

___ *Depict* means   A. to hide.   B. to show.   C. to predict.

4 detrimental
(dĕ′trə-mĕn′təl)
-adjective

- Do you think all television is **detrimental** to children, or are some programs a positive influence on them?
- The gases from automobiles and factories have been so **detrimental** to the environment that some of the damage may be permanent.

___ *Detrimental* means   A. useful.   B. new.   C. damaging.

5 implicit
(ĭm-plĭs′ĭt)
-adjective

- When the gangster growled, "I'm sure you want your family to stay healthy," Harris understood the **implicit** threat.
- Although it's never been said, there's an **implicit** understanding that Carla will be promoted when Earl finally retires.

___ *Implicit* means   A. playful.   B. modern.   C. unspoken.

6 inhibition
(ĭn′hə-bĭsh′ən)
-noun

- A two-year-old has no **inhibitions** about running around naked.
- Sarah's family is openly affectionate, with no **inhibitions** about hugging or kissing in public.

___ *Inhibition* means   A. an inner block.   B. a habit.   C. a purpose.

7 ironic
(ī-rŏn′ĭk)
-*adjective*

● It's **ironic** that Loretta is such a strict mother, because she was certainly wild in her youth.

● "The Gift of the Magi" is a short story with an **ironic** twist: A woman sells her long hair to buy a chain for her husband's watch, while her husband sells his watch to buy ornaments for her hair.

___ *Ironic* means   A. unexpected.   B. inadequate.   C. reasonable.

8 rupture
(rŭp′chər)
-*verb*

● If the dam were to **rupture**, the town would disappear under many feet of water.

● The bulge in the baby's stomach was caused by a muscle wall that had **ruptured** and would have to be repaired.

___ *Rupture* means   A. to heal.   B. to exist.   C. to come apart.

9 saturate
(săch′ə-rāt′)
-*verb*

● Most people like their cereal crunchy, but Teresa lets hers sit until the milk has **saturated** every piece.

● Studying history for three hours **saturated** my brain—I couldn't have absorbed one more bit of information.

___ *Saturate* means   A. to protect.   B. to empty.   C. to fill.

10 vindictive
(vĭn-dĭk′tĭv)
-*adjective*

● If a woman refuses to date my older brother, he becomes **vindictive**. One way he takes revenge is to forward her all his junk e-mail.

● After she was given two weeks' notice, the **vindictive** employee intentionally infected all the office computers with a virus.

___ *Vindictive* means   A. sympathetic.   B. spiteful.   C. puzzling.

Matching Words with Definitions

Following are definitions of the ten words. Clearly write or print each word next to its definition. The sentences above and on the previous page will help you decide on the meaning of each word.

1. _____ A holding back or blocking of some action, feeling, or thought

2. _____ Having a vague or hidden meaning; mysterious

3. _____ Suggested but not directly expressed; unstated, but able to be understood

4. _____ Inclined to seek revenge; vengeful

5. _____ To represent in pictures or words; describe

6. _____ To burst or break apart

7. _____ Lacking something essential; inadequate; insufficient

8. _____ To soak or fill as much as possible

9. _____ Harmful; causing damage

10. _____ Opposite to what might be expected

CAUTION: Do not go any further until you are sure the above answers are correct. Then you can use the definitions to help you in the following practices. Your goal is eventually to know the words well enough so that you don't need to check the definitions at all.

Sentence Check 1

Using the answer line provided, complete each item below with the correct word from the box. Use each word once.

A. cryptic	B. deficient	C. depict	D. detrimental	E. implicit
F. inhibition	G. ironic	H. rupture	I. saturate	J. vindictive

_____   1. A person can be intelligent and yet be ___ in common sense.

_____   2. When the pressure in the gas pipe became too great, the pipe ___(e)d.

_____   3. Isn't it ___ that the richest man in town won the million-dollar lottery?

_____   4. Even something as healthful as vitamins can be ___ to your health when taken in very large amounts.

_____   5. Becky's usual lack of ___ was evident the day she came to class barefoot.

_____   6. In the novel *Oliver Twist*, Charles Dickens ___s life in an English orphanage as truly pathetic°, with little food and no love.

_____   7. The clans, or families, of ancient Scotland were extremely ___. If anyone from another clan harmed one of their members, the others would take full revenge.

_____   8. The fifth-grade assignment was written in double talk. Everyone laughed as the students tried to make out the teacher's ___ message.

_____   9. The aroma of Gretchen's perfume so ___(e)d the air in the car that Steve coughed and rolled down a window.

_____   10. Although it's not written in teachers' contracts, there is a(n) ___ understanding that teachers will spend time preparing lessons and responding to students' work.

NOTE: Now check your answers to these items by turning to page 179. Going over the answers carefully will help you prepare for the next two practices, for which answers are not given.

Sentence Check 2

Using the answer lines provided, complete each item below with **two** words from the box. Use each word once.

_____
_____   1–2. Water-balloon fights are fun until a balloon ___s against your clothes, and they get ___(e)d with cold water.

_____
_____   3–4. Most viewers find the painting, with its dozens of dots on a white background, to be ___. However, it's possible to figure out what the painting ___s by mentally connecting the dots.

_____
_____   5–6. I feel it's a waste of energy to retaliate° when someone has injured me, but my sister is always trying to get even with people. Her ___ attitude is ___ to her relationships with family and friends.

_____   7–8. It's ___ that the book *Live Simply on Little Money* has made the author
_____   wealthy, since a(n) ___ message of the book is that the author himself
                          requires little money.

_____   9–10. Gerry feels people should "lose their ___s" and do whatever they feel like
_____   doing, but I think people who are totally ___ in self-control have poor
                            manners.

Final Check: *A Nutty Newspaper Office*

Here is a final opportunity for you to strengthen your knowledge of the ten words. First read the following selection carefully. Then fill in each blank with a word from the box at the top of the previous page. (Context clues will help you figure out which word goes in which blank.) Use each word once.

My therapist says it's (1)_____ to my mental health to keep my thoughts bottled up inside of me, so I'll drop all (2)_____s and tell you about the newspaper office where I work.

Let me attempt to describe my managing editor first. It's sort of (3)_____ that Ed is in communications because I've never met anyone harder to talk to. Although he's a proponent° of clear expression, Ed communicates as unclearly as anyone I know. For example, if I say, "How are you doing today, Ed?" he'll give me some (4)_____ response such as "The tidal pools of time are catching up with me." I used to think there might be some deep wisdom (5)_____ in Ed's incoherent° statements, but now I just think he's a little eccentric°.

Then there's Seymour, our sportswriter. Seymour is perfectly normal except that he has unexplained fits of crying two or three times a week. In the middle of a conversation about the baseball playoffs or the next heavyweight title fight, Seymour suddenly goes into a frenzy° of crying and (6)_____s handfuls of Kleenex with his tears.

Now, I don't mean to (7)_____ our office as a totally depressing place. It is not entirely (8)_____ in excitement, but even our excitement is bizarre°. It is usually provided by Jan, a (9)_____ typesetter who, whenever she feels injured by Ed, takes revenge in some horrible but entertaining way. One of her favorite types of reprisal° is sneaking fictional items about him into the society column. I'll never forget the time Ed was in the hospital after his appendix (10)_____(e)d. He almost broke his stitches when he read that he was taking a vacation at a nudist colony. The article infuriated° him so much that he probably would have sued the newspaper for libel°—if he didn't work there himself.

Scores   Sentence Check 2 _____%   Final Check _____%

Enter your scores above and in the **Vocabulary Performance Chart** on the inside back cover of the book.

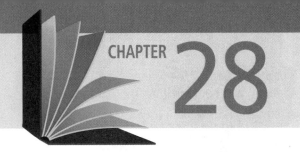

constrict	habitat
exhaustive	pragmatic
fallible	pretentious
formulate	reconcile
genial	vile

Ten Words in Context

In the space provided, write the letter of the meaning closest to that of each **boldfaced** word. Use the context of the sentences to help you figure out each word's meaning.

1 constrict
(kən-strĭkt′)
-*verb*

● The summer highway construction will **constrict** traffic by confining it to only two lanes.

● For centuries in China, girls' feet were **constricted** with binding to keep them from growing to normal size. Women's feet were considered most attractive if they were less than four inches long.

___ *Constrict* means   A. to expand.   B. to repair.   C. to squeeze.

2 exhaustive
(ĭg-zô′stĭv)
-*adjective*

● Don't buy a used car without putting it through an **exhaustive** inspection. Check every detail, from hood to trunk.

● My teacher recommended an **exhaustive** thousand-page biography of Freud, but who has time to read such a thorough account?

___ *Exhaustive* means   A. smooth.   B. detailed.   C. narrow.

3 fallible
(făl′ə-bəl)
-*adjective*

● "I know we all are **fallible**," the boss told his workers. "But do you have to make so many of your mistakes on company time?"

● When they are little, kids think their parents can do no wrong; but when they become teenagers, their parents suddenly seem **fallible**.

___ *Fallible* means   A. optimistic.   B. friendly.   C. imperfect.

4 formulate
(fôr′myə-lāt′)
-*verb*

● The author first **formulated** an outline of his plot and then began writing his mystery.

● Before stepping into his boss's office, Toshio had carefully **formulated** his case for a raise.

___ *Formulate* means   A. to develop.   B. to question.   C. to accept.

5 genial
(jēn′yəl)
-*adjective*

● I was worried that my grandmother's treatment at the nursing home might be harsh, so I was relieved when the nurses and aides turned out to be very **genial**.

● Stacey found her first dance instructor so rude and unpleasant that she changed to a more **genial** one.

___ *Genial* means   A. good-looking.   B. practical.   C. good-natured.

6 habitat
(hăb′ĭ-tăt)
-*noun*

● Many people believe that wild animals should be allowed to remain in their natural **habitats** and not be captured and put in zoos.

● Mosses can live in a large variety of humid **habitats**, from very cold to very hot.

___ *Habitat* means   A. a pattern.   B. a plan.   C. a territory.

7 pragmatic
(prăg-măt′ĭk)
-adjective

● We always called my sister "Practical Polly" because she was the most **pragmatic** member of the family.

● When Vince was single, he spent most of his money on travel. Now that he has a family to support, he must spend his money in more **pragmatic** ways.

__ *Pragmatic* means   A. sensible.   B. patient.   C. pleasant.

8 pretentious
(prē-tĕn′shəs)
-adjective

● Dana's classmates don't like her because she's so **pretentious**. It's hard to like someone who acts as if she knows it all.

● My aunt marked her husband's grave with a large, **pretentious** monument, as though he were a member of a royal family.

__ *Pretentious* means   A. overly imaginative.   B. important-seeming.   C. cruel.

9 reconcile
(rĕk′ən-sīl′)
-verb

● When my grandfather died, we worked hard to **reconcile** Grandma to the fact that he was really gone.

● After his third wreck in six months, Ahmed **reconciled** himself to living somewhere along a bus line and doing without a car.

__ *Reconcile to* means   A. to bring to accept.   B. to frighten about.   C. to hide from.

10 vile
(vīl)
-adjective

● My sister loves a certain cheese that has the **vile** odor of something that fell off a garbage truck.

● When I finally get around to cleaning out the refrigerator, I always find some **vile** moldy leftovers at the back of a shelf.

__ *Vile* means   A. threatening.   B. natural.   C. nasty.

Matching Words with Definitions

Following are definitions of the ten words. Clearly write or print each word next to its definition. The sentences above and on the previous page will help you decide on the meaning of each word.

1. _____ To bring (oneself or someone else) to accept

2. _____ The natural environment of an animal or a plant

3. _____ Making a show of excellence or importance, especially when undeserved

4. _____ Capable of making an error

5. _____ To make smaller or narrower, as by squeezing or shrinking

6. _____ Covering all possible details; complete; thorough

7. _____ Friendly, pleasant, and kindly

8. _____ Offensive to the senses, feelings, or thoughts; disgusting

9. _____ To plan or express in an orderly way

10. _____ Practical

CAUTION: Do not go any further until you are sure the above answers are correct. Then you can use the definitions to help you in the following practices. Your goal is eventually to know the words well enough so that you don't need to check the definitions at all.

Sentence Check 1

Using the answer line provided, complete each item below with the correct word from the box. Use each word once.

A. constrict	B. exhaustive	C. fallible	D. formulate	E. genial
F. habitat	G. pragmatic	H. pretentious	I. reconcile	J. vile

_____ 1. The local diner serves the world's most ___ beef stew, full of big globs of fat.

_____ 2. Why is Debra acting so unfriendly today? She's usually so ___.

_____ 3. My mother was forced to ___ herself to my independence when I moved into my own apartment.

_____ 4. Bright light ___s the pupils of our eyes, letting in less light. Darkness makes them wider, letting in more light.

_____ 5. My supervisor told me that if I wished to work on an independent project, I should first ___ a detailed plan of my idea.

_____ 6. For her term paper on orchids, Waneta did ___ research, covering every aspect of the flower's growth and marketing.

_____ 7. ___ about his intelligence, Norm tries to impress people by using big words.

_____ 8. Children's stories sometimes mistakenly show penguins at the North Pole. The birds' ___ is actually near the South Pole.

_____ 9. "It would be more ___," my brother said, "if you went to the grocery once a week for a larger order rather than going daily for just a few items."

_____ 10. When the auto mechanic said, "Well, I'm ___ like everyone else," I responded, "Yes, but your mistake almost got me flattened by a truck."

NOTE: Now check your answers to these items by turning to page 179. Going over the answers carefully will help you prepare for the next two practices, for which answers are not given.

Sentence Check 2

Using the answer lines provided, complete each item below with **two** words from the box. Use each word once.

_____
_____ 1–2. "You want me to be perfect, but that's impossible!" I cried. "___ yourself to the fact that every one of us is ___." It wasn't until then that my mother realized how detrimental° her criticism had been to our relationship.

_____
_____ 3–4. Wildlife experts ___(e)d a plan to preserve what little remains of the gorilla's natural ___. Continued loss of that territory will jeopardize° these magnificent animals and could even result in the demise° of the species.

_____ 5–6. My uncle was not at all ___ about fiscal° matters. He would spend household money on videotapes and ___-smelling cigars and leave the family without any extra cash.

_____   7–8. When our pet python escaped, we quickly made a(n) ___ search throughout
_____   the house and grounds. We found him wrapped around our dog, about to ___
                                the poor mutt to death.

_____   9–10. At the sales seminar, employees were taught to be ___ with customers and
_____   never to seem ___, no matter how much they knew. Customers like warm,
                                 amiable° salespeople, not ones who show off.

Final Check: *Roughing It*

Here is a final opportunity for you to strengthen your knowledge of the ten words. First read the following selection carefully. Then fill in each blank with a word from the box at the top of the previous page. (Context clues will help you figure out which word goes in which blank.) Use each word once.

"Whose brilliant idea was this, anyway?" Sara asked. "If people were intended to sleep on the ground and cook over a fire, we wouldn't have beds and microwave ovens."

"Stop complaining," Emily said. "At least *you've* got on dry clothes. You didn't end up walking through some (1)_____ mud because your canoe overturned. And you didn't have a(n) (2)_____ partner who claimed to know everything about canoeing but actually didn't know enough to steer around a rock."

"So I made a mistake," George said. "We're all (3)_____."

"Well," Emily responded, "your mistake has lost us our tent. And our sleeping bags and clothes are saturated° with muddy water."

Then Doug spoke up. "It's no big deal. We didn't plan for this, so let's improvise°. Sara and I will lend you clothes, and you two can squeeze into our tent."

"Squeeze is right, " said Emily. "Four in one tent won't work—it just isn't feasible°. We'll be so (4)_____(e)d that we won't be able to exhale."

"It's your choice," said Doug. "Decide if you want to be in a crowded tent or sleep out in this wild-animal (5)_____."

Sara couldn't resist adding, "If you had just listened to me this time and had been a bit more (6)_____ when planning for this trip, we wouldn't be in such a mess. You would have written a(n) (7)_____ list of what we would need, from A to Z. Then you would have (8)_____(e)d a clear plan for who would take what. Then we wouldn't be out here with two corkscrews but no plastic to wrap our belongings in."

"Let's just stop complaining before this degenerates° into a shouting match. Instead, let's try to be a little more (9)_____ with one another," said Doug. "Right now, we need to (10)_____ ourselves to our imperfect situation and not let it detract° so much from our vacation that we forget to have a good time."

Scores	Sentence Check 2 _____%	Final Check _____%

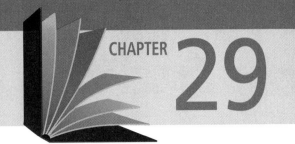

avid	mediate
dwindle	muted
esteem	nurture
evoke	pacify
legacy	transient

Ten Words in Context

In the space provided, write the letter of the meaning closest to that of each **boldfaced** word. Use the context of the sentences to help you figure out each word's meaning.

1 avid
(ăv′ĭd)
-*adjective*

___ *Avid* means

- Suki, an **avid** reader, enjoys nothing more than a good science-fiction novel.
- Artie is such an **avid** sports fan that he has two televisions tuned to different sporting events so he doesn't miss any action.

A. likable.   B. devoted.   C. helpful.

2 dwindle
(dwĭn′dəl)
-*verb*

___ *Dwindle* means

- As the number of leaves on the tree **dwindled**, the number on the ground increased.
- Chewing nicotine gum helped Doreen's craving for cigarettes to **dwindle**. She smoked fewer and fewer cigarettes each day until she quit altogether.

A. to make sense.   B. to drop suddenly.   C. to decrease.

3 esteem
(ĕ-stēm′)
-*noun*

___ *Esteem* means

- When Mr. Bauer retired after coaching basketball for thirty years, his admiring students gave him a gold whistle as a sign of their **esteem**.
- The critics had such **esteem** for the play that they voted it "Best Drama of the Year."

A. concern.   B. admiration.   C. curiosity.

4 evoke
(ē-vōk′)
-*verb*

___ *Evoke* means

- Music can **evoke** powerful feelings. A sweet violin solo often moves its listeners to tears.
- The smells of cider and pumpkin pie **evoke** thoughts of autumn.

A. to bring out.   B. to shelter.   C. to follow.

5 legacy
(lĕg′ə-sē)
-*noun*

___ *Legacy* means

- Ana's great-grandfather, grandmother, and mother were all musicians. She must have inherited their **legacy** of musical talent because she's an excellent piano and guitar player.
- One of the richest **legacies** that my mother handed down to me is the love of nature. I've inherited her interests in growing flowers and in hiking.

A. a memory.   B. a high hope.   C. an inherited gift.

6 mediate
(mē′dē-āt′)
-*verb*

___ *Mediate* means

- My father refused to **mediate** quarrels between my sister and me. He would say, "Settle your own fights."
- Each of the farmers claimed the stream was part of his property. Finally, they agreed to let the town council **mediate** their conflict.

A. to avoid.   B. to settle.   C. to observe.

7 muted
(myōo'təd)
-*adjective*

● When I put in my earplugs, the yelling from the next apartment becomes **muted** enough so that it no longer disturbs me.

● The artist used **muted** rather than bright colors, giving the painting a quiet, peaceful tone.

__ *Muted* means   A. soft.   B. temporary.   C. boring.

8 nurture
(nûr'chər)
-*verb*

● Although I often forget to water or feed my plants, my sister carefully **nurtures** her many ferns and violets.

● Many animals feed and protect their babies, but female fish, in general, do not **nurture** their young. The female only lays the eggs, which are guarded by the male until they hatch.

__ *Nurture* means   A. to inspect.   B. to seek out.   C. to care for.

9 pacify
(păs'ə-fī')
-*verb*

● When I'm feeling nervous or upset, I often **pacify** myself with a soothing cup of mint tea.

● Not only did I anger Roberta by calling her boyfriend "a creep," but I failed to **pacify** her with my note of apology: "I'm sorry I called Mel a creep. It's not always wise to tell the truth."

__ *Pacify* means   A. to amuse.   B. to encourage.   C. to soothe.

10 transient
(trăn'shənt)
-*adjective*

● The drug's dangers include both permanent brain damage and **transient** side effects, such as temporarily blurred vision.

● Julia wants a lasting relationship, but Rico seems interested in only a **transient** one.

__ *Transient* means   A. dull.   B. short-lived.   C. hard to notice.

Matching Words with Definitions

Following are definitions of the ten words. Clearly write or print each word next to its definition. The sentences above and on the previous page will help you decide on the meaning of each word.

1. _____ Softened; toned down; made less intense
2. _____ Temporary; passing soon or quickly
3. _____ Enthusiastic, devoted; eager
4. _____ To make calm or peaceful
5. _____ To draw forth, as a mental image or a feeling
6. _____ To gradually lessen or shrink
7. _____ To settle (a conflict) by acting as a go-between
8. _____ High regard; respect; favorable opinion
9. _____ To promote development by providing nourishment, support, and protection
10. _____ Something handed down from people who have come before

CAUTION: Do not go any further until you are sure the above answers are correct. Then you can use the definitions to help you in the following practices. Your goal is eventually to know the words well enough so that you don't need to check the definitions at all.

Sentence Check 1

Using the answer line provided, complete each item below with the correct word from the box. Use each word once.

A. **avid**	B. **dwindle**	C. **esteem**	D. **evoke**	E. **legacy**
F. **mediate**	G. **muted**	H. **nurture**	I. **pacify**	J. **transient**

_____ 1. When my newborn nephew starts to scream, his parents ___ him by rocking him and singing softly.

_____ 2. The photos in my album ___ many fond memories of my high-school friends.

_____ 3. If you study too long at one sitting, your concentration will eventually begin to ___.

_____ 4. At the party, Cara and I kept our conversation ___ so that no one would overhear us.

_____ 5. You must ___ a child with love and respect as well as with food and shelter.

_____ 6. Part of the charm of spring is that it's ___. It comes and goes so quickly that we can't wait for its return.

_____ 7. To show his ___ for her singing, the talent agent sent Mary flowers after she performed in a local theater.

_____ 8. My cousin Bobby is the most ___ collector I know. He collects almost anything, from baseball cards to beer cans.

_____ 9. Shakespeare's plays, a priceless ___ from the sixteenth and seventeenth centuries, have been enjoyed by generation after generation.

_____ 10. Rather than go to court, Mr. Hillman and the owner of the gas station agreed to have a lawyer ___ their disagreement.

NOTE: Now check your answers to these items by turning to page 179. Going over the answers carefully will help you prepare for the next two practices, for which answers are not given.

Sentence Check 2

Using the answer lines provided, complete each item below with **two** words from the box. Use each word once.

_____
_____ 1–2. Becky's ___ for Gerald turned out to be ___. She discovered that he used drugs and could not condone° his habit, so she broke up with him.

_____
_____ 3–4. Leo is such a(n) ___ chef that his enthusiasm for cooking never ___s. He's been known to cook with great zeal° for ten straight hours.

_____
_____ 5–6. Loud music upsets our canary, but ___ tones ___ her.

_____   7–8. It is necessary to ___ a human infant because it is the biological ___ of newborn mammals to be unable to survive on their own. Parental care is indispensable°.

_____

_____   9–10. In the Bible, King Solomon ___s a dispute between two women, each of whom contends° that a child is her own. To end the impasse°, the king suggests that the child be cut in two. This thought ___s horror in one of the women. The king then knows she is the real mother.

_____

Final Check: *Getting Scared*

Here is a final opportunity for you to strengthen your knowledge of the ten words. First read the following selection carefully. Then fill in each blank with a word from the box at the top of the previous page. (Context clues will help you figure out which word goes in which blank.) Use each word once.

Do you remember trying to scare yourself and everybody else when you were a kid? For instance, maybe you were a(n) (1)_____ roller-coaster rider, closing your eyes and screaming and loving every minute. Afterward, you would (2)_____ your still nervous stomach by quietly sipping an ice-cold Coke. If a short roller-coaster ride gave you too (3)_____ a thrill, there was always the long-term fear of a horror movie. If the horrors it depicted° were vile° enough, you might be scared about going to bed for the next three months.

And remember popping out from behind corners and yelling "Boo!" at your brother? The fight that followed ("You didn't scare me one bit." "Did too." "Did not." "Did too.") would go on until a grown-up (4)_____(e)d the conflict. (Parents always seemed to be there to settle disputes among siblings° or to (5)_____ and reassure you at times when you needed support.)

At other times, you and your friends probably sat around a campfire late at night, engaging in your favorite nocturnal° activity—telling ghost stories. Thrilled with the horror of it all, you spoke in voices so (6)_____ they were almost whispers. The storyteller who gained the most (7)_____ was the one who could (8)_____ the greatest terror in others. If anybody's fear started to (9)_____, this expert would build it up again with the most effective story in the campfire repertoire°, the story of the ghost in the outhouse, a (10)_____ handed down from older brothers and sisters to younger ones. This traumatic° story always made you so scared that you needed to go to the outhouse. But fearing the ghost there, how could you?

| Scores | Sentence Check 2 _____% | Final Check _____% |

Enter your scores above and in the **Vocabulary Performance Chart** on the inside back cover of the book.

CHAPTER 30

aloof	longevity
ambivalent	magnitude
augment	mundane
dispel	obscure
explicit	render

Ten Words in Context

In the space provided, write the letter of the meaning closest to that of each **boldfaced** word. Use the context of the sentences to help you figure out each word's meaning.

1 aloof
(ə-lōof′)
-adjective

- Some people say that the British are **aloof**, but the British people I've met seem warm and open.
- I knew that Tyrell was upset with me about something because he was **aloof** even when I tried to be friendly.

___ *Aloof* means   A. motivated.   B. lazy.   C. cold.

2 ambivalent
(ăm-bĭv′ə-lənt)
-adjective

- "Because I'm **ambivalent** about marriage," Earl said, "I keep swinging back and forth between wanting to set the date and wanting to break off my engagement."
- I'm **ambivalent** about my counselor. I appreciate her desire to be helpful, but I dislike her efforts to interfere in my life.

___ *Ambivalent* means   A. meaning well.   B. having mixed feelings.   C. experienced.

3 augment
(ôg-mĕnt′)
-verb

- Why are women so willing to **augment** their height by wearing high heels when this kind of footwear is so bad for their feet?
- Because Jamila needed additional money, she **augmented** her salary by typing term papers for college students.

___ *Augment* means   A. to add to.   B. to risk.   C. to cover up.

4 dispel
(dĭ-spĕl′)
-verb

- Vickie's sweet note of apology was enough to **dispel** the slight anger Rex still felt toward her.
- I tried to **dispel** my friend's fears about her blind date that evening by telling her that my parents met on a blind date.

___ *Dispel* means   A. to cause.   B. to eliminate.   C. to communicate.

5 explicit
(ĕks-plĭs′ĭt)
-adjective

- Even though the instructions were **explicit**, we were still unable to put the bookcase together.
- My parents were very **explicit** about what I could and could not do during their three-day absence. They presented me with a detailed list!

___ *Explicit* means   A. brief.   B. mysterious.   C. specific.

6 longevity
(lŏn-jĕv′ĭ-tē)
-noun

- Toyotas and Hondas are known for their **longevity**, often outlasting more expensive cars.
- The animal with the greatest **longevity** is the giant land tortoise, which can live several hundred years.

___ *Longevity* means   A. form.   B. long life.   C. size.

164

7 magnitude
(măg′nĭ-tōōd′)
-*noun*

● Numbers in the billions and trillions are of too great a **magnitude** for most people to grasp.

● When the bank teller realized the **magnitude** of his error, he panicked at the thought of being held responsible for the loss of so large a sum of money.

___ *Magnitude* means   A. a great amount.   B. a time.   C. a length.

8 mundane
(mŭn-dān′)
-*adjective*

● Because Usha teaches belly dancing every day, it is simply one more **mundane** activity to her.

● The most **mundane** activities can turn into extraordinary events. For instance, I met my best friend while washing my clothes at the laundromat.

___ *Mundane* means   A. exciting.   B. painful.   C. commonplace.

9 obscure
(ŏb-skyōōr′)
-*adjective*

● The chemist didn't express his theory clearly, so it remained **obscure** to all but a few scientists.

● The police easily discovered who committed the murder, but even to the best psychiatrists, the killer's motives remained **obscure**.

___ *Obscure* means   A. unimportant.   B. unclear.   C. known.

10 render
(rĕn′dər)
-*verb*

● Don't let the baby near your term paper with that crayon, or she will **render** it unreadable.

● Phyllis added so much red pepper to the chili that she **rendered** it too hot for anyone to eat.

___ *Render* means   A. to remember.   B. to make.   C. to wish.

Matching Words with Definitions

Following are definitions of the ten words. Clearly write or print each word next to its definition. The sentences above and on the previous page will help you decide on the meaning of each word.

1. _____ To drive away as if by scattering; cause to vanish

2. _____ Size; greatness of size or amount

3. _____ Ordinary; everyday

4. _____ Stated or shown clearly and exactly

5. _____ Having conflicting feelings about someone or something

6. _____ To cause (something) to become; make

7. _____ Not easily understood; not clearly expressed

8. _____ Cool and reserved; distant in personal relations

9. _____ To increase; make greater, as in strength or quantity

10. _____ Length of life; life span

CAUTION: Do not go any further until you are sure the above answers are correct. Then you can use the definitions to help you in the following practices. Your goal is eventually to know the words well enough so that you don't need to check the definitions at all.

Sentence Check 1

Using the answer line provided, complete each item below with the correct word from the box. Use each word once.

A. **aloof**	B. **ambivalent**	C. **augment**	D. **dispel**	E. **explicit**
F. **longevity**	G. **magnitude**	H. **mundane**	I. **obscure**	J. **render**

_____   1. The best writers can describe something ___ so that it doesn't seem ordinary at all.

_____   2. The architect decided to add another pillar to the building to ___ its support.

_____   3. "Russell seems ___ toward me," Janice said, "as if he both likes and dislikes me."

_____   4. Recent research suggests that our parents' ___ doesn't necessarily affect how long we will live.

_____   5. When I'm frightened, I try to appear ___ because looking cool and distant helps me feel in control.

_____   6. The essence of my science teacher's genius is that he is able to make complicated, ___ ideas clear to students.

_____   7. "If you keep walking on the backs of your shoes like that, you will ___ them as flat as the floor," Anya's mother said.

_____   8. If Claude proposes marriage to Jean, he will ___ any doubts she may still have as to whether or not he really loves her.

_____   9. "I try to make my test questions as ___ as possible," said Mr. Baines, "so that my students will know exactly what answers I'm looking for."

_____   10. I began to realize the ___ of the insect population when I read that there are more kinds of insects living today than all other kinds of animals in the world.

NOTE: Now check your answers to these items by turning to page 179. Going over the answers carefully will help you prepare for the next two practices, for which answers are not given.

Sentence Check 2

Using the answer lines provided, complete each item below with **two** words from the box. Use each word once.

_____
_____   1–2. When asked about his ___, ninety-year-old Mr. Greene gives a(n) ___ recipe for a long life: eat well, exercise, and stay away from hospitals. "It's ironic°," he explains, "that I got the worst infection of my life at a hospital."

_____
_____   3–4. Harriet was able to ___ the family income by working overtime. Although her fiscal° worries dwindled,° her problems with her husband and children increased in ___ as a result.

_____
_____   5–6. I'm ___ about playing with our rock band. The music is a source of elation° for me, but I'm afraid it will ___ me deaf one of these days.

_____ 7–8. Gail sometimes appears cold and conceited, but she is ___ only toward people whom she strongly dislikes. With all others, her usual genial° and modest manner soon ___s any impression that she is haughty°.

_____ 9–10. "Does the idea that we don't always see things as they really are seem ___ to you?" the teacher asked. "If so, it will become clearer if you relate it to the ___ experience of looking down a road. Doesn't it look narrower in the distance than it really is?"

Final Check: *My Sister's Date*

Here is a final opportunity for you to strengthen your knowledge of the ten words. First read the following selection carefully. Then fill in each blank with a word from the box at the top of the previous page. (Context clues will help you figure out which word goes in which blank.) Use each word once.

I remember watching my older sister, Ruth, as she removed the last spiked curler from her hair. We gaped° at the result. She somehow had (1)_____(e)d her hair limp as spaghetti. When Ruth started to cry, I tried to pacify° her with my usual gentleness: "Why are you such a crybaby about some stupid guy?"

The guy was Steven Meyer. He and Ruth were going to a high-school dance. She'd had a crush on him for years, for reasons that were (2)_____ to me. (I had never been able to discern° what she saw in him.)

When Ruth began to (3)_____ her makeup by applying some more powder, she gave a terrifying scream that probably reduced my (4)_____ by at least a year. She informed me between sobs that a pimple had just appeared on her nose, making her "look like a vile° witch." I studied her face, expecting a pimple of truly amazing (5)_____. Instead, I spotted a tiny speck. I tried to (6)_____ Ruth's worries: "So, it makes you look like a witch. Don't you want to look bewitching?" But she just began to cry again. I took this opportunity to go downstairs and wait for Steven Meyer.

He arrived a half hour before Ruth was ready. In the interim°, while waiting for Ruth, we talked, and I tried to figure out exactly what Ruth saw in him. Finally, she appeared. Trying to look (7)_____, she came downstairs very slowly, wearing a cool, distant expression.

When Ruth returned home later that night, her comment about the evening was both curt° and (8)_____: "Totally rotten." She contended° that Steven, far from being extraordinary, had turned out to be deficient° in personality—"the most (9)_____ sort of person in the world." It seemed Ruth had bypassed feeling (10)_____ about Steven and gone straight from love to hate.

It's just as well, since I've been married to Steven for ten years now.

Scores   Sentence Check 2 _____%   Final Check _____%

Enter your scores above and in the **Vocabulary Performance Chart** on the inside back cover of the book.

The box at the right lists twenty-five words from Unit Five. Using the clues at the bottom of the page, fill in these words to complete the puzzle that follows.

aloof
ambivalent
avid
constrict
depict
dispel
fallible
feign
furtive
genial
implicit
ironic
mediate
mundane
muted
nurture
obscure
pathetic
pragmatic
punitive
saturate
sibling
smug
sneer
vivacious

ACROSS

4. To make smaller or narrower, as by squeezing or shrinking
6. Pitifully inadequate or unsuccessful
7. To soak or fill as much as possible
9. Overly pleased with one's own cleverness, goodness, etc.; self-satisfied
13. Having conflicting feelings about someone or something
17. Enthusiastic and devoted
19. Cool and reserved
21. Suggested but not directly expressed
22. Not easily understood or clearly expressed
23. To settle (a conflict) by acting as a go-between
24. A sister or brother

DOWN

1. Lively; full of enthusiasm
2. Giving or involving punishment; punishing
3. Done or behaving so as not to be noticed; secret; sneaky
5. To promote the development of by providing nourishment, support, and protection
7. To show or express contempt or ridicule
8. Practical
10. Softened; toned down; made less intense
11. Friendly, pleasant, and kindly
12. To pretend; give a false show of
14. Ordinary; everyday
15. Opposite to what might be expected
16. Capable of making an error
18. To represent in pictures or words; describe
20. To drive away as if scattering; cause to vanish

PART A

Choose the word that best completes each item and write it in the space provided.

_____ 1. Dean is so ___ that he refers to his position of hamburger cook at a fast-food restaurant as "chef."

      A. punitive   B. transient   C. pretentious   D. muted

_____ 2. Peter hasn't been ___ about quitting his job, but he's hinted at it.

      A. explicit   B. avid   C. fallible   D. punitive

_____ 3. In talking with the social worker, the abused child ___ a life of horror.

      A. depicted   B. implored   C. intimidated   D. nurtured

_____ 4. When my brother complained about a shortage of cash, his ___ message was "Can you lend me some money?"

      A. smug   B. avid   C. implicit   D. vivacious

_____ 5. The poker gang laughed when Mom asked to join their game, but their ___ for her rose as she won the first four hands.

      A. esteem   B. longevity   C. legacy   D. magnitude

_____ 6. While driving home three hours after her curfew, Lucille ___ an excuse she hoped her parents would believe.

      A. formulated   B. dispelled   C. ruptured   D. intimidated

_____ 7. After a(n) ___ search during which I crawled around my entire apartment, my "missing" contact lens fell out of my eye.

      A. exhaustive   B. fiscal   C. pretentious   D. vindictive

_____ 8. Jerome deserves his excellent grades, but he doesn't have to be ___ and say, "Naturally, I got straight A's again."

      A. obscure   B. deficient   C. smug   D. muted

_____ 9. It's ___ that my rich uncle is so stingy and my parents, who aren't rich, are always lending money to family members.

      A. exhaustive   B. ironic   C. furtive   D. pragmatic

_____ 10. Although he had heard about his grandmother's aches and pains a million times, Dennis ___ interest whenever she complained to him.

      A. implored   B. feigned   C. mediated   D. intimidated

(Continues on next page)

PART B

On the answer line, write the letter of the choice that best completes each item.

_____ 11. "I'm not **fallible**," my older sister insists. She means that she never makes
    A. money.
    B. meals.
    C. mistakes.
    D. good grades.

_____ 12. The **habitat** of a cactus is
    A. very prickly.
    B. capable of storing water.
    C. grayish-green.
    D. the desert.

_____ 13. A **mundane** experience, in most people's opinion, would be
    A. grocery shopping.
    B. meeting one's future spouse.
    C. sky-diving.
    D. having major surgery.

_____ 14. "This new comedy show is **devoid** of humor," wrote the television critic, meaning that the show
    A. is always funny.
    B. is funny some of the time.
    C. completely lacks humor.
    D. is going to win an award.

_____ 15. When Isaac **implored** his sister to lend him ten dollars, he
    A. blackmailed her into lending him the money.
    B. demanded that she lend him the money.
    C. refused her offer to lend him the money.
    D. begged her to lend him the money.

_____ 16. A person who begins honking and yelling, "Go, go!" at other drivers the second a traffic light turns green is **deficient** in
    A. vision.
    B. rudeness.
    C. patience.
    D. speed.

_____ 17. A reliable way to **infuriate** a teacher is to
    A. skip class, refuse to do assignments, and talk back rudely in class.
    B. hold the door open for him or her and offer to help clean up the classroom.
    C. take education courses in college and eventually get a student-teaching assignment.
    D. ask for clarification when you do not understand an assignment.

_____ 18. Roger realized Anitra's interest in him had **dwindled** when she began to
    A. ask his friends if he was dating anyone special.
    B. object to his seeing other women.
    C. come up with excuses to call him at home.
    D. avoid his phone calls and visits.

_____ 19. When my father **mediates** a quarrel, he
    A. intentionally angers the people involved because he wants them to fight.
    B. helps settle the quarrel by acting as a go-between.
    C. takes one person's side in order to make the other one even angrier.
    D. refuses to become involved in the quarrel in any way.

_____ 20. Although Vanessa developed a crush on her classmate Josh, the feeling was **transient** because
    A. she asked him out on a date.
    B. Josh was in all her classes.
    C. she soon met the boy she called her "true love."
    D. Josh returned Vanessa's feelings.

Score   (Number correct) _____ x 5 = _____%

PART A

Complete each item with a word from the box. Use each word once.

A. **ambivalent**	B. **condone**	C. **contemplate**	D. **evoke**	E. **feasible**
F. **fiscal**	G. **inhibition**	H. **jeopardize**	I. **legacy**	J. **magnitude**
K. **muted**	L. **reconcile**	M. **sibling**		

_____ 1. To make the bright green a more ___ shade, the painter added a few drops of black.

_____ 2. Music in a minor key often ___s sad feelings in the listener.

_____ 3. No one realized the ___ of Nora's depression until she tried to kill herself.

_____ 4. Isabel has ___ feelings about her job. She loves the work but hates her boss.

_____ 5. Why ___ dropping out of school when you've got only two semesters to go?

_____ 6. It isn't ___ to grow roses in our back yard. There's too much shade back there for roses.

_____ 7. Rosa has ___(e)d her son's temper tantrums for so long that he thinks they're acceptable behavior.

_____ 8. My love of the outdoors is a(n) ___ from my grandfather, who often hiked in the mountains.

_____ 9. The company is in such bad ___ shape that over half the employees will soon lose their jobs.

_____ 10. Dick ___(e)d his chances of getting the job when he addressed the interviewer by the wrong name.

_____ 11. My ___s will be coming from California and Arkansas to celebrate our parents' twenty-fifth anniversary.

_____ 12. At first, Tiffany was reluctant to sit in Santa Claus's lap, but she overcame her ___s when she saw that he was handing out candy canes.

_____ 13. As the wedding drew near, Brenda had to ___ herself to the fact that her son would marry a woman she disliked.

(Continues on next page)

PART B

Write **C** if the italicized word is used **correctly**. Write **I** if the word is used **incorrectly**.

_____ 14. *Saturate* the washcloth by wringing it out.

_____ 15. I asked Sal to *augment* the stereo because it was giving me a headache.

_____ 16. An *avid* reader, Judy spends much of her time enjoying newspapers, magazines and books.

_____ 17. Sonia *sneered* at the rock star who was her idol and asked him to autograph her CD.

_____ 18. Being a *pragmatic* person, my brother values music and poetry more than practical things.

_____ 19. Barry didn't let his children stay up late last night because he didn't want to set a *precedent* for future nights.

PART C

On the answer line, write the letter of the word that is the **synonym** of the boldfaced word.

Example: ___A___ dwindle   A. lessen   B. increase   C. turn

_____ 20. **aloof**   A. angry   B. friendly   C. reserved

_____ 21. **nurture**   A. starve   B. establish   C. nourish

_____ 22. **render**   A. make   B. prevent   C. return

PART D

On the answer line, write the letter of the word that is the **antonym** of the boldfaced word.

Example: ___B___ dwindle   A. lessen   B. increase   C. turn

_____ 23. **genial**   A. unpleasant   B. kindly   C. inborn

_____ 24. **pathetic**   A. admirable   B. required   C. sorry

_____ 25. **intimidate**   A. delay   B. frighten   C. encourage

Score   (Number correct) _____ x 4 = _____ %

Enter your score above and in the **Vocabulary Performance Chart** on the inside back cover of the book.

Each item below starts with a pair of words in CAPITAL LETTERS. For each item, figure out the relationship between these two words. Then decide which of the choices (A, B, C, or D) expresses a similar relationship. Write the letter of your choice on the answer line.

_____ 1. INTROVERT : SHY ::
    A. firefighter : brave   C. showoff : modest
    B. timid : shyness   D. recipe : ingredients

_____ 2. SIBLING : BROTHER ::
    A. niece : aunt   C. parent : father
    B. baby : infant   D. twins : triplets

_____ 3. VIVACIOUS : SLUGGISH ::
    A. lively : active   C. spirited : cheerleader
    B. curious : interested   D. passionate : uncaring

_____ 4. FURTIVE : SPY ::
    A. tall : mouse   C. dishonest : criminal
    B. sly : sneaky   D. tiptoe : walk

_____ 5. GAPE : AMAZING ::
    A. smile : sad   C. yawn : exciting
    B. laugh : humorous   D. interrupt : conversation

_____ 6. PUNITIVE : PENALTY ::
    A. liberating : shackles   C. instructive : lesson
    B. punishing : reward   D. verdict : evidence

_____ 7. CRYPTIC : CODE ::
    A. spicy : carrot   C. wealthy : beggar
    B. encouraging : cheerleader   D. mystical : magical

_____ 8. DETRIMENTAL : SMOKING ::
    A. beneficial : exercise   C. snakebite : antidote
    B. physician : health   D. harmful : medicine

_____ 9. RUPTURE : PIPE ::
    A. sweep : dustcloth   C. inhale : exhale
    B. dirt : shovel   D. malfunction : computer

_____ 10. VINDICTIVE : FORGIVING ::
    A. neglectful : attentive   C. expensive : costly
    B. local : nearby   D. take : revenge

(Continues on next page)

_____ 11. CONSTRICT : SHRINK ::

    A. commonplace : usual   C. fracture : bone

    B. vanish : appear   D. fire : ash

_____ 12. GENIAL : GRUMPY ::

    A. gentle : mild   C. selective : picky

    B. elegant : awkward   D. legible : readable

_____ 13. VILE : SPOILED FOOD ::

    A. rude : good manners   C. shiny : new coin

    B. striped : long lines   D. medicine : bitter taste

_____ 14. ESTEEM : ROLE MODEL ::

    A. admiration : enemy   C. respect : fondness

    B. familiarity : stranger   D. contempt : bully

_____ 15. MUTED : BLARING ::

    A. coarse : rough   C. functional : useless

    B. quiet : silence   D. external : outside

_____ 16. PACIFY : ENRAGED ::

    A. calm : asleep   C. preach : sermon

    B. heal : wounded   D. delay : tardy

_____ 17. DISPEL : FALSE RUMOR ::

    A. expose : conceal   C. sneeze : cold

    B. seal : crack   D. enclose : container

_____ 18. EXPLICIT : OBSCURE ::

    A. frequent : rare   C. expire : lapse

    B. usual : everyday   D. sow : seeds

_____ 19. MUNDANE : ORDINARY ::

    A. stone : diamond   C. sparkling : shiny

    B. bright : night   D. childish : adult

_____ 20. MAGNITUDE : MOUNTAIN ::

    A. agility : tortoise   C. magnify : microscope

    B. dampness : desert   D. sweetness : candy

Score   (Number correct) _____ x 5 = _____%

Appendixes

A. Limited Answer Key

IMPORTANT NOTE: Be sure to use this answer key as a learning tool only. You should not turn to this key until you have considered carefully the sentence in which a given word appears.

Used properly, the key will help you to learn words and to prepare for the activities and tests for which answers are not given. For ease of reference, the title of the "Final Check" passage in each chapter appears in parentheses.

Chapter 1 (Joseph Palmer)

Sentence Check 1

1. adamant
2. encounter
3. malign
4. amiable
5. amoral
6. epitome
7. absolve
8. antagonist
9. animosity
10. eccentric

Chapter 2 (Telephone Salespeople)

Sentence Check 1

1. dilemma
2. wary
3. inclination
4. curt
5. sabotage
6. demoralize
7. subsequent
8. irate
9. zeal
10. retort

Chapter 3 (A Cruel Sport)

Sentence Check 1

1. tangible
2. obsolete
3. acclaim
4. adjacent
5. escalate
6. engross
7. exploit
8. methodical
9. terminate
10. elicit

Chapter 4 (Bald Is Beautiful)

Sentence Check 1

1. infirmity
2. implication
3. infringe
4. succinct
5. sparse
6. innovation
7. revitalize
8. subjective
9. inequity
10. deterrent

Chapter 5 (No Luck with Women)

Sentence Check 1

1. mercenary
2. allusion
3. altruistic
4. assail
5. euphemism
6. taint
7. appease
8. syndrome
9. arbitrary
10. banal

Chapter 6 (A Taste of Parenthood)

Sentence Check 1

1. audience
2. sympathetic
3. childhood
4. pendant
5. quartet
6. nonessential
7. happily
8. unicycle
9. annually
10. hypertension

Chapter 7 (Accident and Recovery)

Sentence Check 1

1. calamity
2. ponder
3. flagrant
4. comprehensive
5. conventional
6. persevere
7. rehabilitate
8. turmoil
9. fluctuate
10. venture

Chapter 8 (Animal Senses)

Sentence Check 1

1. enhance
2. attest
3. dispatch
4. exemplify
5. enigma
6. nocturnal
7. discern
8. orient
9. mobile
10. attribute

Chapter 9 (Money Problems)

Sentence Check 1

1. predominant
2. concurrent
3. constitute
4. prerequisite
5. nominal
6. decipher
7. recession
8. default
9. confiscate
10. hypothetical

Chapter 10 (The New French Employee)

Sentence Check 1

1. suffice
2. sinister
3. vulnerable
4. intricate
5. implausible
6. sanctuary
7. incoherent
8. scrutiny
9. degenerate
10. intercede

Chapter 11 (A Cruel Teacher)

Sentence Check 1

1. immaculate
2. blight
3. gloat
4. blatant
5. contrive
6. garble
7. retaliate
8. gaunt
9. qualm
10. plagiarism

Chapter 12 (It's Never Too Late)

Sentence Check 1

1. exclaimed
2. biorhythm
3. patricide
4. homeward
5. inflexible
6. forceful
7. semiprivate
8. finalists
9. humanitarian
10. humiliated

Chapter 13 (Learning to Study)

Sentence Check 1

1. Intermittent
2. devastate
3. incorporate
4. indispensable
5. incentive
6. rigor
7. squander
8. curtail
9. digress
10. succumb

Chapter 14 (The Mad Monk)

Sentence Check 1

1. intrinsic
2. alleviate
3. virile
4. cynic
5. infamous
6. covert
7. revulsion
8. speculate
9. benefactor
10. demise

Chapter 15 (Conflict Over Holidays)

Sentence Check 1

1. aspire
2. benevolent
3. diversion
4. mandatory
5. abstain
6. deficit
7. dissent
8. affiliate
9. agnostic
10. lucrative

Chapter 16 (Dr. Martin Luther King, Jr.)

Sentence Check 1

1. Conversely
2. extrovert
3. poignant
4. prevalent
5. contend
6. proponent
7. charisma
8. contemporary
9. traumatic
10. quest

Chapter 17 (Relating to Parents)

Sentence Check 1

1. prone
2. congenial
3. flippant
4. prompt
5. rapport
6. impasse
7. relentless
8. perception
9. reprisal
10. rationale

Chapter 18 (Held Back by Fears)

Sentence Check 1

1. boyish
2. Wisdom
3. discouraged
4. immobile
5. produced
6. magnified
7. duplicate
8. psychoanalyst
9. intensify
10. claustrophobia

Chapter 19 (Interview with a Rude Star)

Sentence Check 1

1. comprise
2. redundant
3. haughty
4. libel
5. glib
6. benign
7. blasé
8. facade
9. condescend
10. pseudonym

Chapter 20 (The Nightmare of Gym)

Sentence Check 1

1. detract
2. ominous
3. averse
4. elation
5. nullified
6. endow
7. expulsion
8. disdain
9. divulge
10. mortified

Chapter 21 (Skipping Church)

Sentence Check 1

1. latent
2. designate
3. deviate
4. credible
5. interim
6. cursory
7. secular
8. improvise
9. shun
10. simulate

Chapter 22 (A Model Teacher)

Sentence Check 1

1. waive
2. commemorate
3. deplete
4. transcend
5. complacent
6. niche
7. menial
8. diligent
9. consensus
10. empathy

Chapter 23 (My Talented Roommate)

Sentence Check 1

1. bizarre
2. repertoire
3. falter
4. conducive
5. gist
6. hamper
7. viable
8. paradox
9. frenzy
10. flaunt

Chapter 24 (Fascinating Courses)

Sentence Check 1

1. actor
2. geochemistry
3. omnipresent
4. asterisk
5. director
6. theologian
7. misplace
8. contradict
9. Monogamy
10. populated

Chapter 25 (Cal and His Sisters)

Sentence Check 1

1. vivacious
2. implore
3. devoid
4. introvert
5. jeopardize
6. sibling
7. infuriate
8. sneer
9. intimidate
10. smug

Chapter 26 (Shoplifter)

Sentence Check 1

1. gape
2. contemplate
3. precedent
4. feasible
5. condone
6. fiscal
7. furtive
8. pathetic
9. feign
10. punitive

Chapter 27 (A Nutty Newspaper Office)

Sentence Check 1

1. deficient
2. rupture
3. ironic
4. detrimental
5. inhibition
6. depict
7. vindictive
8. cryptic
9. saturate
10. implicit

Chapter 28 (Roughing It)

Sentence Check 1

1. vile
2. genial
3. reconcile
4. constrict
5. formulate
6. exhaustive
7. Pretentious
8. habitat
9. pragmatic
10. fallible

Chapter 29 (Getting Scared)

Sentence Check 1

1. pacify
2. evoke
3. dwindle
4. muted
5. nurture
6. transient
7. esteem
8. avid
9. legacy
10. mediate

Chapter 30 (My Sister's Date)

Sentence Check 1

1. mundane
2. augment
3. ambivalent
4. longevity
5. aloof
6. obscure
7. render
8. dispel
9. explicit
10. magnitude

B. Dictionary Use

It isn't always possible to figure out the meaning of a word from its context, and that's where a dictionary comes in. Following is some basic information to help you use a dictionary.

How to Find a Word

A dictionary contains so many words that it can take a while to find the one you're looking for. But if you know how to use guidewords, you can find a word rather quickly. *Guidewords* are the two words at the top of each dictionary page. The first guideword tells what the first word is on the page. The second guideword tells what the last word is on that page. The other words on a page fall alphabetically between the two guidewords. So when you look up a word, find the two guidewords that alphabetically surround the word you're looking for.

● Which of the following pair of guidewords would be on the page with the word *skirmish*?

    skimp / skyscraper   **skyward / slave**   **sixty / skimming**

The answer to this question and the questions that follow are given on the next page.

How to Use a Dictionary Listing

A dictionary listing includes many pieces of information. For example, here is a typical listing. Note that it includes much more than just a definition.

> **driz•zle** (drĭz′əl) *v.* **-zled, -zling.** To rain gently and steadily in fine drops.
> — *n.* A very light rain. —**driz′zly,** *adj.*

Key parts of a dictionary entry are listed and explained below.

Syllables. Dots separate dictionary entry words into syllables. Note that *drizzle* has one dot, which breaks the word into two syllables.

● To practice seeing the syllable breakdown in a dictionary entry, write the number of syllables in each word below.

    glam•our _____   **mi•cro•wave** _____   **in•de•scrib•a•ble** _____

Pronunciation guide. The information within parentheses after the entry word shows how to pronounce the entry word. This pronunciation guide includes two types of symbols: pronunciation symbols and accent marks.

Pronunciation symbols represent the consonant and vowel sounds in a word. The consonant sounds are probably very familiar to you, but you may find it helpful to review some of the sounds of the vowels—*a, e, i, o,* and *u.* Every dictionary has a key explaining the sounds of its pronunciation symbols, including the long and short sounds of vowels.

Long vowels have the sound of their own names. For example, the *a* in *pay* and the *o* in *no* both have long vowel sounds. Long vowel sounds are shown by a straight line above the vowel.

In many dictionaries, the *short vowels* are shown by a curved line above the vowel. Thus the *i* in the first syllable of *drizzle* is a short *i.* The pronunciation chart on the inside front cover of this book indicates that the short *i* has the sound of *i* in *ill.* It also indicates that the short *a* has the sound of *a* in *apple,* that the short *e* has the sound of *e* in *end,* and so on.

● Which of the words below have a short vowel sound? Which has a long vowel sound?

    drug _____   **night** _____   **sand** _____

Another pronunciation symbol is the *schwa* (ə), which looks like an upside-down *e*. It stands for certain rapidly spoken, unaccented vowel sounds, such as the *a* in *above*, the *e* in *item*, the *i* in *easily*, the *o* in *gallop*, and the *u* in *circus*. More generally, it has an "uh" sound, like the "uh" a speaker makes when hesitating. Here are three words that include the schwa sound:

in•fant (ĭn′fənt)   **bum•ble** (bŭm′bəl)   **de•liv•er** (dĭ-lĭv′ər)

● Which syllable in *drizzle* contains the schwa sound, the first or the second? _____

Accent marks are small black marks that tell you which syllable to emphasize, or stress, as you say a word. An accent mark follows *driz* in the pronunciation guide for *drizzle,* which tells you to stress the first syllable of *drizzle.* Syllables with no accent mark are not stressed. Some syllables are in between, and they are marked with a lighter accent mark.

● Which syllable has the stronger accent in *sentimental*? _____

sen•ti•men•tal (sĕn′tə-mĕn′tl)

Parts of speech. After the pronunciation key and before each set of definitions, the entry word's parts of speech are given. The parts of speech are abbreviated as follows:

noun—*n.*   pronoun—*pron.*   adjective—*adj.*   adverb—*adv.*   verb—*v.*

● The listing for *drizzle* shows that it can be two parts of speech. Write them below:

_____   _____

Definitions. Words often have more than one meaning. When they do, each meaning is usually numbered in the dictionary. You can tell which definition of a word fits a given sentence by the meaning of the sentence. For example, the word *charge* has several definitions, including these two: **1.** To ask as a price. **2.** To accuse or blame.

● Show with a check (✓) which definition (1 or 2) applies in each sentence below:

The store charged me less for the blouse because it was missing a button.   1 ___   2 ___

My neighbor has been charged with shoplifting.   1 ___   2 ___

Other information. After the definitions in a listing in a hardbound dictionary, you may get information about the *origin* of a word. Such information about origins, also known as *etymology,* is usually given in brackets. And you may sometimes be given one or more synonyms or antonyms for the entry word. *Synonyms* are words that are similar in meaning to the entry word; *antonyms* are words that are opposite in meaning.

Which Dictionaries to Own

You will find it useful to own two recent dictionaries: a small paperback dictionary to carry to class and a hardbound dictionary, which contains more information than a small paperback version. Among the good dictionaries strongly recommended are both the paperback and the hardcover editions of the following:

The American Heritage Dictionary
The Random House College Dictionary
Webster's New World Dictionary

Answers to the Dictionary Questions

Guidewords: *skimp/skyscraper*
Number of syllables: 2, 3, 5
Vowels: *drug, sand* (short); *night* (long)
Schwa: second syllable of *drizzle*

Accent: stronger accent on third syllable *(men)*
Parts of speech: noun and verb
Definitions: 1; 2

C. Topics for Discussion and Writing

NOTE: The first three items for each chapter are intended for discussion; the last three, for writing. Feel free, however, to either talk or write about any of the items.

Chapter 1 (Joseph Palmer)

1. Do you ever watch TV programs in which real-life **antagonists** appear and **malign** each other as the audience cheers and shouts? What do you think of these shows?

2. Think of some **amiable** people you know and also people who seem to feel a lot of **animosity** toward others. How do their relationships with others differ? Why might they deal with others as they do?

3. Do you think **amoral** people are born that way? Or is there another explanation for why some people have no conscience?

4. Write a paper on a point of view about which you are **adamant**. For example, you might feel strongly that children should be given a voice in certain family decisions. Or you might stubbornly insist that the government should offer free health care for all citizens regardless of age or income. In your paper, explain your reasoning.

5. Select a person in entertainment, sports, or politics who you think is the **epitome** of something—for example, the epitome of courage or talent or kindness. Write a paper in which you describe this person and give evidence for your opinion. You might begin with a sentence such as this: *Former President Jimmy Carter is the epitome of service to humankind.*

6. Who is the most **eccentric** person you have ever had an **encounter** with? Write a paper about two or three unusual things this person has done.

Chapter 2 (Telephone Salespeople)

1. Do you enjoy salespeople who make their sales pitches with great **zeal**? Or does such enthusiasm make you **wary**? Give an example of a strong sales pitch you've heard recently, either in person, on TV, or on the radio.

2. Have you had to deal with classmates or coworkers who were frequently **curt**? Do you **retort** sarcastically to make them realize how rude they are? Is there a better way to handle such a situation?

3. When you are faced with a difficult **dilemma**, what is your **inclination**: to make a decision quickly, or to put off deciding as long as possible? For instance, how have you decided to take one course instead of another, or choose one job or project instead of another?

4. When has a careless comment from someone **demoralized** you? How did you react? Judging from your **subsequent** conversations with that person, did he or she mean to make you feel bad? Write a paper explaining the comment and the context in which it was given, how the comment affected you, and how you eventually came to view it.

5. What in your day-to-day life really makes you **irate**? Write about a situation (or person) that regularly angers you.

6. Do you know, or know about, a person who acts in self-destructive ways, creating problems for himself or herself? Write about a person who **sabotages** his or her own life. Here's a sample main idea for your paper: *My brother has sabotaged his own future by thinking only of the present.*

Chapter 3 (A Cruel Sport)

1. Do people who wear fur **exploit** animals, or are they making appropriate use of resources? Do you feel the same way about people who wear leather and eat meat?

2. Have you ever been in a conversation that was at first calm but then **escalated** into an angry argument? How did you (or the other person involved) eventually **terminate** the fight?

3. Name a book or movie that truly **engrossed** you and that you think is deserving of **acclaim**. What specifically about the book or movie **elicits** such admiration from you?

4. Pretend you're an advice columnist. One of your readers writes, "Dear _____, Occasionally, on the bus I take to work (or school), an attractive person sits in the seat **adjacent** to mine. How can I make contact?" Write a humorous, **methodical** plan for this reader to follow in order to meet the attractive stranger.

5. Will calculators and computer spell-check programs make basic math and spelling **obsolete**? Write a paper in which you defend one of these two points: (1) Public schools should stop spending so much time on math and spelling, or (2) Despite the common use of calculators and computer spell-check programs, public schools should continue to emphasize math and spelling.

6. Select one of the following types of people: an athlete, a musician, an artist, a slob, a neat freak, a pack rat, or an animal lover. Write a paper in which you describe this imaginary person's apartment. What **tangible** evidence in the apartment would give hints of the owner's identity?

Chapter 4 (Bald Is Beautiful)

1. Have you ever noticed barriers to wheelchairs in your town? If you had to use a wheelchair, would you feel not being able to enter shops, restaurants, and theaters was just one of those things you had to get used to? Or would you feel it was an **inequity** that should be corrected?

2. In recent years, we have seen more and more people willing to put their divorces, lawsuits, family problems, dating lives, and even marriages on television for the entertainment of strangers. What are the **implications** of this trend in TV entertainment—for both the participants and the audience?

3. With the move of many businesses to malls, many old business areas have boarded-up buildings and only **sparse** attractions for local residents. What are a few things that could be done to **revitalize** such an area in your town?

4. What **innovations** might make your school a better place? Write a few suggestions in the form of a memo to school administrators. Be as **succinct** as possible—the officials are busy people.

5. Do any of the campaigns against teenage smoking, drinking, and drug use actually succeed as **deterrents**? Write a paper explaining your view.

6. Abortion is a topic about which people have strong, highly **subjective** views. How far do you feel anti-abortion protesters should be allowed to go? Should they be able to picket abortion centers, for instance, as long as they do not interfere with traffic? How about protesters who **infringe** on the ability of others to obtain abortions by blocking the entrance to such a center? Write a paper about your thoughts.

Chapter 5 (No Luck with Women)

1. Which is the most **banal** TV show you've ever seen? Explain your choice by naming one or two ways in which the show lacks originality.

2. Are there rules and regulations at your school or workplace that seem **arbitrary**? Why do you think such seemingly unreasonable rules exist? Whom might they be intended to **appease**?

3. As you were growing up, what topics did people in your family consider unpleasant or offensive? Did family members tend to use **euphemisms** and make only vague **allusions** to these subjects? Or did they speak about them directly? Give an example to illustrate your point.

4. Who is the most **mercenary** of your friends or acquaintances? At the other end of the scale, which of your friends or acquaintances is the most **altruistic**? Write a paper that describes both people and indicates which one you prefer and why.

5. Do you sometimes feel **assailed** by homework, tests, and other school demands? Write a humorous paper about "Tired Student **Syndrome**," describing the symptoms of this imaginary "disease."

6. Has anyone ever spread a rumor about you that has **tainted** your reputation? If not, have you seen someone else's reputation damaged by rumors? Write about the rumor and its effects.

Chapter 7 (Accident and Recovery)

1. Pretend the superintendent of a prison for youthful criminals wants to **rehabilitate** the inmates and has consulted you. With your classmates, brainstorm ideas for such a program. The program can be as **comprehensive** as you like, involving any kind of treatment or education you think might help these young people turn their lives around.

2. Whom can you think of whose clothing and appearance are quite **conventional**? On the other hand, whom can you think of whose clothing and appearance show a **flagrant** disregard for what is considered normal? Describe in detail the two people's appearances, and suggest why they might have decided to look or dress as they do.

3. Think of someone you admire because of a risk he or she has taken. Perhaps the person gave up a steady but boring job to do something he or she really believed in, or maybe the person **ventured** failure by going back to school after being out of it for some time. What happened? In your opinion, is the person happy he or she took that risk?

4. Do you know anyone whose life seems to involve one **calamity** after another? Write a paper about this person, giving examples of events that have caused his or her life to be in **turmoil**. Do you think that the person has more than his or her share of bad luck? Or does he or she somehow contribute to the problems?

5. Think of a situation in your life in which you were tempted to give up, but kept trying. Perhaps you've struggled with a class, a sport, a personal relationship, or a job. In a paper, describe the situation and explain what made you **persevere** instead of giving up. Alternatively, write about such a situation in the life of someone you know.

6. Write about a difficult decision you've had to make. Describe how your thoughts **fluctuated** as you **pondered** what course of action to take. What did you finally decide to do, and why?

Chapter 8 (Animal Senses)

1. Which appeals to you more: living your life in one community where you'd "put down roots," or living a more **mobile** life, moving from place to place? Explain which way of life you'd prefer and why.

2. Think of a time when a friend has done something to **enhance** his or her appearance. Did you **discern** the change right away, or did it take some time? How did you react to the change?

3. Everyone seems to know at least one "Odd Couple," two people who seem so different that their attraction to one another is an **enigma**. Whom do you know, or know about, who **exemplify** such a mismatched couple? Why might they be together?

4. If you could design your own town, what **attributes** would it include? Write a paper listing and explaining some characteristics you feel would contribute to good lives for residents and make it easy for newcomers to **orient** themselves.

5. Choose a place you are familiar with both during the day and at night. Write a paper contrasting the place's daytime and **nocturnal** appearances. What sights, sounds, and other sensations might one experience at each time of day? You might describe, for instance, how a place that is unattractive in daylight becomes more attractive at night, when its ugliness is hidden. Or you might describe a place that is pleasant during the day but scary after dark.

6. Choose a character trait of one of your relatives. Then write a paper in which you **attest** to this trait's influence on your family life. For example, you might write about how your sister's bad temper has ruined some family activities or how your uncle's sense of humor has helped others get through some bad times. Add interest to your paper by using colorful descriptions and quotations.

Chapter 9 (Money Problems)

1. What, in your mind, **constitutes** lying? Does it occur only when a person says something he or she knows is not true? What about this **hypothetical** situation? Bill has a paper due the next day. The library is closed, and he doesn't have a computer at home. He says to his friend Ned, "I sure wish I knew someone who could let me use his computer." Ned says, "Good luck," and goes home. Then someone mentions to Bill that Ned has a computer at home. Later, Bill accuses Ned of lying, and Ned responds, "I never said I didn't have a computer. You never asked." Did Ned lie?

2. In your career as a student, what book have you been required to read that you found hardest to **decipher**? What was so difficult about it, and what (if anything) did you finally get out of it?

3. During a **recession**, soup kitchens, homeless shelters, and places that distribute donated clothing and food are very active. If you were in charge of such a place, would you provide services to the unemployed free of charge, or do you think it would be better to charge **nominal** fees? Explain your answer.

4. Imagine that you face two **concurrent** job offers: one paying $100,000 a year, and the other giving you the opportunity to travel for a year at someone else's expense. You can't accept both offers. There is no guarantee that either job will be available to you if you don't take it now. Write about the choice you would make and why you would make it.

5. What do you think are the **predominant** reasons so many people **default** on their car and house payments? Write a paper listing two or three of those reasons and explaining some ways to avoid failing to make such payments.

6. We often hear about situations in which authorities have **confiscated** children, taking them out of abusive or neglectful situations and placing them in foster homes. These situations might be avoided if people were better prepared for the enormous responsibility of parenthood. Write a paper in which you explain two or three helpful **prerequisites** for people thinking about having children.

Chapter 10 (The New French Employee)

1. Which is easier to get away with—a simple lie or an **intricate** one? Give examples.

2. When you see the relationship between two friends or family members **degenerate**, what do you think is your best response? Should you **intercede** on behalf of the person you think is in the right, or should you keep your distance? Use situations from your experience to illustrate your points.

3. What are some **implausible** excuses you've heard (or perhaps given!) for not completing homework? Did any **suffice** to satisfy the teacher?

4. In school, people who are different in any way are often **vulnerable** to teasing, criticism, and even attack. Write a paper about a person you've known who was targeted for abuse because he or she was in some way different. Did anyone come to this person's defense?

5. Foster homes should be **sanctuaries** for children who, for whatever reasons, cannot stay in their own homes. Tragically, foster parents may have **sinister** motives for taking in children. Pretend that you are in charge of checking out would-be foster parents. Write a paper about the kind of **scrutiny** you would give them before approving them. You might begin with a main idea such as this: *If I were in charge of checking out would-be foster parents, I'd look for three things.*

6. Some people find it easy to speak up in public, while others tend to be **incoherent** when trying to speak in a group. Which are you? Write a paper about at least one experience that shows how easy or difficult speaking up in public is for you. If you like, use exaggeration to achieve a humorous tone.

Chapter 11 (A Cruel Teacher)

1. Why do you think **plagiarism** is considered such a bad thing in school and elsewhere? What is the most **blatant** case of plagiarism you've heard about?

2. After you have (or someone else has) **retaliated** against someone who has hurt or offended you, how do you usually feel? Do you **gloat**, bragging that you've gotten back at him or her? Or do you have some **qualms** about having sunk to that person's level? Give an example.

3. Telephone messages are easy to **garble**. Describe a time that a message you've left—or one you've received—was so jumbled that its meaning became confused.

4. How strongly are young people influenced by images on TV and in magazines? For instance, do very slender models and actresses encourage young girls to become unhealthily **gaunt**? Write a paper about a few ways young people imitate what they see in the media. Use detailed examples to support your points.

5. Where do you fall on the neatness scale? Are you a total slob? Does it drive you crazy if your room or house is anything less than **immaculate**? Write a humorous paper describing your housekeeping methods. Your main point might be stated something like this: *My housekeeping methods are weird but effective.*

6. What, in your opinion, is the single biggest **blight** on society today? Drugs? Guns? Child abuse? Pollution? Something else? Write a paper in which you explain your opinion as well as one or two solutions you've **contrived** for dealing with the problem.

Chapter 13 (Learning to Study)

1. Describe a time when you tried to **curtail** a bad habit, such as eating too much, smoking, or biting your nails. Did it help to provide yourself with **incentives**, such as rewarding yourself with new jeans if you'd lose five pounds?

2. When you imagine losing all your belongings in a fire, you realize what is **indispensable** to you. If such a tragedy occurred and you could rescue only one object, what would it be? What are two other objects it would **devastate** you to lose?

3. Describe your perfect vacation. Where would it take place, and what activities would you **incorporate** into it?

4. "Youth is wasted on the young," one writer said, meaning young people (in the eyes of their elders, anyway) often **squander** their opportunities. What opportunity do you wish you had made better use of? What happened to keep you from taking full advantage of the situation—did you **succumb** to laziness, the bad example of friends, or something else? Write a paper about an opportunity you missed.

5. Write a paper that describes a mentally or physically exhausting experience you have had. Use sharp details to make the reader feel the **rigor** of the experience. Don't **digress** into other topics, such as why you were there or who else was with you. Simply write about the difficulty.

6. Who is the most effective teacher you have ever had? Write a paper that explains what made him or her so good. Also mention whether you always appreciated him or her, or whether your good opinion was **intermittent**—interrupted by periods when you thought the teacher was, for example, too tough or unfair.

Chapter 14 (The Mad Monk)

1. In your opinion, what really makes a male **virile**? Is it how he looks? How he treats other people? How he handles his responsibilities? What qualities are **intrinsic** to a manly male?

2. While most people regard accused killers with **revulsion**, it is a strange fact that some women are fascinated by them. **Infamous** characters such as O. J. Simpson and Charles Manson receive love letters, even offers of marriage, from such women. **Speculate** on the reasons such men attract women's attention.

3. Have you had a favorite pet that died? What led to its **demise**? Explain what made the pet so special to you.

4. **Cynics** say that no one does anything simply to be kind. Write a paper that either agrees with or contradicts that view. If you hold the opposing view, offer the example of someone who has served as a **benefactor** to you, or to someone else, without expecting a reward.

5. What's the best way you know to **alleviate** the blues? Write a paper on a way (or ways) you cheer yourself up. Include a colorful example of each method you mention.

6. Children often carry on **covert** activities. For example, they may hide the fact that they use a flashlight to read under the blanket when they should be sleeping. Or they may try to keep adults from learning that they've skipped school. As a young child, what secret activities did you take part in? Write a paper describing one or more such activities. Tell what the experiences were like for you and what methods you used to keep from being caught. If you ever *were* caught, explain how you were caught and what the consequences were.

Chapter 15 (Conflict Over Holidays)

1. When you were younger, were there rules about **mandatory** behavior in your household that created **dissent** between you and your parents? What were they?

2. What career do you **aspire** to? Does that career attract you primarily because it is **lucrative**, or are there other reasons you are drawn to it?

3. Tell about your daily diet. Does it have a **deficit** of certain kinds of food? Too much of others? What do you consider a healthy diet for someone your age?

4. Who is the most **benevolent** person you know? Write a paper about that person and his or her acts of generosity, describing one or more such acts in detail.

5. What role does television play in your life? Is it an occasional **diversion**, a constant companion, or something in between? How much of a problem would it be for you to **abstain** from watching it for a week? A month? Write a paper describing television's role in your life and how you think you'd manage if you had to give it up.

6. Are you **affiliated** with any groups, such as social clubs, study groups, or volunteer organizations? Write a paper explaining the group's role in your life. What type of group is it? Why did you join? What activities are you involved in? Has your view of the group changed since you've joined it?

Chapter 16 (Dr. Martin Luther King, Jr.)

1. Which famous athletes and entertainers would you say have **charisma**? In your opinion, are the people who have that quality necessarily **extroverts**, or can a quiet person be magnetic and charming as well?

2. What do you think of NASA's **quest** for a way to put astronauts on Mars and maybe even to establish a human colony there? Are you a **proponent** of further space exploration, or do you think the government's money could be better spent in other ways?

3. Describe the most **poignant** book, movie, or television show that you've read or seen lately. Include details that show just what was so touching about it.

4. What **traumatic** event do you remember from your childhood? **Conversely**, what is one of your happiest childhood memories? Write a paper about either event, telling what happened and explaining what made the event so painful or happy for you.

5. Who is a **contemporary** figure that you greatly admire? Write a paper in which you explain which qualities in that person you particularly respect. Begin with a main idea similar to this: *I admire and respect _____ largely because of two of his/her special qualities.*

6. What do you **contend** are the two best reasons for going to college? Write a paper explaining and defending your point of view.

Chapter 17 (Relating to Parents)

1. Brothers and sisters, even those who are usually on **congenial** terms, sometimes tease and play tricks on one another. If you had a brother or sister (or a cousin or close friend) when you were younger, did you sometimes do things to annoy him or her? What was the **reprisal**, if any?

2. People's **perceptions** of behavior often differ. For instance, have you ever been accused of being **flippant** when you were in fact being serious? Do people sometimes think you're grouchy when you're not feeling that way at all? Explain. How do you convince people of your true intent or feelings?

3. With whom in your family do you have the best **rapport**? How is communicating with that person different from talking with other members of your family?

4. Write a paper about a time when you and another individual—perhaps a friend, a coworker, or a family member—had a disagreement and reached an **impasse**. What happened next? What was your **rationale** for how you acted?

5. Imagine that you have a friend who has a self-destructive habit. Perhaps he or she is **relentless** about smoking, drinking, overeating, or taking drugs. Write a paper about two or three techniques you might try in order to **prompt** your friend to give up the unhealthy habit.

6. When you are faced with a decision, are you **prone** to make it quickly—or to put it off as long as possible? Think about, for instance, how long it takes you to select which classes to sign up for, what gifts to buy, when to get a haircut, and whether to ask someone out on a date. Write a paper in which you give examples of your usual decision-making style.

Chapter 19 (Interview with a Rude Star)

1. Should celebrities have the same protection from **libel** as people who aren't famous? Since celebrities invite fame and the media attention that comes with it, is it unrealistic for them to complain when the media publish things they don't like?

2. Today's families **comprise** a bigger variety of relationships than ever. Take a poll in your class, asking your classmates, "What types of relationships does your family include?" How many families include a mother, a father, and their biological children? How many others include stepparents, step-siblings, half-siblings, adopted children, foster children, and single parents? What conclusions can be drawn?

3. People who appear to be "stuck up" are sometimes shy and unsure of themselves, and actually quite friendly once you get to know them. Can you think of a person who seemed **haughty** to you at first, but who turned out to have quite a **benign** personality? How did you discover the truth about this person?

4. Think of an activity that you once believed was great fun, but about which you've become **blasé**. At what point did it cease being fun and original? Why do you think your opinion of it changed? Write quickly, without thinking much about your choice of words. Then look carefully at your paper to find **redundant** parts, if any, and cross them out or reword them.

5. Write a paper describing a building you find impressive—perhaps an old mansion, theater, or museum, or a modern house or storefront with some special appeal. Describe the building's **facade** so your reader can picture it clearly.

6. Every school has its social cliques—groups of students who hang out together because of some shared characteristics. Write a paper that describes several cliques in your school. Was (or is) there a lot of interaction between those cliques, or did (or do) members of one group refuse to **condescend** to mix with members of the others?

Chapter 20 (The Nightmare of Gym)

1. Of all the movies you've ever seen, which would you say had the most **ominous** atmosphere? What made it so ominous?

2. If a troublesome student views school with **disdain**, does it do any good to threaten him with **expulsion**? What might be more effective ways of dealing with students' bad behavior?

3. Is it ever right to **nullify** the results of an election? Under what conditions?

4. We all have memories of special childhood occasions when we were filled with **elation**. Write a paper describing such an occasion in your childhood. Include any details and explanations needed for your reader to understand why the experience filled you with such joy or pride.

5. Although the details may be embarrassing to **divulge**, write a paper about an experience that really **mortified** you. Be sure to include specific information so that the reasons for your feelings will make sense.

6. Of the people you know, who is **endowed** with the best combination of physical, mental, and/or emotional qualities? Write a paper describing that person. Since no one is perfect, include one or two characteristics that **detract** from the person's otherwise outstanding personality and/or appearance. Your main idea for this paper might be similar to this: *Although Veronica does have her faults, she has a wonderful combination of personal qualities.*

Chapter 21 (Skipping Church)

1. Think of a time you (or someone you know) had to **improvise** a false story to get out of an uncomfortable situation. Was the story **credible** enough to be believed? What happened as a result?

2. Should public schools be completely **secular**, or do you think it's all right to have, for instance, prayer in schools or a teacher talking about his or her religious beliefs? Explain.

3. There are actually people who earn their livings as "life coaches": they advise their clients on issues ranging from school and career choices to their love lives. If you had to **designate** a person you know—or know about—to be your life coach, who would that person be, and why?

4. What would you like to be doing in ten years? What will you do in the **interim** in order to make that goal happen? In addition, what might you wish to **shun** so that you can achieve your goal? Write a paper that describes your goals and what you plan to do to reach them.

5. Most people have an interest or two they'd like to explore if they had more time and/or money. What's a **latent** interest of yours that you've never really developed? Write a paper explaining that interest and why it appeals to you. Also tell how you might follow this interest one day when you have time for it.

6. Write about a time in your life when you **deviated** from what you knew was right. What happened? How did you feel afterward?

Chapter 22 (A Model Teacher)

1. What are the two **menial** household tasks that you dislike the most? Is there a **consensus** on this question among your classmates?

2. When you imagine the lives of celebrities, surrounded by adoring fans and making incredible amounts of money, it's not hard to understand why these people develop attitude problems. Do you think you could deal with sudden wealth and fame without becoming **complacent**? How might you **transcend** the pressures of being a celebrity and remain a "regular person"?

3. Think about your future. What **niche** do you see yourself filling in ten years? What type of work do you think you'd like to be doing? What could you do now to learn about that activity to see if it's really what you imagine it to be?

4. Write a paper about two people in your life. One is a person for whom you have a lot of **empathy** because you think this person is trying hard to do a good job of managing his or her life. The other is a person who has **depleted** your store of sympathy, perhaps because he or she seems to be a complainer who does little to improve his or her situation. In your paper, contrast how the two people manage their lives and problems.

5. What do you wish you had been more **diligent** about when you were younger? Studying a particular subject? Practicing a musical instrument? Learning an athletic skill? Write a paper describing what you wish you'd worked harder at, and why.

6. Write a paper, humorous or serious in tone, in which you answer the following question: After your death many years from now, your friends and/or family want to **commemorate** your life in some fashion. What would be a suitable celebration held or memorial established in your honor? Your paper might take the form of instructions to your friends and family.

Chapter 23 (My Talented Roommate)

1. Homeless people are sometimes the victims of mental illness or other conditions that make them look, act, and speak strangely. What examples of **bizarre** behavior have you noticed among homeless people? How do passersby tend to react?

2. You may have heard the saying, "If you've got it, **flaunt** it." What does that statement mean? Are there times when that guideline is not appropriate? If the characteristic one wishes to flaunt is modesty, does the saying become a **paradox**?

3. Without going into too much detail, describe the **gist** of your all-time favorite book, movie, or television program. See if you and your classmates can come up with "Ten Best" lists for each of these types of entertainment.

4. Your room/house/apartment is a mess. The phone rings. Someone who means a great deal to you is coming to see you in twenty minutes. You go into a **frenzy** of tidying up. What tricks do you have in your housecleaning **repertoire** to help you make the most of your time? Do you, for example, hide dirty dishes in a closet? Stuff clothes under the bed? Write a description of how you would make your place presentable for the unexpected guest.

5. Think of one problem with your school—an aspect of it that you dislike or that doesn't work well. Write a paper in which you explain the problem and then propose a **viable** solution.

6. You've been asked to help new students at your school succeed. What atmosphere do you find most **conducive** to doing schoolwork? What conditions **hamper** study? Write a paper that contrasts those two situations and makes suggestions for successful studying.

Chapter 25 (Cal and His Sisters)

1. Describe a recent experience that infuriated you. What happened? Why did it make you so angry?

2. Which member of your family (or which of your friends) is particularly vivacious? Which could be called an introvert? How do these very different people get along?

3. Describe someone you know—perhaps a teacher, an employer, a fellow student or teammate—who intimidated you. What did he or she do to make you feel that way? Sneer at your mistakes? Make impossible demands? With your classmates, brainstorm suggestions for dealing with such people.

4. Write a paper about a time you saw a friend or family member involved in something you believed jeopardized his or her well-being, and you tried to help. The danger could have been to your friend's emotional or physical health, reputation, or general happiness. When you implored your friend to think about the behavior, what was his or her response?

5. When we say, "He (or she) is like a brother (or sister) to me," we mean that a person is very close to us and that we understand one another in a special way. Write a paper about someone who is "like a sibling" to you. In your paper, describe the ways in which the relationship is special to you.

6. Of all the classes you have taken or organizations you have joined, which would you say was most devoid of interest or value to you? Write a paper describing what the class or organization was like and why it failed to interest you.

Chapter 26 (Shoplifter)

1. Everyone knows the tendency of drivers to slow down and gape at the scene of an accident. What do you think is the reason for this tendency? What drives people to stare at a horrible sight?

2. Do you condone using physical punishment, such as spanking, for children? Or do you think there are punitive techniques that work more effectively? What would these be? Explain.

3. When you were little, did you ever feign an illness in order to get out of doing something? Were you skillful enough to get away with it, or were your attempts to act sick pretty pathetic?

4. Write a paper comparing two routes your future might take. One route should be quite feasible—a practical, realistic plan. The other should be less realistic, even wildly unlikely, but lots of fun. Use humor to make your paper enjoyable to write and to read.

5. What's your fiscal style? Do you save for a future need? Spend money as soon as you have it? And how did you develop your style—are you following the precedent your family set for you? Write a paper about how you behave with money and why. You might state your main idea like this: *My money-management habits can be improved in a couple of ways.*

6. As you contemplate everything you've done in the current school year, which of your accomplishments are you proudest of? Why? Write a paper about your reasons for choosing this particular accomplishment.

Chapter 27 (A Nutty Newspaper Office)

1. You would think that when people grew up with situations that were **detrimental** to their well-being—for instance, with an abusive parent or with family members who are alcoholics—that they would be determined never to repeat that situation. It's an **ironic** fact, though, that people often do re-create those painful situations when they become adults. Why do you think people tend to repeat behaviors that they themselves have been hurt by? What might be done to help them change?

2. Do you know someone who seems to have an unusual number of **inhibitions**? Maybe the person refuses to do anything in public, such as dance or try a new activity, that might make him or her look silly. Are these people **deficient** in self-confidence, or could there be other reasons for their inhibitions?

3. How are chores divided up in your family? Has the family formally decided who should do what, or is there more of an **implicit** understanding about general areas of responsibility?

4. Write a paper in which you **depict**, hour by hour, a typical school day for you. Which parts of it do you enjoy the most? The least?

5. Have you, or has someone you know, ever been the victim of a **vindictive** act? Write a paper describing what the other person did and why—and what happened as a result.

6. Write about a time when a friend's **cryptic** behavior left you puzzled or disturbed. Perhaps someone with whom you'd been on good terms suddenly began acting unfriendly, or someone seemed busy with an activity he or she wouldn't talk about. Be sure to explain just what was puzzling about the behavior. If you eventually figured out what was going on, include that in your paper as well.

Chapter 28 (Roughing It)

1. When you hear about battles between housing developers and environmentalists concerned about protecting animals' **habitats**, whose side are you usually on? Which do you think is more important: to take care of people's housing needs, or to protect animals' homes? Explain your view.

2. A **pretentious**, know-it-all character appears in many TV comedies and movies. Think of such a character and describe how he or she makes a show of his or her importance.

3. Is there a situation in your life that you're not very pleased with, but you've had to **reconcile** yourself to? For example, maybe someone you care about is friendly with someone you don't care for. Or maybe a relative or employer is grouchy, but there doesn't seem to be much you can do about it. Explain what you've had to do to accept the situation.

4. We are probably all **fallible** in our first judgments of others. Write about a time when your initial judgment of another person was wrong. Perhaps you thought someone was unfriendly at first, but the person turned out to be quite **genial** when you got to know him or her better. Give specific examples of the person's behavior so that your reader can understand your reactions.

5. Think of a minor problem that's annoying you right now—such as a faucet that is leaking, a cat that is scratching the furniture, or your losing an assignment or a library book. In a paper, explain that problem. Then **formulate** a **pragmatic** solution to the problem, and explain that as well.

6. What do you know how to do very well? Paint a room perfectly? Make a divine salad? Buy holiday gifts on a strict budget? Write **exhaustive** directions for doing something you're skilled in so a reader wishing to follow your instruction will benefit from your experience and have no trouble achieving good results.

Chapter 29 (Getting Scared)

1. Think of one legacy—a talent, an interest, a part of your physical appearance or way of behaving—that you've inherited from a relative. Tell about the relative and the legacy you've inherited. Are you glad or sorry that you have this trait in common?

2. What in your opinion are some of the most important things parents can do to nurture their children? Why might these things be so important to a growing child?

3. Have you ever been asked to mediate a disagreement between friends or family members? How did you respond? Were you successful in helping to pacify both people, or did one end up thinking he or she had been treated unfairly? Explain.

4. Write a paper about someone you once liked and respected, but who has lost your esteem. What happened to make your good opinion of this person dwindle?

5. Have you had the opportunity to revisit a place you knew well as a child—perhaps your or a relative's old home, your elementary school, or a place where you used to play? Write a paper about the experience of revisiting that place and the feelings and memories it evoked in you. Were those memories clear and strong, or dim and muted?

6. Write about an interest that you were avid about at one point in your life—a hobby or subject in which you were deeply involved. How did you become interested in it? Have you retained that interest, or was it transient?

Chapter 30 (My Sister's Date)

1. When have you faced a decision about which you were ambivalent? What made the decision so difficult? Did something finally happen to render the decision a little easier for you?

2. Do you enjoy reading material that is new and challenging, or do you prefer something more mundane? Give examples. Also, what are your techniques for dealing with reading assignments that are somewhat obscure?

3. Is there someone you've been friends with for many years? What do you think has contributed to the longevity of your friendship?

4. Write a description of someone who you think is aloof. Include explicit details about exactly what the person does that makes him or her seem so cool and distant.

5. Imagine that a friend who had dropped out of school was considering going back. But he or she is scared and says, "I don't know if I can succeed." Write a letter to your friend in which you do your best to dispel his or her fears. Include in your letter the point that education augments a person's chances for a successful career.

6. Write a paper about an important decision you've had to make recently. What about the decision made it a matter of great magnitude to you? How did you know it was the right decision?

D. List of Words and Word Parts

NOTE: Word parts are in *italics*.

absolve, 8
abstain, 84
acclaim, 16
adamant, 8
adjacent, 16
affiliate, 84
agnostic, 84
alleviate, 80
allusion, 24
aloof, 164
altruistic, 24
ambivalent, 164
amiable, 8
amoral, 8
animosity, 8
ann, enn, 28
antagonist, 8
appease, 24
arbitrary, 24
aspire, 84
assail, 24
aster-, astro-, 130
-ate, 62
attest, 46
attribute, 46
audi, audio-, 28
augment, 164
averse, 114
avid, 160
banal, 24
benefactor, 80
benevolent, 84
benign, 110
bio-, 62
bizarre, 126
blasé, 110
blatant, 58
blight, 58
calamity, 42
charisma, 88
claim, clam, 62
commemorate, 122
complacent, 122
comprehensive, 42
comprise, 110

concurrent, 50
condescend, 110
condone, 148
conducive, 126
confiscate, 50
congenial, 92
consensus, 122
constitute, 50
constrict, 156
contemplate, 148
contemporary, 88
contend, 88
contra-, 130
contrive, 58
conventional, 42
conversely, 88
cor, cour, 96
covert, 80
credible, 118
cryptic, 152
cursory, 118
curt, 12
curtail, 76
cycl, cyclo-, 28
cynic, 80
decipher, 50
default, 50
deficient, 152
deficit, 84
degenerate, 54
demise, 80
demoralize, 12
depict, 152
deplete, 122
designate, 118
deterrent, 20
detract, 114
detrimental, 152
devastate, 76
deviate, 118
devoid, 144
di-, du-, 96
digress, 76
dilemma, 12
diligent, 122

discern, 46
disdain, 114
dispatch, 46
dispel, 164
dissent, 85
diversion, 85
divulge, 114
-dom, 96
dwindle, 160
eccentric, 9
elation, 114
elicit, 16
empathy, 122
encounter, 9
endow, 114
engross, 16
enhance, 46
enigma, 46
epitome, 9
-er, -or, 130
escalate, 16
esteem, 160
euphemism, 25
evoke, 160
exemplify, 47
exhaustive, 156
explicit, 164
exploit, 16
expulsion, 115
extrovert, 88
facade, 110
fallible, 156
falter, 126
feasible, 148
feign, 148
fin, 62
fiscal, 148
flagrant, 42
flaunt, 126
flex, flect, 62
flippant, 92
fluctuate, 42
forc, fort, 62
formulate, 156
frenzy, 126